T5-BQA-941

THE VEIL OF ISIS.

THE VEIL OF ISIS:

A

SERIES OF ESSAYS ON IDEALISM.

BY

THOS. E. WEBB

Essay Index Reprint Series

BOOKS FOR LIBRARIES PRESS
FREEPORT, NEW YORK

First Published 1885
Reprinted 1972

Library of Congress Cataloging in Publication Data

Webb, Thomas Ebenezer, 1821-1903.
   The veil of Isis.

   (Essay index reprint series)
   Reprint of the 1885 ed., issued in series: Dublin
University Press series.
   1. Idealism. I. Title.
B823.W3 1972   141   72-8522
ISBN 0-8369-7337-2

PRINTED IN THE UNITED STATES OF AMERICA

B
823
.W3
1972

TO

THE RIGHT HON. GERALD FITZ GIBBON,

LORD JUSTICE OF APPEAL IN IRELAND,

IN MEMORY

OF

THE DAYS WHEN HE READ PHILOSOPHY

WITH

THE AUTHOR.

181958

PREFACE.

ACCORDING to a French writer, quoted by Dugald Stewart in his *Dissertation*, the comparative history of philosophical systems is nothing else than a history of the variations of philosophical schools, leaving no other impression upon the reader than an insurmountable disgust at all philosophical researches, and a demonstrated conviction of the impossibility of raising an edifice on a soil so void of consistency as that which philosophy supplies.

I have long come to the conclusion that the general conviction to which this passage gives expression is erroneous, and that even the extent of the variations of opinion on philosophical questions has been greatly exaggerated by those who have written on the subject. It cannot be doubted, as David Hume observes, that the mind is endowed with several powers and faculties, that these powers are distinct from each other, that what is really distinct to the immediate perception may be distinguished by reflection, and consequently that there is a truth or falsehood in all propositions on this subject which

are not beyond the compass of our understanding. If this
be so, there is no reason why philosophers should not arrive
at a practical agreement on such questions as the origin of
our knowledge and ideas, the classification of our mental
faculties, the nature of general reasoning and of reasoning by induction—in short on all the questions which
the term psychology embraces. These are mere questions of
fact; and on all these points we are capable of knowledge
—of knowledge similar in character and certainty to that
which we attain in the study of the phenomena of external nature, supposing what we call external nature to
exist externally, and not to be itself a mere evolution
of the mind.

In point of fact, there is a much more extensive agreement among philosophers upon these interesting questions
than is generally suspected. Their actual agreement is
disguised by a variety of causes. In philosophy, as in
political economy, there are innumerable speculators, who
have set up trade, as it were, without any of that intellectual capital which is found in the accumulated thought
of their predecessors, and whose divergences, for that
reason, may safely be discounted. Of those who have
endeavoured to prepare themselves for their vocation by a
previous course of reading, a large number have studied
the former philosophers in histories of philosophy, themselves compiled from previous histories, which are not histories but misconceptions. Even when great thinkers,
like Hobbes, and Locke, and Hume, are studied in their
own writings, those writings contain so much equivocal

expression, so much misleading metaphor, so many imperfect statements, so many statements apparently conflicting, so many statements in which precision is sacrificed to point, that the real meaning of the author, like a law of nature lying latent in a chaos of phenomena, is only to be elicited by a process of patient induction, to the drudgery of which ambitious spirits are unable to submit. The sense of originality, the reaction against assertion, and the pride of confutation supervene, and thus impelled the highest intelligences are apt to fancy themselves to be opposed to those with whom, if they properly understood them, they would find that they agreed. The very conditions of all philosophical discussion are calculated to aggravate the evil. There is no universal language in philosophy, and to such an extent has mere difference of expression been mistaken for diversity of thought, that the history of philosophy appears to the cynical spectator to be a wild Babel of confusion. Even when a great thinker, like Kant, invents a terminology which is generally adopted, the very novelty of his expression disguises the identity of his thoughts with those which had been previously expressed in more familiar language. Another source of illusion—though even this does not exhaust the tale—requires to be stated. Truth, as I have elsewhere said, is a polygon and not a point; but before the polygon is constructed the sides must be described, and, by a natural prejudice, the philosopher who insists on one aspect of a general question is supposed to ignore the existence or to deny the importance of the rest.

Impressed with these considerations, some years ago I wrote and published the *Intellectualism of Locke* with the object of indicating the fundamental identity of opinion, as far as mere matters of psychology are concerned, which exists between Locke on the one hand and Reid and Kant upon the other. In the present work I have followed out this idea, and have attempted to show that on the great question of the theory of perception Hume is substantially at one with Reid, and that on the still greater question of the transcendental origin of our ideas of physical causation he anticipated both the principle and the results of Kant.

As to those matters which transcend the sphere of consciousness, and which concern, to use the familiar phrase, the mystery of existence, the demonstrated conviction of hopeless disagreement displays a show of reason. But even here there is a tendency towards unanimity among those who are competent to form an opinion on the subject. On the question of the existence of an external world, to take the simplest question of existence, the great thinkers, who have formed an epoch in the history of thought during the last century and a-half, have come to a practical agreement. Berkeley started the question by asking how it is possible for us to know that material substances exist; and having shown that we cannot know this either by sense or reason, declined to believe in the existence of that of which he had no knowledge. Hume, less sceptical than the dogmatic theologian, admitted that the existence of material things must be assumed as a fact in all our reasonings, but contended that if the existence of an external world be based on instinct it is contrary to reason, and that, if referred to reason, it is unsupported by any evidence that reason can accept. Generalized by Kant, the conclusion of Hume assumed a more scientific form, and among the philosophers of the present day there are few who would venture to reject the critical conclusions—that no object external to ourselves is presented to our consciousness; that if an object be not given, its existence cannot possibly be proved; and that if it cannot be proved, its existence must remain for ever a mere object of belief.

Whether the existence of the great realities with which we are concerned is to be regarded as an object of knowledge or as an object of belief is a matter of small practical importance to those who reflect that in the ordinary affairs of life, as in the deepest mysteries of religion, we live by faith and not by sight. But speculative curiosity remains unsatisfied, and where the field of knowledge is closed, the region of hypothesis expands before us. Are the objects of our knowledge distinct from the subject which evolves them? Are those objects three, or two, or one? Is the Deity, for example, to be excluded from the theory of real existence? Is the world, on the other hand, to be regarded as nothing but a phantasm? Is there no real existence to be recognized except the soul? And as to the soul itself, is it anything but a system of vanishing ideas? Is there any substance in existence? The answer involved in each of these questions is a system of metaphysics. But these metaphysical hypotheses, unlike the hypotheses which we form as to physical phenomena, are incapable of verification, and accordingly all thinking men are disposed to agree that mere ontologies are not answers to a question of ascertainable fact, but answers to a riddle which in our present state of existence cannot by possibility be solved.

Yet even here, as it seems to me, we have an element of science. Dugald Stewart has observed that from the limited number of good stories, as they are called, which we possess, the wit of man would seem to be a barrel-organ with only a limited number of tunes. This remark applies with more felicity to metaphysics. In India, in Greece, in Egypt, in Mediæval Europe, in Modern Germany, in England, and in France, we see the constant recurrence of those various guesses at the riddle of existence which are called systems of metaphysical philosophy. They are all based on a limited number of fundamental conceptions, the permutations and combinations of which may be rigorously ascertained. To the curious mind it cannot but be an object of interest to contemplate the sum total of the hypotheses which the human mind is competent to frame on a question which it is incompetent to solve. To know the possibilities of thought is knowledge. It is not by a history of names, however, but by an evolution of conceptions, that such a result is to be attained, and, as an illustration of an idea rather than as the accomplishment of an aim, I have sketched the *Ideal of Systems* which concludes these Essays.

One word may be permitted as to the title of this

book. The Veiled Isis, as we learn from Plutarch, was
the Egyptian symbol of the mystery of being. I have
endeavoured to illustrate the impossibility of solving this
mystery, even in its simplest form, by giving a sketch of
the speculations in relation to the external world which
have occupied thoughtful men for the last century and
a-half. In this attempt I have endeavoured to trace the
forms which idealism has assumed in the hands of the
great masters of speculation; and I trust I may be par-
doned if, instead of styling a work composed amid infinite distractions a History of Philosophy from Locke to
Hegel, I revive an old fashion, and adopt, though at an
immeasurable distance, the precedents set by the *Siris*
of Berkeley and the *Leviathan* of Hobbes.

TRINITY COLLEGE, DUBLIN,
   10th December, 1884.

CONTENTS.

APPENDIX.

Pourtant pouvons nous dire, que le désir d'entendre la verité est un désir de la divinité, mesmement la verité de la nature des dieux, dont l'estude et le prochas de telle science est comme une profession et entrée de religion, et œuvre plus saincte que n'est point le veu et l'obligation de chasteté, ny de la garde et closture d'aucun temple : et si est davantage très agréable à la déesse que tu sers, attendu qu'elle est très sage et très sçavante, ainsi comme la derivation mesme de son nom nous le donne à cognoistre, que le sçavoir et la science luy appartient plus qu'à nul autre, car c'est un mot grec que *ISIS*.

Et en la ville de Sais l'image de Pallas, qu'ils estiment estre Isis, avait une telle inscription :—Je suis tout ce qui a esté, qui est, et qui sera jamais, et n'y a encore eu homme mortel qui m'ait descouverte de mon voile.

Plutarque par Amyot.

THEISTIC IDEALISM:

OR

BERKELEY.

THEISTIC IDEALISM:

BERKELEY.*

———◆———

Visa quaedam mitti a Deo velut ea quae in somnis videantur.

Cic. Acad. ii. 15.

IRELAND may claim the distinction of having produced three philosophers, each of whom formed an epoch in the history of thought. Johannes Scotus Erigena, the founder of the Scholastic System—Hutcheson, the father of the modern School of Speculative Philosophy in Scotland—and Berkeley, the first who explicitly maintained a Theory of Absolute Idealism—were all men of Irish birth, and were marked, in a greater or less degree, by the peculiar characteristics of Irish genius.

It has frequently been observed that the genius of the Irish People is naturally borne to dialectics.

---

* The substance of this Essay was originally given as a lecture from the Chair of Moral Philosophy, and was afterwards published as an article in the *North British Review* for May, 1861.

B

The author of Hudibras, indeed, selects 'the wild Irish' as the types of that mystic learning and occult philosophy which he ridicules in Ralpho. Nor was this the mere fancy of the poet. As early as the time of Charles the Bold, the contemporary chronicler speaks of the multitude of philosophers who, like Scotus, crossed the sea from Ireland. At a later period Bayle speaks of the Hibernians as renowned for able logicians and metaphysicians; and Stewart describes them as distinguished in all the Continental Universities for their proficiency in the scholastic logic. And the facts justify the statement. It was to the uncouth 'Hibernian figures' who prowled about the halls of Oviedo that Lesage describes Gil Blas as addressing himself when bent on disputation. It is an Irish tutor whom Bayle selects as the man to harass a Professor of Salamanca with sorites. It was the Irish at the University of Paris whom Remi describes as 'rampant with reason and on fancies fed.' The Irish logician, in fact, was as ubiquitous as the Irish soldier of fortune, and like the philosophic vagabond in the Vicar of Wakefield—nay, if we are to believe Boswell, like Goldsmith himself— he disputed his way through the Universities of Europe.

The University of Dublin has from the first accommodated itself to the national bent, and given a prominent place in its curriculum to mental science. Its statutes, drawn by Laud, enact that the Isagoge of Porphyry and the Organon, the Physics, and the Metaphysics of Aristotle, should be the text-books of the different classes, and that thrice in the week, at least, their topics should be discussed in public disputation. Aristotle and Porphyry in due time were superseded by Locke; and when the heads of houses were conspiring to ignore the existence of the Essay at Oxford, and when it merely supplied an occasional thesis at Cambridge, it was the recognized text-book of the schools at Dublin. Nor have the graduates of the Irish University been undistinguished in the prosecution of the favourite study. Dodwell, the antagonist of Clarke—Browne, the most original and independent of the followers of Locke—and Berkeley, the forerunner of Hume and Kant—were Fellows of Trinity College.* King, the author of the Treatise on the Origin of Evil—Burke, among his other claims to distinction, the writer of the Essay on the Sublime and Beautiful—and Archer Butler, the historian of Ancient Philosophy—were Scholars of the House. To the present day philosophy still occupies its place of honour, and, without mentioning less celebrated names, it is sufficient to point to the historian of the Rise and Influence of the Spirit of Rationalism in Europe, as a proof that the philosophic spirit is not extinct in the University of Berkeley.

* Lord Macaulay, in his History of England (ch. xiv.), states, that Dodwell was attainted 'by the Popish Parliament in Dublin,' for the 'unpardonable crime of having a small estate in Mayo.' There was a more obvious ground for his attainder. Dodwell was a Fellow of Trinity College, Dublin, though Lord Macaulay seems only to have known him as 'Camdenian Professor of Ancient History at *Oxford.*' But even the remains of Berkeley lie at Oxford, and not at Dublin or at Cloyne.

The estimation in which the character of the illustrious Idealist was held by his contemporaries is well known. Everyone knows how he charmed the fierce misanthropy of Swift—how Pope attributed to him the possession of every virtue under heaven—how Atterbury exclaimed, that till he knew him he did not think that so much understanding, so much knowledge, so much innocence, and such humility, had been the portion of any but the angels. The range of his intellectual accomplishments was almost as wonderful as his virtue was unique. He was an accomplished musician; he was a connoisseur in painting; he was a devoted student of poetry and romance; he was the master of an eloquence which could rouse even the Scriblerus Club into momentary enthusiasm for the mission to Bermuda. At the age of twenty-six, he had already produced the works which were to revolutionise the philosophy of Europe. But the *New Theory of Vision*, and the *Principles of Human Knowledge*, and the *Dialogues* by which they were elucidated, were not the only labours of his life. His *Querist*, to repeat the oft-repeated words of Mackintosh, contains more hints, then original, and still unapplied in legislation and political economy, than are to be found in any equal space. In his *Analyst* he anticipated Hegel in pointing out that seeming inconsistency in the calculus of Newton which Carnot attempted to explain by a compensation of errors, which Lagrange endeavoured to evade by his calculus of functions, and which Euler and

D'Alembert could only obviate by pointing out the
constant conformity of the mathematical conception
with ascertained results. In his *Minute Philosopher*
he shows himself master of the whole domain of
speculation, and, while tracking the free thought of
the day through its various evolutions, exhibits an
exquisite elegance of diction which is unsurpassed
by Addison himself; and finally, in that wonderful
miscellany of physical hypothesis and metaphysical
research, which he denominated *Siris*, he seems to
have been borne aloft into the very atmosphere of
Plato, and has given to the world of speculation a
modern counterpart of the Parmenides and the
Timæus.

The Theory of Vision which established that
' all *visible* things are equally in the mind, and take
up no part of the external space' (s. cxi), was the
natural prelude to the Principles of Human Knowledge which proclaimed that " all the choir of
heaven and furniture of earth—in a word, all those
bodies which compose the mighty frame of the
world, have not any subsistence without a mind "
(*Prin.* vi. xlvi). The conception indeed was no
novelty in the history of thought. It had been
realized in the prophetic trances of the Hebrew
seers, and in the apocalyptic vision of St. John.
The Hindoo sages had maintained that our system
of perception was a mere picture, and that the
world of matter was nothing but *maya,* or illusion.
The Philosophers of the West had long been wavering over a similar conclusion. The Platonists had

held that matter was merely a supposition necessary for the production of the phenomena of sense. The Academics had suggested that the perception of external things might possibly be nothing but a dream presented by the gods. The Alexandrines had intimated that the soul was not in the world, but that the world was in the soul. The speculation at an early period engaged the attention of the Church. The Fathers had been compelled to consider the question in the discussion of Marcion's doctrine of the mere phenomenal nature of the Incarnation. The Schoolmen had asked whether God could not present to sense the species representing an external world, when there was in reality no external world for the species to represent. The founders of the more modern Schools of philosophy had been hovering around the same attractive light. Malebranche had admitted that if God should annihilate the material world, and present corresponding ideas to the mind, the phenomena of sense would be the same. Locke had allowed that the idea might exist, though the reality had no existence. Even Leibnitz, in spite of his Monadology, had confessed, not only that the existence of body was not susceptible of demonstration, but that the world, for aught that philosophy could teach, might be merely a resplendent iris, an image on the glass, a waking dream.

A pure Theistic Idealism, it is true, could not well have been developed in the West before the time of Berkeley, for the Pagan Idealists had no abiding conception of the omnipresence and spirituality of God, and the Catholic philosophers not only accepted the Catholic doctrine of Transubstantiation, but conceived that the existence of the world of matter had been positively revealed by Holy Writ. However this may be, Idealism was the natural product of the age, and of this the history of philosophy affords a curious proof. Three years after the publication of the Principles of Human Knowledge, another thinker combined the idealistic elements with which the speculations of the times were fraught. In his *Clavis Universalis*, Collier, like Berkeley, attempted a demonstration of the nonexistence of the world ; and the perfect correspondence between the independent speculations of the two idealists is one of the most curious facts in the history of thought. It was the correspondence of the clocks of Leibnitz. Collier, like Berkeley, declined to allow the question to be decided by an appeal to Holy Writ with Malebranche, or by an appeal to common sense with Locke. Like Berkeley, he started from the phenomena of vision, and proved that the world of vision could have no existence but in mind. Like Berkeley, he transferred his idealism from the realm of vision to the realm of touch. Like Berkeley, he held not only the non-existence, but the impossibility of the existence, of a world of matter. As to the mode of the production of our ideas, the two philosophers were equally agreed. Both rejected the doctrine of material efflux, and the cognate doctrine of impressed species ; both rejected the hypothesis of seeing all things in God, and also the egoistical idealism which declares that the mind is the creator of its own ideas; both held that our sensible ideas are the immediate effect of the agency of God. In some respects the idealism of Collier is more philosophical than that of Berkeley. He is a more consecutive, if not a more consistent, thinker. He shows what Berkeley omitted to show, the ambiguity of the word *idea*. He anticipates the analysis of Hamilton by raising the question whether the idea exists in the mind as in its proper place, or inheres in it as in its proper subject, or is dependent on it as on its proper faculty. Above all, he shows, in opposition to Berkeley's theory of vision, that the quasi-externality of visual objects is part and parcel of perception, and that it is as much an attribute of the figments of imagination as of the facts of sense.*

But Berkeley and Collier were like the two women grinding at the mill—the one was taken and the other left; and while the name of the one is known to few, except the antiquaries of philosophy, the name of the other marks a philosophic epoch. And yet even Berkeley has been subjected to all the vicissitudes of fame. Though his great work

* This question is fully discussed, and, in my opinion, finally determined by Mr. Abbott, in his work on Sight and Touch. Mr. Abbott satisfactorily shows that if the idea of *outness* is not primarily given it can never be subsequently acquired (chap. v). Mr. Mahaffy takes the same view in his Introduction to Kuno Fischer's Kant, p. xvi. Philosophers who, like Mr, Mill and Professor Fraser, adopt the theory of Berkeley, seem to me, in spite of every artifice of language, to beg the question by assuming *outness* in the medium they employ in their efforts to explain it.

did not, like that of Hume, fall still-born from the press, the speculation which was to revolutionize the philosophy of Europe was at first received with the easy toleration of contempt. According to Swift he made a proselyte of Smalridge, and a few other people of position. But in the world in general he was assailed with the ridicule with which Pyrrho was mocked when he pursued his cook. Brown, the famous opponent of Shaftesbury, tells us, in his Essay on Satire, that ' coxcombs refuted Berkeley with a grin.' But the grin was not confined to coxcombs. Warburton laughed at the idealist as a mere visionary. Arbuthnot could not suppress a sneer ə ' poor philosopher Berkeley,' and described him to Swift as enjoying the idea of health after being brought to death's door by the idea of a fever. Voltaire said it was pleasant to think that ten thousand cannon balls and ten thousand dead men were only so many disagreeable ideas. Johnson looked on the whole ideal system as worthy of no better refutation than that supplied by his memorable kick. Beattie professed to regard the reference of everything to God as something atheistic. Even Reid, who had himself been a Berkeleian, recanted his heresy, did penance as a man of common sense, and recommended his quondam friend the idealist to run his head against a post, and to be clapped into a madhouse for his pains (*Works*, 184). So remote, indeed. was the idealist philosophy from received opinions that even philosophers of a higher mood were unable to accept it. At the instance

of Addison the great *à priori* philosopher of the age
met Berkeley in order to discuss the subject; but
Berkeley complained that Clarke, though he could
not answer him, had not the candour to own himself
convinced.   Berkeley experienced equal difficulty
in convincing the rival philosopher who saw everything God.   He discussed the matter with Malebranche in his cell, but so high did the philosophical excitement rise that the visionary died in
consequence of his interview with the apostle of
ideas.   Hume took a characteristic view of the subject.   All Berkeley's arguments, he said, though
otherwise intended, were in reality sceptical; for
while they admitted of no answer, they produced
no conviction (*Works*, IV. 181)—a remark which
supplies the true justification of Clarke in his re-
fusal to own himself convinced.   But the influence
which Berkeley was destined to exert was far more
powerful than any of his contemporaries suspected.
From his time philosophy ceased to concern itself
with matter.   The authority of the Church was disregarded; the reference to revelation was ignored;
and philosophy became ideal.   It is scarcely too
much to say with Hamann that without Berkeley
there would have been no Hume, as without Hume
there would have been no Kant—and as without
Kant there would have been no Hegel.

But, regarded as a matter of history, the antecedents of a philosophy are as much an object of curiosity as its results; and looking at the subject in
this light, it is not to be denied that the idealism of

Berkeley had its starting point in the philosophy of Locke. Locke had taught that the soul is conscious only of its own ideas (i. i. 8); and that these bounds were ample enough for the capacious mind of man to expatiate in, though it takes its flight further than the stars, and cannot be confined to the limits of the world—though it extends its thoughts beyond the utmost expansion of matter, and makes incursions into the incomprehensible inane (ii. vii. 10). Our ideas of the sensible qualities of matter Locke had conceived to be produced by *impulse*. But how little Hamilton was justified in identifying his doctrine with the materialism of Democritus and Digby (*Disc.* 78. 81) is evident from Locke's qualification of his own remark. He admits that *motion*, according to the utmost reach of our ideas, is able to produce nothing but motion, and that, when we allow it to produce pleasure and pain, or the idea of a colour or a sound, we are fain to quit our reason, go beyond our ideas, and attribute it wholly to the good pleasure of our Maker (ii. iii. 6). In strict accordance with this view, he holds that our knowledge of the existence of spiritual is more certain than our knowledge of the existence of material things. "Whilst I know, by seeing or hearing, &c., that there is some corporeal being without me, the object of that sensation," he says, "I do more certainly know, that there is some spiritual being within me that sees and hears: this, I must be convinced, cannot be the action of bare insensible matter, nor ever could be without an immaterial

thinking being" (II. xxiii. 15). Reid deems it
strange that Locke, who wrote so much upon the
subject, should not see those consequences which
Berkeley thought so obviously deducible from the
doctrine of ideas.   But this is an injustice to Locke's
philosophical acumen. " There can be nothing more
certain," he says, "than that the idea we receive
from an external object is in our minds; this is
intuitive knowledge; but whether there be anything more than barely an idea in our minds,
whether we can thence certainly infer the existence
of anything without us which corresponds to that
idea, is that whereof some men think there may be
a question made, because men may have such ideas
in their minds when no such thing exists, no such
object affects their senses" (IV. ii. 14; IV. xi. 1).
Locke, however, evaded the difficulty, and took
refuge in the arms of common sense. The confidence that our faculties do not herein deceive us,
he said, is the greatest assurance we are capable
of, concerning the existence of material beings (IV.
xi. 3). "If after all," he said, "any one should be so
sceptical as to distrust his senses, and to affirm that
all we see and hear, feel and taste, think and do,
during our whole being, is but the series and delud-
ing appearances of a long dream, whereof there is
no reality, and therefore will question the existence
of all things, or our knowledge of anything; I must
desire him to consider, that, if all be a dream, he
doth but dream that he makes the question, and so
is not much matter that a waking man should

answer him" (IV. xi. 8)—the "evidence is as great as we can desire, being as certain to us as our pleasure or pain, that is, happiness or misery, beyond which we have no concernment either of knowing or being" (*ibid.*).   But the ultimate conclusion of Locke was the very starting-point of Berkeley. The knowledge of our own being, he said, we have by intuition—the existence of a God reason clearly makes known to us—and the knowledge of the existence of any other being we can have only by sensation, for there is no necessary connexion of any other existence but that of God, with the existence of ourselves (IV. xi. 1, 13).

The same point had been reached by the disciples of a different school.   It was a first principle in the philosophy of Descartes, and Leibnitz, and Malebranche, as it was in that of Locke, that the mind is conscious only of its own ideas.   These philosophers, it is true, maintained the existence of a material world without us; but they held that mind and matter are essentially opposed; that, in the words of Norris, they are separated by the whole diameter of existence; and that consequently mind, if left to its own unaided force, can never take cognizance of matter.   To bridge this chasm between mind and matter, different philosophical structures had been framed.   According to the Cartesians, God, on the occasion of the presence of the external object, caused the mind to be so and so affected.   According to Leibnitz, God had so pre-established the independent developments of mind and matter, that there was an everlasting harmony between them. According to Malebranche, God, being cognizant of everything, was cognizant of matter; and being cognizant of matter, admitted man into a participation of his cognition, so that the mind saw material things in God. The theories of Occasional Causes, Pre-established Harmony, and Vision of the Universe in God, thus conducted to the same point as the Hyperphysical Realism of Locke. The *Deus ex machina* was the last resource of all; and all admitted that the world of matter could only be brought into relation with the mind by the intervention, direct or indirect, of God.

Of all the philosophers who preceded Berkeley, the one who approached most nearly to his conclusion was Malebranche. The French metaphysician regarded it as an indisputable fact, that it is only by means of ideas that the unextended mind can become cognizant of extended objects.* He contemptuously rejected the argument for the existence of the external world which is based on common sense. With equal contempt he rejected the theory which maintains that external objects make us aware of

* Mais je parle principalement ici des choses matérielles qui certainement ne peuvent s' unir à notre âme de la façon qui lui est nécessaire afin qu' elle les aperçoive; parce qu' étant étendues, et l'âme ne l' étant pas, il n' y a point de rapports entre eux (*Rech.* L. iii. P. ii., c. i). C'est incontestable qu' on ne peut voir les choses matérielles par elles-mêmes et sans idées (*ibid.*). Par ce mot *idée* je n' entends ici autre chose que ce qui est l'objet immédiat, ou la plus proche de l'esprit quand il aperçoit quelque objet (*ibid.*). On ne s' arrête pas à expliquer plus au long ces belles choses et les diverses manières dont différents philosophes les conçoivent (c. ii). On assure donc qu' il n' est pas vraisemblable que les objets envoient des images ou des espèces qui leur resemblent (*ibid.*).

their existence by the emission of species or entity-ideas. He avowed that according to his way of thinking matter could not even be accepted as the cause of our perceptions or sensations. The experience of delirium and dreams, he said, establishes that there is no necessary connexion between the presence of an idea and the existence of a corresponding thing without. He admitted, as we have seen, that if the world were annihilated, and if God should produce in our minds the ideas which are now produced in them on the presence of external objects, we should perceive everything that we now perceive. How then are we to account for the existence of our sensible ideas? Malebranche considered it evident that these ideas could not be created by the mind itself, for they were not the creatures of the will, and the mind must have had a knowledge of them before it could produce them.* The obvious conclusion would seem to be that the cause of our sensible ideas must be God. But Malebranche recoiled from this conclusion. He was not only a philosopher but a theologian. Having demonstrated God's existence from

---

* Pensez-vous, Ariste, que la matière, que vous ne jugez peut-être pas capable de se remuer d'elle-même, ni de se donner aucune modalité, puisse jamais modifier un esprit, le rendre heureux ou malheureux, lui representer des idées, lui donner divers sentiments ? Pensez-y et répondez moi (*Entret.* vii). Il n' y a point de liaison nécessaire entre la présence d'une idée à l'esprit d'un homme et l'existence de la chose qui cette idée représente, et ce qui arrive a ceux qui dorment ou qui sont en délire le prouve suffisament (*Rech.* L. i. c. x). Dans la supposition que le monde fût anéanti, et que Dieu néanmoins produisît dans notre cerveau les mêmes traces, ou plutôt dans notre esprit les mêmes idées qui s' y produisent de la présence des objets nous verrions les. mêmes beautés (*Entret.* i).

the idea of infinity, he proceeded to demonstrate the existence of the world by a reference to the word of God. The Scriptures, he said, inform us of the Incarnation of our Lord ; the Scriptures inform us that in the beginning God created the heavens and the earth. The existence of the material world being thus established, all that remained was to account for its perception. This Malebranche did on the principles of the Cartesian School. The essence, the primary conception, of matter, he said, was extension; and no extended thing could modify the mind. Declining, therefore, to recognise any secondary qualities in matter, he distinguished our ideas from our sensations; and while he regarded the former as *perceived* by us in God, he regarded the latter as simply *caused* by the Deity in us on the occasion of the presence of external objects.*

But Berkeley treated the system and the scruples of his illustrious predecessor with but scant respect. God, he said, was not a musician, who required to be directed by notes, in order to produce that har-

---

Un homme ne peut pas former l'idée d'un objet s' il ne le connaît auparavant, c'est-à-dire s' il n' en a déja l'idée laquelle ne dépend point de sa volonté. Que s'il en a déja une idée, il connait cet objet, et il lui est inutile d'en former une nouvelle. Il est donc inutile d' attribuer à l'esprit de l'homme la puissance de produire ces idées (*Rech.* L. iii. P. ii. c. iii).

* Lorsque nous apercevons quelque chose de sensible il se trouve dans notre perception sentiment et idée pure.

Le sentiment est une modification de notre âme et c'est Dieu qui la *cause* en nous, et il la peut causer quoiqu' il ne l'ait pas, parce qu' il voit, dans l'idée qu' il a de notre âme, qu'elle en est capable. Pour l'idée qui se trouve jointe avec le sentiment, elle est en Dieu et nous le voyons, parce qu'il lui plaît de nous la *découvrir;* et Dieu joint la sensation à l'idée lorsque les objets sont présents, afin que nous le croyions ainsi, et que nous entrions dans les sentiments et dans les pas-

monious train and composition of sound that is called a tune (*Prin.* lxxi). He protested, in the person of Philonous, that he could not understand how our ideas, which are things altogether passive and inert, can be the *essence*, or any part, or like any part, of the essence or substance of God (*Dial.* ii).* Revelation, he said, had used words in their vulgar acceptation; and the ideal philosophy did not deny the existence of anything which Holy Writ had declared to be existent (*Prin.* lxxxii). In fact, the Scriptures themselves ascribed those effects to the immediate agency of God which the heathen philosophers ascribed to Nature (*Prin.* cl). But the question at issue was one to be determined not by revelation but by reason. And what were the dictates of reason on the subject? They were obvious. If primary and secondary qualities are only 'ideas existing in the mind' (*Prin.* ix), why should we make any distinction between ideas and sensations? If it is possible that we might be affected with all the ideas that we have, although no bodies

---

sions que nous devons avoir par rapport à eux (*Recherche de la Vérité*, L. iii. P. ii. c. vi).

* Il faut bien remarquer qu'on ne peut pas conclure que les esprits voient *l'essence* de Dieu de ce qu'ils voient toutes choses en Dieu de cette manière. L'essence de Dieu, c'est son etre absolu, et les esprits ne voient point en *substance* divine prise absolument, mais seulement en tant que relative aux créatures ou participable par elles (*Rech.* L. iii. P. ii. c. vi).

Demeurons donc en ce sentiment, que Dieu est le monde intelligible ou le lieu des esprits, de même que le monde matériel est le lieu des corps; que c'est de sa *puissance* qu'ils reçoivent toutes leur modifications; que c'est dans sa *sagesse* qu'ils trouvent toutes leur ideés; et que c'est par son *amour* qu'il sont agités de tous leur mouvements réglés (*ibid.*). Locke, in his Examination of Malebranche's Opinion, falls into the same error as Berkeley on this point (*Exam.* 31).

C

existed without which resembled them (*Prin.* xviii),
why might not bodies be regarded as the perceptions of a waking dream? If the world is not
known as object, and cannot be inferred as cause
(*ibid.*), what reason have we to believe in its existence? If, in fine, ' the being of a Spirit infinitely
wise, and good and powerful, is abundantly sufficient
to explain all the appearances of nature' (*Prin.*
lxxii), why should we gratuitously assume the co-
operation or the co-existence of any other cause?
But Berkeley pushed the argument still further. He
contended, not only that we are unable to demonstrate the existence of the world of matter, but that
we are able to demonstrate its non-existence. The
supposition of an external material world, he said,
was unmeaning (*Prin.* xvii)—it was replete with
contradictions (*Prin.* iv. xvii. lxvii)—it could not
even be conceived (*Prin.* xxiii). How can we conceive objects existing unconceived, he asked, and
professed himself willing to put the whole controversy upon that single issue (*Prin.* xxii). True,
the series of sensations of which we are conscious,
he said, must have some thinking substance or substratum to support them (*Prin.* ii), as well as some
active cause by which they are produced and changed
(*Prin.* xxvi). But what is the cause in question?
Not a mere physical antecedent to be found in antecedent ideas; for our ideas are 'visibly inactive'
(*Prin.* xxv). Not corporeal substance; for it had
no existence (*Prin.* ix). Neither could the cause in
question be ourselves; for the ideas perceived by

sense have no dependence on ourselves—they are not the creatures of the will (*Prin.* xxix). The cause must, accordingly, be God. The whole argument is neatly summarized by Hylas:—"I find myself affected with various ideas whereof I know I am not the cause; neither are they the cause of themselves, or of one another, or capable of subsisting by themselves, as being altogether inactive, fleeting, dependent beings; they have therefore some cause distinct from me and them, of which I pretend to know no more than that it is the cause of my ideas" (*Dial.* ii). Hylas, it is true, makes an abortive attempt to identify this primeval cause with *matter;* but the inexorable Philonous asks, 'Though it should be allowed to exist, yet, how can that which is inactive be a cause, or that which is unthinking be a cause of thought?' (*ibid.*). Hylas is coerced into recognizing the agency of *mind.* " From [the mere perceptions of the senses]," says Philonous, " I conclude that there is a mind which affects me every moment with all the sensible impressions I perceive ; and, from the variety, order, and manner of them, I conclude the Author of them to be wise, powerful, and good, beyond comprehension" (*ibid.*). Thus while the *attributes* of the Infinite Mind are collected from a 'contemplation of the contrivance, order, and adjustment of things,' its *existence* is 'necessarily inferred from the bare existence of the sensible world'—and this consideration, in the opinion of Philonous, at once baffles the most strenuous advocate of atheism, and effectually disposes of the wild imaginations of Hobbes, Vanini, and Spinosa (*Dial.* ii).

Whatever may be the force of the argument thus constructed, it is so clear that it might well have been supposed to bid defiance to the powers of misconception. But Berkeley has not escaped the fate which has overtaken philosophers in every age. He has been systematically misunderstood. Mr. Mill has remarked that " he was excelled by none who ever wrote in the clear expression of his meaning, and the discrimination of it from what he did not mean"; yet, he adds, " scarcely any thinker has been more perseveringly misapprehended, or has been the victim of such persistent *ignoratio elenchi*, his numerous adversaries having generally occupied themselves in proving what he never denied, and denying what he never asserted." A singular illustration of the truth of this remark is furnished by the Scottish School. According to Reid, the Idealism of Berkeley was the result of two things—the Ideal Theory which Reid erroneously attributed to the philosophers in general, and the Theory of the Origin of Ideas which he erroneously attributed to Locke. Men, he said, who, like Hume and Berkeley, recognized no ideas but those of sensation and reflection, were compelled to repudiate the idea of substance (*Works*, 322); and anyone who accepted the theory universally received by philosophers concerning ideas would find unanswerable arguments against the existence of the material world (p. 282). In attributing these theories to Berkeley, Reid is followed not only by Stewart and Brown, but by Hamilton and Mansel—nay, stranger still to say, by Mill himself. And yet it is demonstrable that Berkeley held neither of these obnoxious doctrines; and the first duty of an expositor of his philosophy is, to clear his memory from the charge.*

In arguing against the existence of Matter, Berkeley anticipates a distinction which pervades the whole of recent philosophy. The distinction is taken in the following passages extracted from the second of the Dialogues between Hylas and Philonous, in which he popularizes and explains his Principles of Human Knowledge. "Either you perceive the being of matter immediately or mediately," says Philonous—"if *immediately*, pray inform me by which of the senses you perceive it; if *mediately*, let me know by what reasoning it is inferred from those things you perceive immediately." "You neither perceive matter *objectively*," he continues, "as you do an inactive being or idea, nor know it, as you do yourself, by a reflex act : neither do you *mediately* apprehend it by similitude of the one or the other, nor yet collect it by reasoning from that which you know immedi-

---

* As to the Ideal Theory, see Reid's *Works*, i. 282 ; Stewart's *Works*, v. 88, 422 ; Brown's *Works*, ii. 17 ; Hamilton's *Reid*, 288, and *Disc.*, 69 ; Mansel's *Proleg.* 318 ; Mill, *ut infra*. As to the Theory of the Origin of Ideas, see Reid's *Works*, 294, 322 ; Stewart's *Works*, v. 72 ; Brown's *Works*, ii. 187 ; Hamilton's *Lect.* ii. 198 ; Mansel's *Proleg.* 134 ; Mill, *ut infra*. In my *Intellectualism of Locke* I have endeavoured to free the prince of the philosophers of England from the charges to which, like the Irish philsopher, he has been exposed. I have recurred to the subject in note A.

ately." In a word, he says, " I have no immediate *intuition* thereof; neither can I mediately from my sensations, ideas, notions, actions, or passions, *infer* an unthinking, unperceiving, inactive substance, either by probable deduction or necessary consequence." From these passages it is plain that Berkeley anticipates Hamilton's celebrated distinction between Presentative or Immediate and Representative or Mediate Cognition (*Reid,* 804); that he repudiates his theory of Natural Realism ; and that he adopts the Ideal Theory to this extent, that he holds the mind is conscious of nothing but its own ideas.

But what are the *Ideas* of which alone we are thus asserted to be conscious ? According to the Scottish School, the idea of Berkeley is a separate entity—a something numerically distinct from mind—a something which may pass from the mind of man into the mind of God—an essence of the nature of that *tertium quid* which, as Hamilton says, was originally devised to explain the possibility of a knowledge by an immaterial substance of an existence so disproportioned to its nature as a material object. What place a representative idea such as this could have had in a system in which there was nothing to represent it is hard to imagine. Brown clearly perceived that the existence of ideas as separate from the mind is an assumption as gratuitous as the assumption of the external existence of matter itself could have been, and that, in point of fact, permanent and independent ideas are matter under another name (*Lect.* xxiv). He clearly saw that to believe that these entities exist in the mind is to materialize intellect under the pretence of intellectualizing matter (*ibid.*). But critics, when they imagine their author to be preposterously absurd, are too much carried away by their own sense of superiority to entertain the thought that the author, instead of being preposterously absurd, may possibly have been egregiously misconceived. And that, in this respect, Berkeley has been egregiously misconceived is certain. It is true he tells us that "ideas are inert, fleeting, dependent beings, which subsist not by themselves, but are supported by, or exist in, minds, or spiritual substances" (*Prin.* lxxxix). But Philonous has explained his meaning. "When I speak of objects as existing in the mind, or impressed on the senses," he says, "I would not be understood in the gross literal sense, as when bodies are said to exist in a place, or a seal to make an impression upon wax—my meaning is only that the mind comprehends or perceives them, and that it is *affected from without* by some being distinct from itself" (*Dial.* iii). Nor is Berkeley guilty of any inconsistency in this. States of mind exist, and may therefore be called *existences;* they have a being in the mind, and may therefore be properly denominated *beings.* It is true, as Mill remarks, that "when we have occasion for a name which shall be capable of denoting whatever exists, as contradistinguished from nonentity or nothing, there is hardly a word applicable to the purpose, which is not also, and even more familiarly, taken in a sense in which it denotes only substances" (*Log.* i. 51). But Berkeley, when he speaks of ideas as 'existing in the mind,' expressly warns us that they 'subsist not by themselves' (*Prin.* lxxxix). He tells us even that "qualities are in the mind only as they are perceived by it, that is, not by way of *mode* or *attribute*, but only by way of idea" (*Prin.* xlix). Nay, he has himself indicated the -very fallacy pointed out by Mill, and has formally, and repeatedly, explained what is meant by the words *thing, reality, existence,* and *being,* when applied to the objects of sense (*Prin.* iii. lxxxix. cxlii). Nor has he been less explicit as to the meaning which he attaches to the word *idea.** His official statement throughout the Principles of Human Knowledge is, that 'the existence of an idea consists in being perceived' (*Prin.* ii); that it is not 'possible ideas should have any existence out of the thinking minds, or thinking things, that perceive them' (*Prin.* iii); that they are 'mere sensations that exist no longer than they are perceived' (*Prin.* xlvi):

---

* In a note to his *Prolegomena Logica*, Dr. Mansel, after some observations to the flattering character of which I cannot be insensible, professes himself unable to agree with me in regarding Berkeley's theory of ideas as identical with that which represents the idea to be a modification of the mind, and adds that "in Berkeley's system the relation of substance and mode has properly no place" (p. 318). I am not certain that I understand the significance of this last remark. If it means that Berkeley did not regard the idea as a modification of the mental *substance*, I agree with Dr. Mansel. If it means that Berkeley did not regard the idea as a modification of the mental *sensibility*, I conceive it to be erroneous. But if it means that Berkeley did not recognize the *principle* of substance, then, in my opinion, it is not only erroneous, but it is at variance with

and in the explanatory Dialogues, Hylas, as the result of his discussion with Philonous, is compelled to acknowledge that, "upon a fair observation of what passes in his mind, he can discover nothing else but that he is *a thinking being affected with a variety of sensations*" (*Dial.* i).

The first error of the Scottish School being cleared away, it remains to clear away the second. In the Principles of Human Knowledge, Berkeley states it to be self-evident that the sole ' objects of human knowledge' are *ideas*—ideas imprinted on the senses, ideas formed by memory and imagination, or ideas perceived by attending to the passions and operations of the mind (*Prin.* i). But nothing can be an object of knowledge unless it be presented to something which knows, and accordingly Berkeley assumes the existence of ' an incorporeal, active substance or spirit' (*Prin.* xxvi) —'one simple, undivided, active being,' which, ' as it perceives ideas is called the understanding, and as it produces or otherwise operates about them is called the will' (*Prin.* xxvii). Of soul or spirit,

the fundamental principles of Berkeley's philosophy, in which it is laid down that all our sensible ideas must have a cause, and that every cause must be a substance. This is clearly perceived by Professor Maguire, in his masterly tract on Berkeley's Notion of Substance; but as to the nature of Berkeley's *idea*, he says that, "with Dean Mansel and Professor Webb to force it into any one of Hamilton's three forms of Hypothetic Realism is idle, for the phrases *in the mind* and *without the mind* have no reference whatever to locality." But Hamilton's analysis of the possible forms of the representative hypothesis is applied by him to the various forms of Idealism as freely as to Hypothetical Realism itself (*Reid*, 817). 'Berkeley,' he says, ' is one of the philosophers who really held the doctrine of ideas, erroneously, by Reid, attributed to all ' (*Reid*, 288).

Berkeley admits, we can form no *idea* (*ibid.*); nay, he admits that 'such is the nature of spirit, or that which acts, that it cannot be of itself perceived but only by the effects which it produceth' (*ibid.*). Still he contends that 'we have some *notion* of soul, spirit, and the operations of the mind' (*ibid.*); and accordingly he holds that 'human knowledge may naturally be reduced to two heads, that of *ideas* and that of *spirits*' (*Prin.* lxxxvi). But Berkeley goes still further. Not only does he insist that 'we may be said to have some knowledge or notion of our own minds, of spirits and active beings, whereof in a strict sense we have not ideas'; but he also insists that 'in like manner we know and have a notion of relations between things or ideas, which relations are distinct from the ideas or things related, inasmuch as the latter may be perceived by us without our perceiving the former'; and he accordingly concludes that '*ideas*, *spirits*, and *relations* are, all in their respective kinds, the object of human knowledge and subject of discourse' (*Prin.* lxxxix).

In all this there is doubtless much confusion, much variation of statement, much ambiguity of expression; but it may be taken on the whole as certain that Berkeley divided the data of consciousness into two classes, *ideas* and *notions;* that under the head of ideas he comprehended Locke's *ideas of reflection*, and under that of notions those *ideas of relation* which Locke regarded as 'the creations and inventions of the understanding.' Among these conceptions of the understanding Berkeley, like his

master, recognized the notions of essential substance and efficient cause as distinguished from our
notions of a mere permanent collection of qualities
and uniform series of events. It is true that Berkeley—and it is the great defect of his philosophy—
gave no systematic explanation of our notions, and
has even left his views in obscurity as to the mode
in which these notions are evolved. In his Principles he assumes the existence of a substantial cause
to account for the existence of our sensible ideas,
because, as he says, it is '*repugnant* that they should
subsist by themselves' (*Prin.* cxlvi). In his Vindi-
cation of his Theory of Vision, he explains them to
be an 'inference of reason,' as distinguished from
an 'object of sense,' and maintains that 'from our
ideas of sense the inference of reason is good to
power, cause, agent' (sect. xi). In his Siris, however, he is more explicit. He professes to effect a
compromise between the *tabula rasa* of Aristotle and
the *innate ideas* of Plato, and suggests that though
'there are properly no ideas or passive objects but
what were derived from sense,' yet 'there are also
besides these her own acts or operations, such as
notions,' which must be referable to the understanding (*Siris*, 308). For here Berkeley clearly
approximates to Kant. 'As *understanding* perceiv-
eth not,' he says, 'so *sense* knoweth not' (s. 305).
He acknowledges with Kant that sensible objects
'make the first impressions,' and that 'the mind
takes her first flight and spring, as it were, by rest-
ing her foot on these objects' (s. 292); but, with

Kant, he contends that 'the *mind,* her acts and faculties, furnish a new and distinct class of objects, from the contemplation whereof arise certain other notions, principles, and verities,' remote from sense (s. 297) ; and maintains that 'the *mind* contains all, and acts all, and is to all created beings the source of unity and identity, harmony and order, existence and stability' throughout the world (s. 295).

And yet it would be a mistake to identify the psychology of Kant with that of Berkeley. According to Berkeley's official doctrine the mind is purely passive in the reception of its sensible ideas, and therefore contributes nothing to their formation. It does not frame them in any forms of sensibility; it does not combine them into unity by any synthetic power of apperception; it does not anticipate their permanence or their recurrence by any category of the understanding. Time, according to Berkeley, is nothing, abstracted from the succession of ideas (*Prin.* xcviii); space is nothing but the absence of resistance (*Prin.* cxvi). Sensible objects he regarded not as collected together by the mind, but as presented in 'artificial and regular combinations' by their author (*Prin.* lxv). He recognizes the 'foresight' which enables us to regulate our actions for the benefit of life (*Prin.* xxxi); the 'prognostics' which we form as to the permanent coexistence of our ideas (*Prin.* xliv); the 'predictions' which we make concerning the ideas we shall be affected with pursuant to a train of

actions (*Prin.* lix): but the only way in which he
offers to explain these anticipations of experience
is by saying that God operates by the 'established
methods' which we call the laws of nature (*Prin.*
xxx), and that they are derived 'from the experience we have had of the train and succession of
ideas in our minds' (*Prin.* lix). But Berkeley
seems never to have raised the question which was
raised and answered by Hume, and answered still
more explicitly by Kant—How is it that from the
experience we have had we can form any *à priori*
conclusion as to the experience we are about to
have? He seems never to have asked himself why
it is that we form the expectation that God will
continue to act in the future, as we know that he
has acted in the past. He seems never to have
clearly seen that the permanence of the phenomena
of sense and the continuity of their sequences must
be *assumed* in every physical investigation, and that
being necessary assumptions they must be regarded
as *anticipations* of the understanding which antecedent experience may suggest, and which subsequent
experience may confirm, but which no modification
of mere experience can explain.

But if Berkeley does not explain the unity of
human knowledge by the Kantian synthetic unity
of apperception, there can be no doubt that he fully
recognizes in the mind a synthetic unity of *substance;* and his consistent assertion that the soul
must be regarded as a thinking substance should, at
least, have saved him from one of the persistent

misrepresentations to which his philosophy has been
exposed. According to Reid, the argument which
maintains that matter is merely 'a bundle of sensations,' is equally applicable to the mind; and accordingly he gives Hume credit for consistency in
reducing mind itself to a mere 'bundle of thoughts
and passions and emotions' (*Works*, 293). But Reid
failed to observe that while Berkeley recognized the
principle of substance in all its metaphysical reality,
Hume, differing from both him and Locke, ignored it.
He failed to recollect that, while Berkeley held that
matter was a mere bundle of sensations, he held that
it was a mere bundle of sensations in the mind, and
that mind, as the 'substratum of those ideas,' must
of necessity be a substance (*Prin.* vii. xxvi. cxlvi).
If Berkeley denied material substance, it was not
because he thought that material qualities could
exist without a material substratum, but because
he thought that material qualities could not by
any possibility exist without a mind (*Prin.* lxxiii).
But here again Reid's error is without excuse; for
Berkeley anticipated this very objection, and met
it in advance. " In consequence of your own principles," says Hylas to Philonous, "it should follow
that you are only *a system of floating ideas*, without
any substance to support them" (*Dial.* iii). " How
often must I repeat," says Philonous to Hylas,
" that I know, or am conscious of, my own being,
and that I myself am not my ideas, but somewhat
else—a thinking, active principle that perceives,
knows, wills, and operates about ideas?" Philonous

speaks of this fact as known by ' *consciousness*,' as he previously speaks of it as known by a ' *reflex act*,' and by ' *reflection*.' But Berkeley's official doctrine is, that the conception of substance, like the conception of causation, is a *notion* which the mind is compelled by its own necessities to form, since, whatever our ideas may be, ' it is repugnant that they should subsist by themselves' (*Prin.* cxlvi).

But even Mr. Mill is so carried away by the prevailing error, that he falls into the pit which he himself has pointed out. He too occupies himself in proving what Berkeley never denied, and in denying what Berkeley never asserted—nay, he actually charges him for failing to say what he has expressly said. Berkeley, according to Mr. Mill, " supposed that the actual object of a sensible perception, though, on his own showing, only a group of sensations, etc., suspended so far as we are concerned, when we cease to perceive it, comes back literally the same the next time it is perceived by us ; and, being the same, must have existed in another mind. He did not see clearly that the sensations I have to-day are not the *same* as those I had yesterday, which are gone never to return, but are only exactly similar ; and that which has been kept in continuous existence is but a potentiality of having such sensations, such potentiality implying constancy in the order of phenomenon, but not a spiritual substance for the phenomena to dwell in, when not present to my own mind."* But

* *Fortnightly Review* of November, 1872, p. 518.

Berkeley puts the very words of Mill into the mouth of Hylas. "The same idea which is in my mind cannot be in yours, or in any other mind," says Hylas—"doth it not, therefore, follow from your principles that no two can see the same thing, and is not this highly absurd?" "If the word *same* be taken in the vulgar acceptation," replies Philonous, "it is certain (and not at all repugnant to the principles I maintain) that different persons may perceive the same thing, or the same thing, or idea, exist in different minds. Words are of arbitrary imposition; and since men are used to apply the word same where no distinction or variety is perceived—and I do not pretend to alter their perceptions—it follows that, as men have said before, several saw the same thing, so they may, upon like occasions, still continue to use the same phrase without any deviation, either from the propriety of language or the truth of things." "But whether philosophers shall think fit to call a thing the same or no," Philonous continues, "is of small importance. Let us suppose several men together, all endued with the same faculties, and consequently *affected in like sort* by their senses, and who had yet never known the use of language; they would, without question, agree in their perceptions, though, perhaps, when they came to the use of speech—some, regarding the uniformness of what was perceived, might call it the *same* thing; others, especially regarding the diversity of persons who perceived, might

choose the denomination of *different* things "
(*Dial.* iii).*

But the misapprehension of Mill reaches further
than Berkeley's theory of the world; it reduces to
an absurdity his demonstration of the existence of
a God. That demonstration Mackintosh regarded
as the touchstone of metaphysical sagacity. But
what metaphysical sagacity is evinced by the Berkeleian who supposes that Berkeley postulated the
Deity as ' a spiritual substance for the phenomenon
to *dwell in* ' ? The conception of substance undoubtedly plays a conspicuous part in the philosophy of
Berkeley; but in his demonstration of the existence of God the dominant idea is not substance,
but *causation*. Not only does Mill ignore this function of causation—he reproduces in its crudest form
the blunder of Brown as to the nature of Berkeley's sensible ideas. " These," says Brown, " he
evidently considered not as states of the individual mind, but as *separate things* existing in it,

* Collier makes a similar remark.
" When I affirm that all matter exists
in mind, or that no matter is external,
I do not mean that the world, or any
visible object of it, which I, for instance, see, is dependent on the mind
of any other person besides myself;
or that the world, or matter, which
any other person sees is dependent on
mine, or any other person's mind or
faculty of perception. On the contrary, I contend, as well as grant, that
the world which John sees is external
to Peter, and the world which Peter
sees is external to John; that is, I
hold the thing to be the same in this
as in any other case of sensation; for
instance, that of sound. Here, two
or more persons who are present at a
concert of music may, indeed, in some
sense be said to hear the *same* notes
or melody; but yet the truth is, that
the sound which one hears is not the
very same with the sound which another hears, because the souls, or persons, are supposed to be different "
(*Clavis*, p. 6). Compare with this the
corresponding passage in the *Clavis* as
to the mundane idea existing in the
mind of God (p. 79).

and capable of existing in other minds, but in them
alone; and it is in consequence of these assumptions that his system, if it were to be considered as
a system of scepticism, is chiefly defective. But
having, as he supposed, these ideas, and conceiving
that they did not perish when they ceased to exist
in his mind, since the *same ideas* recurred at intervals, he deduced, from the necessity which there
seemed for some Omnipotent Mind, in which they
might exist during the intervals of recurrence, the
necessary existence of the Deity; and if, indeed,
as he supposed, ideas be something different from
the mind itself, recurring only at intervals to
created minds, and incapable of existing but in
mind, the demonstration of some Infinite Omnipresent Mind, in which they exist during these intervals of recurrence to finite minds, must be allowed
to be perfect" (*Lect.* xxiv). But, says Brown,
"the whole force of the pious demonstration, which
Berkeley flattered himself with having urged irresistibly, is completely obviated by the simple denial
that ideas are anything more than the *mind itself
affected in a certain manner;* since in this case our
ideas exist no longer than our mind is affected in
that particular manner which constitutes each particular idea" (*ibid.*).

And yet Berkeley adopts the very words of
Brown. 'I can discover nothing else,' says Hylas,
'but that I am a thinking being *affected* with a
variety of sensations' (*Dial.* i); and it is from
this fact that Philonous concludes 'there is a mind

which *affects* me every moment with all the sensible impressions I perceive' (*Dial.* ii). But what significance could Brown have seen in that form of the demonstration which he considers perfect? Ideas are separate entities, which can exist nowhere but in mind; these ideas perpetually recur; therefore there must be some mind in which they exist during the intervals of their recurrence; therefore there must be a God. What man in his senses could imagine that anyone would be converted to theism by reasoning such as this? The argument attributed by Brown to Berkeley is much the same as the argument attributed by Cicero to Epicurus.* But Epicurus was an atheist, and his argumentation, according to Cicero, was nothing but a make-believe. The only difference between the theory of entity-images and the theory of entity-ideas is one in favour of the former. The materialist made the image flow from God to man, and left us *some* proof of his existence—the immaterialist makes the ideas flow from man to God, and leaves us to postulate a God as a material receptacle for a shoal of fugitive ideas—a receptacle as material as the crystal tank into which gold and silver fish may be conceived as escaping from their crystal bowl.†

---

* Epicurus docet eam esse vim et naturam Deorum, ut primum non sensu, sed mente cernatur ; nec soliditate quadam, nec ad numerum, ut ea quæ ille propter firmitatem στερέμνια appellat, sed imaginibus similitudine et transitione perceptis" (*De Nat.* i. 18). Velleius adds, "cum infinita simillimarum imaginum species ex innumerabilibus individuis existat, et *ad deos affluat*"—the ἀνήριθμον γέλασμα of ideas in the 'pious demonstration' attributed to the Christian idealist by Brown.

† Mansel, who substantially agrees with Brown, states the argument of

Berkeley undoubtedly states that there must be some other mind wherein ideas exist during the intervals of our perception ; but the explanation of this, after what has been already said, is easy. If our sensible ideas are not the spontaneous product of the mind itself, they must be produced from without; if they are produced from without, they must be produced by some cause which has intelligence of the effects which it produces ; and if that cause has intelligence of the effects which it produces, the idea of the effect to be produced must exist and pre-exist in its intelligence, as the idea of the effect to be produced exists and pre-exists in the mind of the musician, the painter, or the poet. It is thus that Malebranche contends that the ideas of all terrestrial things existed in the mind of the Creator before the date of the creation. It is thus that Collier admits the existence of the great mundane idea of created matter by which all things are produced, by which the great God gives sensations

Berkeley in the following form :— "With this argument, which represents God as the efficient cause of our ideas, Berkeley combined another, in which the Deity is regarded as a constantly perceiving mind. Accepting, as allowed on all hands, the opinion that sensible qualities cannot subsist by themselves, and rejecting ·the ordinary hypothesis of their existence in an insensible substratum, he concluded that they must, therefore, exist in a mind which perceives them, and that they have no existence apart from being perceived. If, therefore, they continue to exist when *we* do not perceive them (and that they do so is the irresistible conviction of all men), they must be perceived by some other mind. Hence the continuous duration of things implies the existence of a constantly percipient mind : that is, of God" (*Proleg.* 317). But sensible qualities, according to Berkeley's view, are only sensible ideas, and sensible ideas themselves are nothing but sensations ; and the statement, that sensible qualities, thus understood, continue to exist when *we* do not perceive them, is ambiguous. *Our*

to all his thinking creatures, and by which things which are not are preserved and ordered in the same manner as if they were (*Clavis*, p. 7). It is in this sense that Philonous acknowledges a two-fold state of things—the one ectypal or natural, the other archetypal and eternal; the one created in time, the other existing from everlasting in the mind of God (*Dial.* iii).* But the ideas which existed from everlasting in the mind of God are not the *same* as the ideas which exist for a moment in the mind of man; and the ideas which cease to exist in the mind of man are not the same as the ideas which have no cesser of existence in the mind of God. The eternal existence of objects in the mind of God is, in fact, only another phrase for his eternal knowledge. "All objects," says Philonous, "are eternally known by God, or, which is the same thing, have an eternal existence in his mind; but when things, before imperceptible to creatures, are by a decree of God perceptible to them,

---

sensations cease to exist when our perception of them ceases. *Similar* sensations, it is true, may be experienced by others, and thus, and thus only, things may have a continuous duration. The sensations so experienced require, on Berkeley's theory, the intervention of an efficient cause, which, being intelligent, must be percipient of the effect which it produces; and it is only in this sense that Berkeley contends that the continuous duration of things implies the existence of a constantly perceiving mind.

* Il est indubitable qu' il n' y avait que Dieu seul avant que le monde fût créé, et qu' il n' a pu le produire sans connaisance et sans idée ; que par consequént ces idées, que Dieu en a eues ne sont point différentes de lui-même, et qu' ainsi toutes les créatures, même les plus matérielles et les plus terrestres, sont en Dieu, quoique d'une manière toute spirituelle et que nous ne pouvons comprendre (*Rech.* L. iii. P. ii. c. v). With this compare the proof that our Ideas are not created by the mind (*sup.* p. 15).

then they are said to begin a relative existence with respect to created minds" (*Dial.* iii). It is this relative existence which, in the opinion of Berkeley, constitutes the world to us. So completely relative is that existence, that it is relative not only to the person but to the moment. The world is nothing but successive phenomenon and evanescence. Our ideas have no continuous existence. They disappear to be succeeded by ideas which are similar, but not the same ; and these successive ideas in their similar succession are mere sparkles on the stream of thought—mere bubbles on the river, which glitter in the sun and burst.*

Berkeley carried out this view of the fleeting nature of ideas to its most sublime result. If the world exists only in idea, and if ideas are mere evanescent states of mind, it follows that the Divine Energy is for ever engaged in creating and re-creating worlds. Accordingly, in the opinion of

---

* The following remarks of Ferrier, in his *Institutes of Metaphysic,* are worthy of attention :—" The system of Bishop Berkeley, also, was vitiated by the absence of this analysis, or by the neglect to distinguish the necessary from the contingent conditions of cognition. He falls into the error consequent on the adoption of the first of the alternatives just referred to [that of elevating the senses, considered as elements of cognition, to the same footing of necessity with the ego.] He saw that something subjective was a necessary and inseparable part of every object of cognition. But instead of maintaining that it was the ego, or oneself, which clove inseparably to all that could be known, and that this element must be thought of along with all that is thought of, he rather held that it was the senses, or our perceptive modes of cognition, which clove inseparably to all that could be known, and that these required to be thought of along with all that could be thought of. These, just as much as the ego, were held by him to be the subjective part of the total synthesis of cognition, which could not by any possibility be disconnected. Hence the unsatisfactory cha-

Berkeley, the work of the Creator did not terminate upon the sixth day, but is continued through the ages. The birth of each new creature is the herald of a new creation. Each moment the universe is anew created in every individual mind. Creation never ceases. When Alciphron, in the Minute Philosopher (*Dial.* iv), objects to the notion of Euphranor, that God daily speaks to our senses in a manifest and clear dialect, Crito replies:— "This language hath a necessary connexion with knowledge, wisdom, and goodness. It is equivalent to a *constant creation* betokening an immediate act of power and providence. It cannot be accounted for by mechanical principles, by atoms, attractions, or effluvia. The instantaneous production and reproduction of so many signs, combined, dissolved, transposed, diversified, and adapted to such an endless variety of purposes, ever shifting with the occasions and suited to them, being utterly inexplicable

---

racter of his ontology, which, when tried by a rigorous logic, will be found to invest the Deity—the supreme mind, the infinite Ego—which the terms of his system compel him to place in synthesis with all things, with human modes of apprehension, with such senses as belong to man ; and this, not as a matter of contingency, but as a matter of necessity " (p. 389). How far Berkeley neglects to distinguish the necessary from the contingent conditions of cognition we have already seen. But the final objection made by Ferrier is anticipated by Berkeley, and put into the mouth of Hylas. Philonous replies that though God is 'the cause of our sensations,' and therefore must 'understand' what sensation is, yet he 'perceives nothing by sense,' and cannot possibly be 'affected with sensation' (*Dial.* iii). Malebranche gives a similar reply to the same objection (*Rech.* L. iii. P. ii. c. vi). But though this reply meets Ferrier's objection, it suggests another. If the world in the mind of man is a mere series of sensations, where is the correspondence between the ectypal world existing in the mind of man and the archetypal world existing in the mind of God?

and unaccountable by the laws of motion, by chance, by fate, or the like blind principles, doth set forth and testify the immediate operation of a Spirit or thinking being, and not merely of a Spirit, which every motion or gravitation may possibly infer, but of one wise, good, and provident Spirit which directs, and rules, and governs the world " (s. xiv).

Such is the standpoint of the philosophy of Berkeley. That philosophy recognized the substantial existence of nothing but Spirits, Finite or Divine. It ignored the world of matter; and it ignored the world of entity-ideas. It allowed of no mediation between the human mind and the Divine; it left the soul, as it were, face to face with God. It is true, we did not see God; but everything we saw, and heard, and felt, was an effect of his wisdom—an intimation of his presence. God was not far from every one of us. He upheld everything by the word of his power. His sound was gone out into all lands, and his words into the end of the world. In him we lived, and moved, and had our being. Such, as expressed by himself in the phraseology of Scripture, was the theory of Berkeley. Such was the lofty conception of the great Idealist—a conception the loftiest, perhaps, to which the mind of man, poised on the wings of imagination and intellect, has soared.

The criticism of Kant on the system of his famous predecessor is well known. Berkeley's idealism, he said, was a mere dogmatical idealism (*Kritik*, 166); holding that 'space, together with all

the objects of which it was the inseparable condition, is a thing which is in itself impossible,' he
was constrained to hold that 'the objects in space
are mere products of the imagination' (*ibid.*), and
to 'degrade bodies to mere illusory appearances'
(p. 42). That Berkeley regarded space not as a
form of sensibility which supplied a factor in the formation of our sensible ideas, but as a child of imagination grafted upon sense, we have already seen
(*Siris*, 292). We have seen that he held our sensible ideas to be passive and inert; that he regarded
the world of a sense as a mere picture exhibited to
us by the Omnipresent and Eternal Mind. But still
he maintains that the appearances which are seen
on the theatre of the world are produced by an
artful hand which is concealed behind the scenes,
and that they are imprinted on the senses by a
constantly operating cause in accordance with un-
changing laws (*Prin.* lxiv). It is this that constitutes at once the permanence and the reality of the
world of sense. It is by this that *real things* are distinguished from chimeras (*Prin.* xxxiii). But the objection of Kant recoils in a measure on himself. If
he meets Fichte half way, and insists that sensible
objects are moulded by intuitions of time and space,
of which we are ourselves the source, he at the same
time maintains with Berkeley that the sensations,
without which the intuitions of time and space
would be mere empty forms, are produced by the
ceaseless operations of a Transcendent Cause which
lies beyond the sphere of sense, but which origi-

nates the experience of the permanence and constancy of which the categories are mere anticipations.

There is one point, however, in Berkeley's system in which reality is conspicuously imperilled,
and that is, the existence of *finite spirits* other than
ourselves. This, indeed, is the weak point in every
idealistic system; and Berkeley frankly admits that
it is a weak point in his own.* He grants that 'we
have neither an immediate evidence nor a demonstrative knowledge of the existence of other finite
spirits' (*Dial.* iii). Human agents, he says, are
'marked out and limited to our view by a particular finite collection of ideas' (*Prin.* lvii); and the
knowledge we have of them 'depends on the intervention of ideas by us referred to agents or spirits
distinct from ourselves, as effects or concomitant
signs' (*Prin.* cxlv); but he confesses that it is God
alone who 'maintains that intercourse between
spirits, whereby they are able to perceive the existence of each other' (*Prin.* cxlvii). This immediately suggests a difficulty which it is sufficient to
indicate, and on which it is impossible to dwell.
" In making God the immediate author of all the

---

* Malebranche feels himself compelled to make the admission that, on
the principles of his philosophy, the
existence of finite spirits other than
ourselves is a mere *conjecture:*—De
tous les objets de notre connaissance,
il ne nous reste plus que les âmes des
autres hommes et que les pures intelligences, et il est manifeste que nous
ne les connaissons que par *conjecture.*
Nous ne les connaissons présentement
ni en elles-mêmes ni par leurs idées;
et, comme elles sont différentes de
nous, il n'est pas possible que nous les
connaissions par conscience. Nous *con-
jecturons* que les âmes des autres hommes sont de même espèce que la nôtre
(*Rech.* L. iii. P. ii. c. vii).

motions in nature," says Hylas, "you make him
the author of murder, sacrilege, adultery, and the
like heinous sins" (*Dial.* iii). Philonous answers
that sin does not consist in the outward physical
act, but in the internal deviation of the will; and
that the denial of the existence of any agent but
spirit is 'consistent with allowing to thinking
rational beings, in the production of motions, the
use of limited powers, ultimately, indeed, derived
from God, but immediately under the direction of
their own wills.' But the answer of Philonous
will scarcely be as satisfactory to the reader as it
was to honest Hylas. In one respect, indeed, the
works of man, on the principles of Berkeley, may
be said to take their place among the works of
nature. The creations of genius remain when artist
and architect have passed away. The Transfigura-
tion is as imperishable as any material thing that
can perish, and St. Paul's, while it endures, is as
much a portion of the sense-world as Ben Lomond.
God reproduces their ideas, and makes the creations
of man a portion of his own. But this does not
meet the point of the objection urged by Hylas.
The production of a motion in myself is very different from the production of a pleasurable sensation in another. A motion, on Berkeley's principles, is only an idea (*Prin.* cxi), and on those
principles an idea cannot be the cause of an idea in
ourselves (*Prin.* xxv), and *à fortiori* cannot be the
cause of a sensation in another. Such a sensation,
it is true, may be referred to the preceding motion,

as its 'concomitant sign' (*Prin.* cxlv); but the relation between sign and thing signified is not the
relation of cause and effect (*Prin.* lxv).   Berkeley,
in fact, concedes the point.   'It is evident,' he
says, 'that in affecting other persons the will of
man hath no other object than barely the motion
of the limbs of his body; but that such motion
should be attended by or excite any idea in the
mind of another depends on the will of the Creator'
(*Prin.* cxlvii).   Berkeley thus adopts the theory of
Divine Assistance, and admits that it is God who
causes certain sensations to exist in one on the
occasion of certain volitions in another.

But the great obstacle in the way of the Berkeleian conception of the world is the difficulty of
realizing it in thought.   The boundless abyss of
space with its infinitude of worlds, the immense
geologic periods through which our own world has
existed, the stupendous convulsions of which the
fabric of the earth has been the scene, the mighty
revolutions to which the human race itself has been
subjected ever since its first appearance on the planet, and the mysterious social forces and miraculous
agencies of nature, which are constantly obtrud-
ing themselves upon our wondering gaze—all these
potent realities persistently decline to be superseded
by ideas, and to be relegated to the realms of shade.
But not only does the ideal theory tax the imagination beyond its strength--it positively reverses
all our natural modes of thought.   We have been
accustomed to believe that the world contains the

soul; but we are required to believe that the soul contains the world. We have been accustomed to believe that the body contains the mind; but we must learn to believe that the mind contains the body. We have been accustomed to believe that our fellow-creatures exist without the mind; but we must constrain ourselves to believe that while their souls exist without the mind, their bodies exist within it. Nay, further, we have been accustomed to think that 'the great globe and all that it inhabit' are contained in space; but we have to learn that *within* and *without* are mere relative ideas, and that space is nothing but the absence of resistance. We have been accustomed to believe that we exist in time; but we have to learn that there is no time for us to exist in—that time is nothing abstracted from the succession of our thoughts. All this must be followed out to its rigorous results. If there is no space but only the idea of space, then there is no motion but only the idea of motion. If there is no time but only the idea of time, then there is no duration but only the idea of duration. The mind therefore is motionless amid commotion; it is a mere *punctam stans* amid the lapse of years. These paradoxes Berkeley fearlessly accepts, and transfers them from the Enneads of Plotinus to the Siris (ss. 270, 271). Speculations like these may silence but they do not satisfy the mind. As Hume remarks, they admit of no answer, but they produce no conviction. Their only effect is to cause that momentary amazement and irresolution and confusion which, as the great sceptic remarks, is only scepticism in disguise (*Works*, iv. 181).

For what, in a speculative point of view, is the value of the idealist philosophy? Consider the points which Berkeley endeavours to establish. He maintains the absolute impossibility of matter; he holds that our sensible ideas cannot be generated from within; he contends that the being of a Spirit infinitely wise, good, and powerful, is abundantly sufficient to explain all the appearances of nature (*Prin.* lxxii). That the contrary of this cannot be proved against him may be well conceded. It is possible that the world of matter may have no existence. It is possible that the soul may be endowed with no originative powers of sense. It is possible that all the sensible ideas which we experience may be the result of the immediate agency of God. But possibility is not proof; and what is the proof which Berkeley adduces that these possibilities are facts? To establish his ultimate conclusion he seems to follow a rigorously inductive method. He professes first to ascertain the facts of consciousness, and then by these facts to test the various hypotheses which have been elaborated to explain them. He collects the various anticipations of the mind; he effects the requisite exclusions or rejections; and he seemingly arrives at the necessary conclusion by induction. The cause of sensation, he says, must be either the world, the soul, or God; but it cannot be the world or the soul; therefore it must be God. But this is a mere travesty of the

Baconian process. It is the form of induction without the power. The principles which it assumes are unverified; the very facts by which he affects to exclude the hypotheses which he rejects are incapable of proof.

For how does Berkeley attempt to prove, as a substantive proposition, that there is no material world? In the first place, he assumes as an axiom, that admits of no dispute, that the mind is conscious only of its own ideas. If it be contended, as it is contended by Hamilton, that the mind has a presentative, objective, intuitive knowledge of material things—that the material world is presented as an existing object, and not merely inferred as an efficient or as a co-operative cause—the idealist appeals to consciousness and denies the fact. We do not perceive matter objectively, he says; we have no immediate intuition of its existence; we are conscious only of our own ideas. But, if matter be not given, why may not its existence be inferred? To conceive matter as existing without the mind, says Berkeley, you must conceive it as existing unconceived; and this, he says, is a contradiction in the very terms in which the so-called conception is expressed (*Prin.* xxiii). But if, as Berkeley himself insists, we can conceive God and finite spirits as existing independently of our conceptions, why may we not conceive the world as similarly existing? The question is put by Hylas, and Philonous merely repeats that, as a matter of fact, we neither objectively perceive, nor rationally appre-

hend, the world of matter (*Dial.* iii). But, says
Berkeley, "what are sensible objects but the
things we perceive by sense; and what do we
perceive besides our own ideas, or sensations; and
is it not plainly repugnant that any one of these,
or any combination of them, should exist unperceived?" (*Prin.* iv). But, as Berkeley's first contradiction was a mere quibble, so his second is a
mere begging of the question. ' All extension exists
only in the mind,' he says (*Prin.* lxvii). But why
may we not hold that there is an extension without
corresponding to the idea of extension which is
within? why may we not hold, with Locke, that our
ideas of the primary qualities are resemblances?
Berkeley answers, 'an idea can be like nothing
but an idea; a colour or figure can be like nothing
but another colour or figure' (*Prin.* viii). But if
the ideas of the primary qualities may not be said
to *resemble*, why may they not be said to *represent*,
their objects? Let us concede, however, that the
world is neither given as an *object*, nor to be imagined as a *counterpart* of our ideas. Why may it
not be supposed as the *cause* of our sensations?
That which is inactive and unthinking, says Berkeley, can never be regarded as the cause of thought.
But why? To assert that matter is inactive is
again to beg the question; to assert that that which
is unthinking cannot be the cause of thought, is to
maintain that like can only be produced by like;
and to rely on either proposition is to maintain that
our human conceptions are the measure of the possi-

bilities of things. Matter, though it should be allowed to exist, says Philonous, is conceived as essentially inactive (*Dial.* ii). But what if it be maintained, with Democritus, that the world is a congeries of atoms, each endued with the principle of motion? What if it be maintained, with Strato, that the several parts of matter are endowed with a plastic life, whereby they dispose themselves to the best advantage? What if we hold with Leibnitz that the world is a system of metaphysical units, each an atom of substance with an internal principle of change? What if we hold with Boscovich, that the world is a system of mathematical points, each a centre of attraction and repulsion, each alive with force? What, in fine, if we embrace the theory which has been handed down from Pythagoras to Pope, and say—

All are but parts of one stupendous whole,
Whose body Nature is, and God the soul?

But granting matter to be active, Berkeley rejoins, we must at least admit it to be incapable of thought. And yet what Materialist will concede him this? Even if it be conceded, the conclusion of Berkeley is unproved. How can that which is unthinking, he asks, be considered as a cause of thought? But here again a whole world of speculation is tacitly assumed. Is it certain that like must be produced by like? What if the theory of Heraclitus be correct, and all effect be the result of *opposition*? Why, in any case, assume the truth of the rival principle which Empedocles professed?

E

That principle is not a law of nature—it is not even a law of thought. It is merely one of the oracular utterances of the great Sicilian—*divini pectoris ejus*—which was accepted as readily by Lucretius in the interests of materialism as it was by Berkeley in support of the theory that there is no such thing as matter.

But there is a psychological difficulty in the way of Berkeley which aggravates the difficulties in the way of his ontologic demonstration. He admits that his system is opposed to vulgar notions. He admits that ' it is an opinion strangely prevailing amongst men, that houses, mountains, rivers, and, in a word, all sensible objects, have an existence natural or real distinct from their being perceived by the understanding' (*Prin.* iv). He admits that men ' act as if the immediate cause of their sensations, which affects them every moment, and is so nearly present to them, were some senseless unthinking being' (*Prin.* liv). Even Mr. Mill, when he reduces the whole material world to ' a permanent possibility of sensation,' is compelled, in like manner to admit that ' the majority of philosophers fancy that it is something more, and that the world at large would, if asked the question, undoubtedly agree with the philosophers' (*Exam.* 235). Berkeley boldly refers the belief to the vast number of prejudices and false opinions which are everywhere embraced with the utmost tenacity by the unreflecting portion of mankind (*Prin.* lv); and endeavours to explain it by the knowledge that our ideas are

'imprinted from without' (*Prin.* lvi)—by the belief that sensible qualities exist without the mind
(s. lxxiii)—by 'a nicer strain of abstraction' (s. v)—
by the fact that 'we are apt to think every noun
substantive stands for a distinct idea' (s. cxvi).*
It is strange that Berkeley, whose whole system is
based on our natural belief in the principles of
substance and causation, should thus attempt to
explain away a belief which is equally natural, and
to banish it to the region of prejudice and false
opinion. Mill, who is quite as dogmatic, is more
consistent. When challenged on the point, he is not
content with resolving the most powerful belief of
the human race into 'the tendency of the human
mind to infer differences of things from differences
of names' (*Exam.* 235). He resolves our idea of
substance into 'the tendency to mistake mental
abstractions, even negative ones, for substantive
realities' (p. 236); he resolves our idea of causation
into 'our tendency to believe, that a relation which
subsists between every individual item of our experience and some other item, subsists also between
our experience as a whole and something not within
the sphere of our experience' (p. 237); and he
triumphantly adds, that 'if all these considerations
put together do not completely explain and account
for our conceiving these possibilities as a class of
independent and substantive entities, he knows
not what psychological analysis can be conclusive'
(p. 238). But what are all these tendencies on

* On Berkeley's views as to Abstract Ideas, see Note B.

which Mill so vigorously insists? If they are natural and necessary tendencies, then, as natural and
necessary, they are in reality a form of those innate
principles which he as strenuously assails; if they
are neither natural nor necessary, then he gratuitously substitutes arbitrary principles of error for a
natural principle of belief, which can never be demonstrated to be false. For the belief in the existence
of matter cannot be compared to the theory that the
earth is flat or to the theory that the sun revolves
around the earth. The existence of the antipodes
and the revolution of the planet are susceptible of
proof. The non-existence of the world of material
things cannot be proved; and till a proof of its
non-existence is supplied by philosophy, the belief
of mankind will ever stand in the way of Idealism—
Idealism can neither explain it, nor refute it, nor
remove it.

Berkeley argues that the being of a Spirit infinitely powerful and wise and good is abundantly
sufficient to explain all the appearances of nature
(*Prin.* lxxii). Mill, in like manner, insists that
'where there is a known cause adequate to account for a phenomenon there is no justification for
ascribing it to an unknown one' (*Exam.* 233). It is
strange that two philosophers who deal so freely
with the laws of human belief should appeal so
confidently to the *Law of Parcimony*—the one to
establish the existence of an ontologic fact, the
other to establish the truth of the merest psycho-
logic guess. It is true that entities are not to be

multiplied in vain. It is true that neither more nor more onerous causes are to be assumed than are necessary to account for the phenomena. That has been the language of philosophers from Hamilton to Occam. But this so-called law of parcimony is a mere regulative principle of thought; it is not a law of logic, and still less is it a law of things. No one has contended more vigorously than Mill that a hypothesis is not to be received as probably true, merely because it accounts for all the known phenomena, when this is a condition which other hypotheses may satisfy as well (*Log.* ii. 20). Estimated by this standard, what is the value of the hypothesis that all our sensible ideas are inspired by God? Grant that it accounts for all the phenomena of nature, there are other hypotheses which equally explain them. It possesses no claim upon our intellectual assent which is not equally possessed by the theories of Physical Influence, of Occasional Causes, of Pre-established Harmony, of the Vision of the Universe in God; while these various theories possess at least one advantage over that of Berkeley, inasmuch as they do not bid defiance to the primeval instinct of the human race.

But the Law of Parcimony is a two-edged weapon in the hands of Berkeley. If we assume the existence of spirit as substance and as cause, why may we not regard *the Soul* as sufficient to account for all the appearances of nature? Berkeley contends that 'the ideas actually perceived by sense have no dependence on the will' (*Prin.* xxix.

cxlvi).   But this overlooks one of the most important of philosophical distinctions—that between spontaneity and volition.   It is well known that far
below the surface of consciousness and will, in the
depths of our mental being, there are agencies at
work which manifest their presence only by the
effects which they produce.   Our instincts, our
tendencies, our appetites, affections and desires,
our very capacities of receiving sensations from
without, if indeed our sensations are to be regarded as determined from without, are instances
of this.   The principle is recognized by Berkeley
himself as one of the fundamental principles of
human knowledge.   The conceptions of causality
and substance are recognized by him as notions
which form part of the necessary and yet spontaneous development of the intellect of man.   Why,
then, may not our sensible ideas be the necessary
and yet spontaneous development of our capacities of sense ? and why may not their very
necessity be regarded as an indication of their
subjective source ?   As Malebranche advanced half
way to Berkeley by acknowledging our sensations
to be caused by God, while he contended that our
ideas of extension are perceived in Him; so Kant,
advanced half way to Fichte, by insisting that our
intuitions of space originate within, while he contended that our sensations are determined from
without.   But why may not the sensations which
supply the matter, as well as the intuitions which
supply the form, originate within ?   Why may not

the phenomena of sense be regarded as the mere
spray and sparkle thrown up by some central fount
of intuition ? Why may not the Soul be regarded
as the creator of the world, which, *ex hypothesi*,
exists within ? It is said the world is peopled. But
if we believe in the existence of finite spirits, we
believe as strongly in the existence of their material
bodies ; in fact, it is from believing in the existence
of their material bodies that we believe in the existence of finite spirits. But as we might possess all
the ideas which we possess, though no external
bodies resembling them existed, so we might possess
all the ideas which we refer to finite spirits, though
there were no finite spirits in existence. Berkeley,
in effect, concedes we might. It is God alone, he
says, who maintains that intercourse between spirits,
whereby they are able to perceive the existence of
each other (*Prin.* cxlvii). But why should philosophy have recourse to God for this ? A soul which
could create the world within, and then project it
outward, could surely people its creation. For what
says Cudworth ? " There is also another more in-
terior plastic power in the soul, if we may so call it,
whereby it is formative of its own cognitions, which
itself is not always conscious of ; as when, in sleep
or dreams, it frames interlocutory discourses betwixt itself and other persons, in a long series, with
coherent sense and apt connexions, in which often-
times it seems to be surprised with unexpected
answers and repartees, though itself were all the
while the poet and inventor of the whole fable "

(*Works*, i. 247). See, then, how Berkeley's argument from dreams and frenzies recoils upon himself; see how the law of parcimony serves him.
" From my own *being*," says Philonous, " and
from the dependency I find in myself and my
ideas, I do, by an act of reason, necessarily infer
the existence of a God, and of all created things
in the mind of God " (*Dial.* iii). But what are
we to understand by necessary inference, by act of
reason? Men cannot believe in the existence of
a God more firmly than they believe in the existence of the world; and rejecting the most powerful
of the spontaneous beliefs of humanity, Berkeley
cannot consistently appeal to common sense. By
necessary inference, therefore, he must mean either
mathematical demonstration, or logical contradiction. That the mathematical method has no application in metaphysics is shown conclusively by
Hume and Kant. Where then is the logical contradiction in the Egoistical doctrine, that there is
originally but one substance, the Ego, and that in
this one substance all possible accidents, all possible
realities, are placed. If we may idealize matter,
why may we not deify the mind? On the principles of Berkeley, there is no answer to Fichte
when he relies on the law of parcimony; there is
no answer even when he contends that the notion
of God as a particular substance is contradictory
and impossible (*Schwegler*, 274).

The Idealism of Berkeley is a bold effort to solve
the mystery of existence—an ingenious guess at the

eternal riddle of the sphinx—an abortive attempt to lift the impenetrable veil. It gives philosophical expression to a vague and floating fancy which will ever haunt the intellects of subtle and refining men. But it is utterly incapable of proof, and it assumes principles which, if we follow them, conduct us to that vast abyss in which man sees nothing reflected but his ignorance and terror.

Compare for a moment the rival theories of Berkeley and Malebranche. The points of contact between the systems of these famous philosophers are many; and yet each point of contact suggests a point of contrast. Both of them believed that though the mind is conscious of nothing but its own ideas, it is able to reach the existence which lies beyond the sphere of self. But while the Oratorian recognized the existence of the three great ontological realities, the Anglican recognized the existence of but two. Both of them believed that the being and attributes of God are susceptible of demonstration. But while the Cartesian endeavoured to demonstrate these momentous facts from our idea of infinity, the follower of Locke endeavoured to demonstrate them from the existence and co-ordination of our sensible ideas. Both of them were devout believers in the infallible authority of revelation. But while the Catholic, following the tradition of his Church, clung to the literal interpretation of Scripture, and held that in the beginning God created the heavens and the earth; the Protestant, exercising his right of private judgment, adopted a different method of interpretation, and held that the creation spoken of by Moses was a mere metaphysical creation. Each agreed that naturally we have no objective knowledge of the world of matter. But, while the one admitted its existence on the supposed authority of revelation, the other rejected its existence on the supposed authority of reason. Each admitted that, to explain the generation of our sensible ideas, we must have recourse to God. But while the one identified himself with God as the Universal Substance, the other recognized him rather as the Primeval Cause. Both agreed that God is the cause of our sensations. But while Malebranche, following the footsteps of Parmenides and Plato, identified our ideas of the primary qualities with the conceptions of the reason; Berkeley, pursuing the path of Protagoras, identified those ideas with sensation, and referred them exclusively to sense. Identifying all our sensible ideas with transient and mutable sensation, Berkeley regarded them all as modifications of the mind of man; identifying our ideas of the primary qualities with eternal and immutable conceptions, Malebranche regarded these as cognitions of the mind of God. Hence while the idea of Berkeley was a state of the mind of man subjectively produced by God, the idea, as distinguished from the sensation, of his rival was an act of the mind of God objectively perceived by man. The system of the one was, accordingly, the creation by God of an ideal universe in man; the system of the other was the vision by man of an actual universe in God.

But the moment that Malebranche thus attained reality, he was confronted by a perilous dilemma. Is the Divine idea numerically distinct from that of the human being who perceives it ? The cognition of an act beyond the sphere of self is as difficult to realize as the cognition of a world of matter. Is the human idea identical with the divine ? The world of matter, it is true, is gained, but forthwith the phantom of Pantheism stares us in the face. Nor did the Catholic philosopher recoil in the presence of the dreaded apparition. He believed in the impersonality of reason. He believed in the existence of the Universal Being. He held that God is the place of spirits, as space is the locus of material things. He held that in God we really lived, and moved, and had our being. And so the Vision of Malebranche dilated into Pantheism, and all human personality disappeared. The existence of God, it is true, was not lost in the hallucinations of self ; but all self, all individuality, was lost in the abyss of God.*

---

* Il est absolument nécessaire que Dieu ait en lui-même les idées de tous les êtres qu'il a créés, puisqu' autrement il n'aurait pas pu les produire, et qu'ainsi il voit tous ces êtres en considerant les perfections qu'il renferme, auxquelles ils ont rapport. Il faut de plus savoir que Dieu est très-étroitement uni à nos âmes par sa présence, de sorte qu'on peut dire qu'il est *le lieu des esprits*, de même que les espaces sont en un sens le lieu des corps. Ces deux choses étant supposées, il est certain que l'esprit peut voir ce qu'il y a dans Dieu qui représente les êtres créés, puisque cela est très-spirituel, très-intelligible et très-présent à l'esprit. Ainsi l'esprit peut voir en Dieu les ouvrages de Dieu, supposé que Dieu veuille bien lui découvrir ce qu'il y a dans lui qui les représente (*Rech*. L. iii. P. ii. c. vi).

Ce qu'ils voient en Dieu est très-imparfait, et Dieu est très-parfait. Ils voient de la matière divisible, figurée, etc., et en Dieu il n' y a rien qui soit divisible ou figuré ; car *Dieu est tout être*, parce qu'il est infini et

Berkeley endeavoured to avoid the precipice which overhangs the Pantheistic gulf, but the path which his philosophy pursued lay in an equally perilous direction. Whatever the result of his philosophy may be, Malebranche, at all events, accomplished his original design. He shared in the divine intelligence; he incorporated himself with the divine substance; he became part of God. In doing this he transcended himself; he grasped reality; he attained the object. Berkeley attempted to reach external existence by the principle of causality. But the principle of causality is, at best, a mere principle of reason; and a principle of reason is essentially subjective; and how can a subjective principle give us an objective fact? The eagle, however powerful his pinion, cannot soar out of, cannot outsoar, himself. The mind, however powerful its principles, cannot, by their aid alone, transcend the mind. Let it mount into the heavens, or plunge into the abyss, it is still the soul, and nothing but the soul—the soul concentrated in itself and its beliefs. It may *believe*, but what is the value of belief on the principles

qu'il comprend tout; mais il n'est aucun être en particulier. Cependant ce que nous voyons n'est qu'un ou plusieurs êtres en particulier; et nous ne comprenons point cette simplicité parfaite de Dieu qui renferme tous les êtres (*ibid.*).

The resemblance between the system of Malebranche and that of Spinosa was the subject of a correspondence between Malebranche and Dortous de Mairan. Malebranche expressed himself horrified at the idea that any resemblance between the two systems should be detected. But as M. Simon remarks: 'Avait-il quelque conscience confuse des rapports de sa philosophie avec celle de Spinosa? Ou cette profonde horreur venait-elle seulement de l'existence d'un analogie qui l'irritait contre Spinosa sans qu'il en reconnût le motif?'

The words with which M. Simon closes his Introduction to his edition of Berkeley ? Repudiating the belief in matter, and reducing it to a mere series of sensations—repudiating the belief in space, and reducing it to the mere absence of resistance—repudiating the belief in time, and reducing it to the mere succession of ideas—how can Berkeley, with any degree of plausibility, insist on the belief that every quality must be supported by a substance, and that every change must be produced by an efficient cause ? But even if the validity of the principles of substance and causation be conceded—if it be conceded that the soul is at once a substance and a cause—the concession is in vain. The being of a Spirit powerful, and wise, and good may be sufficient to account for all the phenomena presented to the mind ; but then comes the Egoist, with his irreverent and inexorable law. You have the principle of causality—why postulate the existence of any cause beyond yourself ? If the soul can create the world, and people it with finite spirits, why may not it create the Infinite himself ? The Infinite is the mere imagination of the finite—God, like the giant phantom of the Hartz, is the mere

of the works of Malebranche, are equally applicable to Berkeley, who, notwithstanding the vast stimulus which he has given to speculation, has been assailed by the same shallow wit which said of Malebranche—

> He who in God sees all things pass,
> Sees he not there that he's an ass ?

Un méchant vers de Faydit—

> Lui qui voit tout en Dieu,
> N'y voit pas qu'il est fou ?

eut une fortune immense. Il est com-mode pour le vulgaire de se débarasser ainsi du fardeau de l'admiration, et d'avoir pitié des hommes de génie ! Ce fou de Malebranche est une de nos grandes gloires nationales ; ses visions métaphysiques sont une école de sagesse et de profonde philosophie, et plaise à Dieu, pour l'honneur de la philosophie et les progrès de l'esprit humain, qu'il puisse naître encore des rêveurs comme lui ! (*Oeuvres de Malebranche*, i. 27).

self-projection of the soul—God is nothing but the moral order. Here, then, we find ourselves at the opposite end of the diameter of thought. Flying from Malebranche, we are met by Fichte. The Pantheism of the one philosopher is exchanged for the Panegoism of the other. The world of matter fades into a dream; all finite spirits vanish; God is a mere vision of the night; and the soul is left the solitary of the universe—the universe is absorbed in self.

But even this utter desolation is not the end. The substantial existence of the soul is inferred by Berkeley from the principle of substance, just as the existence of God is inferred by him from the principle of causation. But if the finite spirit is a substance, the infinite spirit is a substance also; and this suggests a problem the existence of which Berkeley does not seem to have suspected. What is the relation of the two substances, which in kind are one? Is the finite substance part and parcel of the infinite? We then have a single absolutely infinite substance, but it is the substance of Spinoza. Is the finite substance additional to the infinite? The infinite then ceases to be infinite, and we are involved in a contradiction more dangerous than any attributed to Newton. But what is true of the principle of causality is true of the principle of substance also; it is only a belief insisted on by one who disregards beliefs. In fact Berkeley admits that it will be found no easy task to abstract the *existence* of a spirit from its *cogitation* (*Prin.* xcviii).

Here, then, the theological idealist reaches the position where Hume and Hegel are entrenched, and proclaims the identity of thought with being. In the system of Berkeley this element lies latent; but in the system of Hume it is evolved, developed, and avowed. Hume denies the existence, not only of corporeal, but of incorporeal substance (*Works*, i. 33). He maintains that 'the idea of existence is the very same with the idea of what we conceive to be existent' (i. 96). He holds that 'our perceptions may exist separately, and have no need of anything else to support their existence' (i. 299). He boldly asserts that man is 'nothing but a bundle or collection of different perceptions, which succeed each other with an inconceivable rapidity, and are in a perpetual flux and movement' (i. 321). It is true that, in his Essays, the work which he expressly desired to be regarded as alone containing his philosophical opinions, he does not repeat these various assertions. But his earlier creed has survived him, and is the creed of his disciples. Following in the footsteps of Berkeley, Mill defines matter to be a permanent possibility of sensation (*Exam.* 233); following in the footsteps of Hume, he defines mind to be a permanent possibility of feeling (p. 241). Claiming to be a Berkeleian, he discards the ministering principles of the philosophy of Berkeley, causality and substance. He accepts the doctrine that the mind is a mere series of sensations—a series which is destitute of substance—a thread of consciousness, which, though it may be prolonged for ever, is not a thread, but an abstraction (*Exam.* 246).

This, then, is the result in which the philosophy of Berkeley ends. The philosophy which was to banish atheism, and idolatry, and irreligion from the world; the philosophy which was to renovate the sciences, which was to purify morals, which was to spiritualize religion, which was to bring man face to face with God—this high and aspiring philosophy but ends in this. Denying all objective knowledge of existence, it restricts itself to the region of belief; denying the most powerful of beliefs, it enters upon the desert waste of speculation, with no guide but the wandering gleam, the *ignis fatuus* of fancy. Led by this delusive light, it glides past the Pantheism of Malebranche; it traverses the Panegoism of Fichte; it ends in the Nihilism of Mill. Bereft of all metaphysical aid, it sees nothing in the world but self; in self it sees nothing but sensation. It beholds all reality, all existence, fade away. It recognises nothing but images, which are images of nothing. The conception of the poet is realised—

And Nought is everything, and everything is Nought.

PROBLEMATICAL IDEALISM:

OR

HUME.

PROBLEMATICAL IDEALISM:

OR

HUME.

———◆———

Haec autem est una contentio quae adhuc permanserit; nam illud, nulli rei assensurum esse sapientem nihil ad hoc controversiam pertine-bat; licebat enim nihil percipere et tamen opinari, quod a Carneade dicitur probatum.—CIC. ACAD. ii. 24.

WHEN David Hume, at the age of twenty-seven, was concluding the Treatise which contained the germ of the Kritik of the Pure Reason, he professed him-self to be affrighted and confounded with the forlorn solitude in which he was placed by his philosophy. He fancied himself some strange, uncouth monster, who had been expelled all human converse, and left utterly abandoned. " Everyone keeps at a dis-tance," he said, "and dreads the storm which beats upon me from every side. I have exposed myself to the enmity of all metaphysicians, logicians, mathematicians, and even theologians; and can I wonder at the insults I must suffer? I have

declared my disapprobation of their systems; and
can I be surprised if they should express a hatred of
mine, and of my person? When I look abroad, I
foresee on every side dispute, contradiction, anger,
calumny, and detraction" (*Works*, i. 335).

Never was expectation more fully realized;
never was prophecy more literally fulfilled. It
is true that the Treatise of Human Nature, like
the Kritik of the Pure Reason, fell apparently
' dead-born' from the press. It is true that, to
take Hume's own account of the matter, it did not
even reach such distinction as to excite a murmur
among ' the zealots.' But the dead birth of the new
philosophy was only a case of suspended animation,
and the absence of the murmur was only the prelude to the storm. Never since the days when, in
the words of Warburton, the whole Church militant
was thundering on the steel cap of the philosopher
of Malmesbury, had there been developed so fierce a
manifestation of general dislike as was roused by
the philosophy of Hume. The effect on the for-
tunes of the philosopher was injurious enough. He
was denounced before the General Assembly of the
Church of Scotland. He was rejected as a candi-
date for the Chair of Morals in the University of
Edinburgh. He was compelled to resign his ap-
pointment of Librarian to the Faculty of Advocates.
Even his fast friend, Lord Hertford, was afraid to
take him to Ireland when he was appointed to
the Lord Lieutenancy, and left the obnoxious
philosopher as Secretary of the Embassy at Paris.

Among the Parisian freethinkers and fine ladies, Hume, to use his own description of his course of life, ate nothing but ambrosia, drank nothing but nectar, breathed nothing but incense, and trod on nothing but flowers. But among his own country-men, again to use his own expression, he was looked on as a monster. As the type of the sentiments with which he was regarded by his contemporaries, we may take Johnson and the literary circle of which he was the centre. The contemptuous lan-guage in which Johnson habitually indulged, when speaking of him, is familiar to every reader of Bos-well. The philosopher, whom Reid acknowledged as his master, and who aroused Kant from his dog-matic slumber, was derided as a mere sciolist. He was a shallow fellow, a vain creature, a mere imi-tator of Voltaire. He was an enemy of the human race, from whom all the courtesies of contro-versy might be lawfully withheld. He was to be jostled down as a chimney-sweep; he was to be knocked on the head like a highwayman; he was to be treated with as little ceremony as a detected de-bauchee. He had only *lumiéres* enough to light him on his way to hell. This was the language habitu-ally employed by the most eminent literary man of the age, when speaking of the philosopher who was known in foreign society as 'the good David,' who was delineated by Mackenzie as 'the good La Roche,' who was acknowledged even by Boswell to be better than his books, and who was said by the author of the *Wealth of Nations* to have approached as nearly to the ideal of a perfectly wise and good man as the imperfection of humanity would permit.

Nor has Hume's philosophy escaped the detraction to which his character has been exposed. The great thinker, who determined the whole subsequent development of European thought, has been described as a paradoxical philosopher, who believed that there could be no belief. Upon the principles he borrowed from Locke and Berkeley, Hume, according to Reid, reared a system of absolute scepticism, which leaves no rational ground to believe any one proposition rather than its contrary (*Works*, 295). Hume, says Stewart, ended where Descartes began, and considered no one proposition as more certain, or even as more probable, than another (*Works*, i. 437). The great speculator, says Mackintosh, aimed at proving that from the structure of the understanding we are doomed for ever to dwell in absolute and universal ignorance (*Works*, i. 136). In fact, the scepticism attributed to Hume by the Scottish School was that which the doctor expounds to Sganarelle :—Notre philosophe ordonne de ne point énoncer de proposition décisive, de parler de tout avec incertitude, de suspendre toujours son jugement. Sir William Hamilton, it is true, offers to explain away this ultra-Pyrrhonian doubt. "Hume," he says, " as a legitimate sceptic, could not assail the foundations of knowledge in themselves; his reasoning is from their subsequent contradiction to their original falsehood; and his principles, not established by himself, are accepted only as princi-

ples universally conceded in the previous schools "
(*Disc.* 87). But even this, as we shall see, involves
an error as palpable as that of Mackintosh, of
Stewart, and of Reid. The only member of the
Scottish school who seems to have formed any just
conception of the scope of Hume's philosophy was
Brown. On the question of the existence of an external world he saw that Hume was, in reality, at
one with Reid (*Works*, ii. 89). But even Brown
should have gone still further, for it may be demonstrated that on all the leading questions of philosophy Hume was in reality at one with Kant.

The *Treatise of Human Nature* was principally
composed a La Flèche—the little town in Anjou, in
the Jesuits' College of which Descartes received his
education. Planned before he was twenty-one,
composed before he was twenty-five, and published
before he was twenty-seven, the Treatise anticipating, as it does, the problem, the method, the
solution, and the results, which Kant proclaimed
in the Kritik at the age of sixty, must ever be
regarded as one of the miracles of precocious genius.
The leading doctrines of the Treatise of Human
Nature, as is well known, were subsequently reproduced in the *Inquiry concerning Human Understanding*,
which Hume, in his advertisement, desired might be
regarded as alone containing his philosophical sentiments and principles. But the general complexion
of the two productions is the same—qualis decet
esse sororum—and the elder bears the palm. The
Treatise is immortal, though disowned. It em-

bodies one of the permanent types of philosophical opinion. Men may differ as to the justice of the conclusions at which it arrived; but its importance is to be estimated by the influence which it exerted rather than by the information which it conveyed. It imparted a stimulus more powerful than science. Its dogmatism dispelled the idealistic dreams of Reid. Its scepticism disturbed the dogmatic sleep of Kant. Its attempt to construct a universe of thought without any metaphysical admixture is the true antecedent of the absolute of Hegel. And, finally, its nihilistic idealism, and empirical conception of geometry, repudiated by Hume himself in his Inquiry, have, in our own time, been revived and offered to the world as a discovery in philosophy by Mill.

It is by a comparison with Kant that the true philosophical position of Hume is best determined. Paradoxical as the assertion may appear, until it is shown to be the truth, Hume was to Kant what Quesnai was to Smith, and what Copernicus or Kepler was to Newton. With inferior powers of analysis, with less genius for system, with a lower tone of enthusiasm, and with a feebler interest in science, Hume rivalled his illustrious successor, in the clearness of his insight into the nature of the problem to be solved, and the justness of his conception of the method of solution. In every direction he approached, and on many of its most important points he actually reached, the position which was assumed by Kant. In fact his Treatise of Human

Nature may be described as the Kritik of the Pure Reason in its rudimentary and undeveloped state. It was the *premier ébauche* of that great design ; and, if it had proceeded from the same author, might be considered in the same light (to borrow a metaphor from an early and forgotten critic of the Treatise) as a juvenile work of Milton, or the first manner of Raphael, compared with the masterpieces of their genius when matured by time.

The tone of sad but lofty eloquence with which Kant commences his Kritik of the Pure Reason is familiar to every student of philosophy. Metaphysics, once the queen of the sciences, he said, had been deposed. Like Hecuba—modo maxima rerum—she was condemned to poverty and exile. Like Rome, once the mistress of the world, she had been destroyed by internecine feuds, and was the spoil of the barbarians. She was the object of universal indifference, contempt, and scorn. With an eloquence less lofty, and perhaps with a feeling less profound, the predecessor of Kant indulges in a strain of similar reflection. Philosophy, he said, was in a most unsatisfactory condition. The very rabble out of doors might judge, from the noise and clamour which they heard, that all was not going well within (i. 5). The victory in the field of speculation was not gained by the men-at-arms, but by the trumpeters and drummers of the army (i. 6). The philosophers, like the angels, had covered their eyes and obscured their vision with their wings (i. 339). Popular superstitions, like robbers chased from the

open country, had fled into the forest, and lay in
wait to break in upon every unguarded avenue of
the mind (iv. 10).   But Hume, like Kant, perceived
that the metaphysical spirit was immortal in the
mind of man.   It was vain, he said, to hope that
men, from frequent disappintment, would abandon
such airy speculations (iv. 10).   The motive of blind
despair could have no place in science.   Every ad-
venturous genius would find himself stimulated,
rather than discouraged, by the failure of his predecessors (iv. 11).   "The only expedient from which
we can hope for success in our philosophic researches," he says in the Treatise, " is to leave the
tedious, lingering method, which we have hitherto
followed, and instead of taking now and then a castle
or village on the frontier, to march up directly to
the capital or centre of these sciences, to human nature itself; which being once masters of, we may
everywhere else hope for an easy victory" (i. 8).
"The only method of freeing learning at once from
these abstruse questions," he says in his later work,
"is to inquire seriously into the nature of human
understanding, and show, from an exact analysis of
its powers and capacity, that it is by no means fitted
for such remote and abstruse subjects" (iv. 11).
It is only 'after deliberate inquiry' that we can
reject 'the most uncertain and disagreeable part
of learning' (*ibid.*); and 'we must submit to this
fatigue,' he says, anticipating the very words of
Kant, 'in order that we may live at ease for ever
after' (*ibid.*).

It is true that a dissertation upon the absolute necessity of self-examination as the preliminary step in mental science was no novelty in the history of thought. Bacon had insisted on a thorough purification of the intellect, before the marriage of the rational and the empirical faculties could be celebrated for the glory of God and for the benefit of man. Hobbes had proclaimed that philosophy, the child of the world and the mind, was all within; and that it was the function of the thinker, as it was that of the statuary, to remove the superfluous mass, and not to make the image, but to find it. Locke, with still greater distinctness, had enounced the true method of philosophical inquiry; and his sense of its importance had suggested the composition of his immortal Essay. He had seen that the first step towards satisfying the curiosity of man, in the remote inquiries into which it was so apt to run, was to take a view of the understanding, to examine its powers, and to ascertain the subjects to which it was adapted. It was in vain, he said, that we let loose our thoughts into the vast ocean of being; it was in vain that we chased the horizon of knowledge, that ever fled before us. Our prime object should be to consider the capacities of our understandings; to discover the extent of our knowledge; to determine the line which sets the bound between the dark and the enlightened parts of things, between what is and what is not comprehensible by us; and we should then with less scruple acquiesce in the avowed ignorance of the one, and employ our thoughts and discourse with more advantage and satisfaction on the other.

In his examination of human nature, the first thing which attracted the observation of Hume was the profound difference which subsists between its practical and its speculative interests. 'Nature, by an absolute and uncontrollable necessity,' he says in the Treatise, when speaking of Scepticism with regard to Reason, 'has determined us to judge, as well as to breathe or feel; nor can we any more forbear viewing certain objects in a stronger and fuller light, upon account of their customary connexion with a present impression, than we can hinder ourselves from thinking, as long as we are awake, or seeing the surrounding bodies, when we turn our eyes towards them in broad sunshine.' 'Whoever has taken the pains to refute the cavils of this total scepticism,' he adds, 'has really disputed without an antagonist, and endeavoured by arguments to establish a faculty, which nature has antecedently implanted in the mind, and rendered unavoidable' (i. 240). His view of Scepticism with regard to the Senses is as clear as his view of Scepticism with regard to Reason. 'The sceptic,' he says, 'still continues to reason and believe, even though he asserts that he cannot defend his reason by reason; and by the same rule he must assent to the principle concerning the existence of body, though he cannot pretend, by any arguments of philosophy, to maintain its veracity. Nature has not left this to his choice, and has doubtless es-

teemed it an affair of too great importance to be
trusted to our uncertain reasonings and speculations.
We may well ask, what *causes* induce us to believe
in the existence of body? but it is in vain to ask
whether there be body or not. That is a point
which we must take for granted in all our reasonings' (i. 245). This distinction of itself dispels a
cloud of error. It shows that the Scepticism of
Hume is not the contradiction of Mackintosh—'a
belief that there can be no belief' (*Works*, i. 137);
for the utmost it can be reduced to is a belief
that there can be no knowledge. It shows, moreover, that a considerable portion of the subsequent
philosophy of common sense and natural belief was
a mere *ignoratio elenchi*. Hume himself defines his
philosophical position. 'My practice you say refutes
my doubts,' he says, in speaking of our belief in
what is called the uniformity of nature—'but you
mistake the purport of my question. As an *agent*, I
am quite satisfied in the point; but as a *philosopher*,
who has some share of curiosity—I will not say
scepticism—I want to learn the foundation of this
inference' (iv. 47).

But in point of fact Hume does not even entertain the belief that there can be no knowledge; for
nothing can be more dogmatic than the tone which
he adopts when, as a philosopher, he proceeds to
lay the foundations of his system. 'It cannot be
doubted,' he says, 'that the mind is endowed with
several powers and faculties; that these powers are
distinct from each other; that what is really dis-

tinct to the immediate perception may be distinguished by reflection ; and consequently that there is
a truth and falsehood in all propositions on this subject, and a truth and falsehood which lie not beyond
the compass of human understanding' (iv. 12). Nor
did Hume despair of discovering the laws to which
our mental phenomena are subjected. Astronomers,
he said, had long contented themselves with proving,
from the phenomena, the true motions, order, and
magnitude of the heavenly bodies, till a philosopher
at last arose who seems, from the happiest reasoning, to have at last determined the laws and forces
by which the revolutions of the planets are governed
and directed. The like, he said, had been per-
formed with regard to other parts of nature ; and
there was no reason to despair of equal success in
our inquiries concerning the mental powers and
economy, if prosecuted with equal capacity and
caution (iv. 14).

In investigating the domain of Human Nature,
Hume occupies the idealist position at the very outset. "It is universally allowed by philosophers,"
he says, "and is, besides, pretty obvious in itself,
that nothing is ever really present with the mind
but its perceptions, or impressions and ideas, and
that external objects become known to us only by
those perceptions they occasion" (i. 97). And he
does not shrink from the logical consequence of
this. "Since nothing," he says, "is ever present
to the mind but perceptions, and since all ideas are
derived from something antecedently present to the

mind, it follows that it is impossible for us so much as to conceive or form an idea of anything specifically different from ideas and impressions. Let us fix our attention out of ourselves as much as possible; let us chase our imagination to the heavens, or to the utmost limits of the universe; we never really advance a step beyond ourselves, nor can conceive any kind of existence but those perceptions which have appeared in that narrow compass. This is the universe of imagination, nor have we any idea but what is there produced " (i. 97).

Such being the universe of imagination, let us see how Hume proceeds to determine the 'mental geography' of this ideal realm. All the perceptions of the human mind, he says, resolve themselves into two distinct kinds, which he calls impressions and ideas (i. 15). By the term *impression*, he would not be understood to express the manner in which our lively perceptions are produced in the soul, but merely the perceptions themselves (i. 16). These impressions might be divided into two kinds, those of sensation and those of reflection (i. 22). " The first kind," he says, " arises in the soul originally, from unknown causes—the second is derived in a great measure from our ideas" (*ibid.*). An impression first strikes upon the senses—of this impression there is a copy taken by the mind, and this we call an *idea*—the idea, when it returns upon the soul, produces passions, emotions, and desires, which may be called impressions of reflection—these, again, are copied by the memory and imagination, and become ideas (*ibid.*). Ideas are thus the copies of impressions. This is the cardinal point of Hume's philosophy. "Every one," he says, "may satisfy himself in this point by running over as many ideas as he pleases. But if anyone should deny this universal resemblance, I know no way of convincing him but by desiring him to show a simple impression which has not a corresponding idea, or a simple idea which has not a corresponding impression. If he does not answer this challenge, as it is certain he cannot, we may, from his silence and our own observation, establish our conclusion." "The full examination of this subject," he says, "is the subject of the present treatise; and therefore we shall here content ourselves with establishing one general proposition—That all our simple ideas, in their first appearance, are derived from simple impressions, which are correspondent to them, and which they exactly represent" (i. 18).

In professing to have established this general proposition, Hume, it is evident, is so far from sceptically accepting his premises from Locke, that he dogmatically rejects one of Locke's most important doctrines. Locke, it is true, holds that the simple ideas, which are the 'materials' of our knowledge, are suggested and furnished by sensation and reflection; but he also recognizes certain relative ideas, such as those of substance and causation, which are 'superadded' to these materials by the action of the understanding, and which, in his controversy with Stillingfleet, he terms 'rational ideas.' But Hume refused to follow Locke in this. He dogmatically lays it down as an 'obvious principle' that 'reason alone can never give rise to any original idea,' and this dogma determined the whole subsequent course of his philosophy, and constitutes its most conspicuous blemish.

Mr. Hodgson, in his Metaphysical Essay on Time and Space, attributes to Hume the merit of being one of those philosophers who have kept closest to phenomena themselves, without mixing up with their analysis any considerations of their possible origin or causes; but in doing this, he says, he produced a picture of the universe as if it were 'unconnected,' 'incoherent,' and 'the work of chance'; and this was especially the case with his theory of causation (p. 33). Curiously enough, Hume anticipated this very objection, and was most anxious to avert its force. "Were ideas entirely loose and unconnected," he says, "*chance* alone would join them; and it is impossible the same simple ideas should fall regularly into complex ones, as they commonly do, without some bond of union among them, some associating quality, by which one idea naturally introduces another" (i. 26).

The faculty by which our simple ideas are combined is the *Imagination;* and the principles of association by means of which it combines them are resemblance, contiguity, and causation (i. 26). "It is plain," says Hume, "that in the course of our thinking, and in the constant revolution of our

ideas, our imagination runs easily from one idea to
any other that resembles it, and that this quality
alone is to the fancy a sufficient bond and association. It is likewise evident that as the senses, in
changing their objects, are necessitated to change
them regularly, and take them as they lie contiguous to each other, the imagination must, by long
custom, acquire the same method of thinking, and
run along the parts of space and time in conceiving
its objects. As to the connexion of cause and effect
we shall have occasion afterwards to examine it to
the bottom, and therefore shall not at present insist
upon it" (i. 27). "Here," says Hume, "is a kind
of attraction, which in the mental world will be
found to have as extraordinary effects as in the
natural "—" its effects are everywhere conspicuous;
but as to its causes, they are mostly unknown, and
must be resolved into original qualities of human
nature, which I pretend not to explain" (i. 29).

But in Hume's philosophy, as in Kant's, the
work of the imagination is only preliminary to the
work of the *Understanding* proper. "Among the
effects of this union or association of ideas," he
says, "there are none more remarkable than those
complex ideas, which are the common subjects of
our thoughts and reasoning, and generally arise
from some principle of union among our simple
ideas" (i. 29). These complex ideas, following the
example of Locke, he divides into modes, substances,
and relations (*ibid.*). Modes are artificial and arbi-

trary combinations (i. 34). 'The idea of a substance is nothing but a collection of simple ideas that are united by the imagination,' and are 'supposed to be closely and inseparably connected by the relations of contiguity and causation' (i. 33). This is evidently Kant's synthesis of the imagination. But if anyone wishes to see how nearly Hume approached the Kantian position, we must examine his analysis of philosophical relations.

"It may, perhaps, be esteemed an endless task," says Hume, "to enumerate all those qualities which make objects admit of comparison, and by which the ideas of *philosophical relation* are produced" (i. 30). "But," he continues, "if we diligently consider them, we shall find that, without difficulty, they may be comprised under seven general heads, which may be considered as the sources of all philosophical relation" (*ibid.*). These seven general heads are Resemblance—Identity—the relations of Space and Time—the relations of Quantity and Number—the relations of Quality and Degree—the relation of Contrariety—and the relation of Causes and Effects (i. 30, 98). These relations are the *Categories* of Hume. The defects of his analysis are patent. It is guided by no definite preconception. It mingles analytic principles such as identity and contrariety with synthetic principles, such as quantity and quality and relation proper. It makes no distinction between the forms of space and time and the categories of substance and causation. It excludes substance from the list of relations, and treats of it under an independent head.* But it is quite evident that, whatever may be its defects, this analysis of philosophical relations contains the germ of Kant's Analytic of Conceptions, and that the relations of Hume are the categories of Kant in their rudimentary or embryo condition.

But Hume not only gives an Analytic of Conceptions—he gives an Analytic of the Principles in which they are embodied. In his chapter on *Knowledge* he divides the seven relations into two classes—' into such as depend entirely on the ideas which we compare together, and such as may be changed without any change in the ideas' (p. 98). If we follow out this distinction, "it appears," he says, "that of these seven philosophical relations there remain only four which, depending solely on ideas, can be the objects of knowledge and certainty. These four are resemblance, contrariety, degrees in quality, and proportions in quantity and number. Three of these relations are discoverable at first sight, and fall more properly under the province of intuition than demonstration" (i. 99), which, as we shall see, is restricted to the relations of quantity and number (iv. 190). "This," says Hume in his chapter on *Probability*, "is all I think necessary to observe concerning those four relations which are the foundation science; but as to the

---

* Kant, however, admits that substance is to be regarded as a category, not because it is itself relative, but because it is the condition of relation (p. 140); and he also admits that substance is more easily recognized through the conception of action than through that of permanence (p. 151).

other three, which depend not on the idea, and may
be absent or present while that remains the same, it
will be proper to explain them more particularly.
These three relations are identity, the situations in
time and place, and causation" (i. 103). Of these
the most important is causation, for "it is only
causation which produces such a connexion as to
give us assurance from the existence or action of
one object that it was followed or preceded by any
other existence or action. Nor can the other two
relations ever be made use of in reasoning, except
so far as they either affect or are affected by it'
(i. 104). With reference to the principles thus
established, Hume gives a second challenge to philosophers—to adduce any proposition which is intuitively certain besides those which he admits.
" Anyone who would assert it to be intuitively certain," he says, " must deny these to be the only infallible relations, and must find some other relation
of that kind to be implied in it, which it will then
be time enough to examine " (i. 110).

It is evident from this that while Hume rejects
what is roughly called Locke's Theory of the Origin
of Ideas, he accepts his Theory of the Origin of
Knowledge, which distinguishes between certain
and universal knowledge on the one hand, and experimental knowledge on the other (iv. iii. 29), and
which bases the latter on ' experience ' and refers
the former to ' intuitive evidence ' and to ' reason '
(iv. xii. 9). But whether we have regard to our
conceptions or to the principles which they suggest,

whether we consider Hume's theory of ideas or his theory of knowledge, Locke's philosophy supplies an answer to the double challenge of Hume, and shows at once that all our ideas are not copied from our impressions, and that the relations of quantity and number are not the only principles of which we may be intuitively certain.

Of the creatures and inventions of the understanding which were recognised by Locke, he places in the forefront of his philosophy the idea of *Substance* which all our ideas of substances suppose. "When we talk or think of any particular sort of corporeal substances," he says, "though the idea we have of them be but a complication or collection of those several simple ideas of sensible qualities which we used to find united in the thing," yet, "because we cannot conceive how they should subsist alone, nor one in another, we suppose them existing in, and supported by, some common subject" (ii. xxiii. 4). This was the supposition of we know not what, which in the Indian story underlay the tortoise which supported the elephant which sustained the world (s. 2). All this was foolishness to Hume. "The opinions of the philosophers about substance and accident," he said, "are like the spectres in the dark, and are derived from principles which, however common, are neither universal nor unavoidable in human nature" (i. 290). 'We have no idea of substance' he said, 'distinct from that of a collection of particular qualities' (i. 33). He repeats his challenge. "I desire those philosophers," he says, "who pretend we have an idea of the substance of our minds, to point out the impression that produces it, and tell distinctly after what manner that impression operates, and from what object it is derived" (i. 298). His "conclusion" is "that since all our perceptions are different from each other, and from everything else in the universe, they are also distinct and separable, and may be considered as separately existing, and may exist separately, and have no need of anything else to support their existence" (i. 299).

Or take the idea of *Causation,* which plays as prominent a part in the philosophy of Hume as the idea of substance does in that of Locke. According to Hume, every impression of sensation 'arises in the soul originally from unknown causes' (i. 22). This is a recognition of the non-sensuous cause of our sensations, the nescio quid of Kant. How, then, does Hume account for the idea of *Efficient Causes*? Hume is undoubtedly entitled to the credit of seeing that, as far as the external senses are concerned, we only find that one fact is followed by another (iv. 74). He is entitled to the credit of having shown, by an exhaustive analysis, that we have no intuition of efficiency, either in the consciousness of motion, or in the consciousness of effort, or in the conscious- ness of volition, whether exerted on the object, or the organ, or the will (*ibid.*). But why may we not form the conception of an efficiency of which we have no intuition? Hume's challenge to the philosophers was 'to show a simple impression which has not a corresponding idea, or a simple idea which has not a corresponding impression' (i. 18). The philosopher produces the conception— the simple idea, as Hume calls it—of efficient cause. Again, what is Hume's reply? "As we can have no idea of anything which never appeared to our outward sense or inward sentiment," he says, "the necessary conclusion seems to be, that we have no idea of connexion and power at all, and that these words are absolutely without any meaning whatsoever" (iv. 87). Hume challenges the philosophers to produce any proposition that is intuitively certain besides those of mathematics. The philosopher produces the principle which asserts that whatever began to exist must have a cause of existence; and Hume replies, that 'anyone who would assert it to be intuitively certain must deny these to the only infallible relations,' which are unalterable so long as the ideas to which they relate remain the same (i. 110). Here it is evident that Hume only eludes his adversary by shifting in a circle. "I believe," says Hume, referring to Locke's celebrated chapter upon Power, "that the most general and most popular explication of this matter is to say, that finding from experience that there are several new productions in matter, such as the motions and variations of body, and concluding there must somewhere be a power capable of producing them, we arrive at last, by this reasoning, at the idea of power and efficiency" (i. 208). "But," says Hume, "to be convinced that this explication is more popular than philosophical, we need but reflect on two very obvious principles :—*first*, that reason alone can never give rise to any original idea ; and *secondly*, that reason, as distinguished from experience, can never make us conclude that a cause or productive quality is absolutely requisite to every beginning of existence " (i. 209, 227).

Whether any particular intelligence can conceive a collection of qualities as existing without essential substance, or can conceive the collection as beginning to exist without an efficient cause, is one of those questions which that particular intelligence must determine for itself. Locke found himself unable to form such a conception, and recognized substance and causation as 'relative ideas.' Berkeley found himself unable to form such a conception, and admitted substance and causation into his philosophy as 'notions.' Hume protested he could conceive what was inconceivable to Berkeley and to Locke. Rejecting the Berkeleian notion, he consistently rejected the Berkeleian theory in both its aspects. Ignoring the conception of efficiency, he saw no necessity for ascribing our ideas to the Deity as *cause ;* and ignoring the conception of inhesion, he saw no necessity for looking on the mind as the *substance* in which ideas must subsist.

In thus confining himself to the phenomena of the mind, analyzing their laws, and excluding all consideration of their efficient causes and of their subjects of inherence, Hume developed a system of psychological idealism without any metaphysical admixture whatsoever. Recognizing nothing in the world but mind, and recognizing nothing in the mind but a system of perceptions, he regarded perception as the sole existence. " There is no impression nor idea of any kind of which we have any consciousness or memory," he says, " that is not conceived as existent; and it is evident that, from this consciousness, the most perfect idea and assurrance of *being* is derived" (i. 95). " From hence," he continues, " we may form a dilemma, the most clear and conclusive that can be imagined, viz., that since we never remember any idea or impression without attributing existence to it, the idea of existence must either be derived from a distinct impression, conjoined with every perception or object of our thought, or must be the very same with the idea of the perception or object " (*ibid.*). His determination is, that " the idea of existence is the very same with the idea of what we conceive to be existent" (i. 96). He thus reaches the conclusion which Parmenides, from a different starting-point, had reached—

ταὐτὸν δ᾽ ἐστὶ νοεῖν τε καὶ οὕνεκέν ἐστι νόημα.

He teaches the doctrine which was taught by Plotinus in the Alexandrian schools. He anticipates, in fine, the famous postulate of Hegel, and proclaims the identity of thought and being.

But if being is identical with thought, the greater is the necessity for thinking. If the ideas of body, which form so large a portion of the system of perceptions, which is called the mind, are mere 'collections,' there must be some process of thinking to collect them. If the mind is but a system of perceptions linked together by the relation of cause and effect, even in its mere psychological aspect, that relation must be thought. Nor does Hume evade his obligations in this respect, for the main characteristic of his philosophy is his theory of *Physical Causation.* It is here that he is most conspicuously on the track of Kant. He anticipates the Kantian view in stating that "the only relation that can be traced beyond our senses, and informs us of existence and objects which we do not see or feel, is causation" (i. 104)—that "it is only causation which produces such a connexion as to give us assurance from the existence or action of one object that it was followed or preceded by any other existence or action" (*ibid.*). He anticipates the Kantian view in stating that the relation of cause and effect is the only relation which involves the idea of a 'necessary connexion' (i. 206). Again he anticipates the Kantian view when he proclaims that this idea of necessary connexion can never be discovered in the object. "I turn the object on all sides," says Hume, " in order to discover the nature of this *necessary connexion,* and find the impression, or impressions, from which its idea may be derived. When I cast my eye on the known qualities of objects, I immediately discover that the relation of cause and effect depends not in the least on *them.* When I consider their relations, I can find none but

those of contiguity and succession, which I have
already regarded as imperfect and unsatisfactory.
Shall the despair of success make me assert that I
am here possessed of an idea, which is not preceded
by any similar impression ?   This would be too
strong a proof of levity and inconsistency ; since
the contrary principle has been already so firmly
established as to admit of no further doubt, at least,
till we have more fully examined the present difficulty " (i. 108).

Hume accordingly devotes himself to the investigation of the origin of this idea.   In this investigation he resolves to " proceed like those who, being
in search of anything that lies concealed from them,
and not finding it in the place they expected, beat
about all the neighbouring fields, without any certain view or design, in hopes their good fortune will
at last guide them to what they search for" (i. 108).
Like Kant, he resolves to reverse the process.   Instead of regarding the conception as conforming to
the object, he asks whether the object might not possibly be regarded as conforming to the conception.
"Having found," he says, "that after the discovery
of the constant conjunction of any objects, we always
draw an *inference* from one object to another, we
shall now examine the nature of that inference, and
of the transition from the impression to the idea ";
and " perhaps," he says, " it will appear in the end
that the necessary connexion depends on the inference, instead of the inference's depending on the
necessary connexion' (i. 123).

The argument by which Hume proceeds to establish this position so completely corresponds with that of Kant that it might well be mistaken for an extract from the Kritik. What is the authority for our inference that objects are necessarily connected, and that the future will be a reproduction of the past? According to Hume, " there can be no *demonstrative* arguments to prove that those instances of which we have had no experience resemble those of which we have had experience "; for " we can at least conceive a change in the course of nature, which sufficiently proves that such a change is not absolutely impossible' (i. 123). Neither, according to Hume, can the proposition be proved by any arguments from *probability ;* for " probability is founded on the presumption of a resemblance betwixt those objects of which we have had experience, and those of which we have had none ; and therefore it is impossible this presumption can arise from probability," inasmuch as " the same principle cannot be both the cause and effect of another "— an axiom which Hume regards as ' the only proposition concerning that relation which is either intuitively or demonstratively certain' (i. 124). But arguments from probability are only arguments from *experience*, and Hume treats the argument from experience thus :—" Should it be said that we have experience that the same power continues united to the same object, and that like objects are endowed with like powers, I would renew my question, why from this experience we form any conclusion be-

yond those past instances of which we have had experience ?   If you answer this question in the same
manner as the preceding, your answer gives still
occasion to a new question of the same kind, even
in infinitum, which clearly proves that the foregoing reasoning had no just foundation" (i. 126).
But not only does Hume propose the Kantian
question and pursue the Kantian method, but he
arrives at the Kantian conclusion.   He doubts not
but his sentiments will be treated by many as extravagant and ridiculous (i. 222), but his conclusion
is that " the necessity of power, which unites causes
and effects, lies in the *determination of the mind* to
pass from the one to the other," just " as the necessity which makes two times two equal to four, or
three angles of a triangle equal to two right ones,
lies only in the act of the understanding by which
we consider and compare these ideas " (i. 220).

So impressed was Hume with the novelty of his
principle and the importance of his discovery that
the object of his Inquiry was little more than to
popularize the theory of the Treatise on this subject
of causation.   It was the main question with which
he was concerned.   "Hume," says Kant, "was
wrong in inferring from the contingency of the
determination according to law, the contingency of
the law itself; and the passing beyond the conception of a thing to possible experience (which is an à
priori proceeding, constituting the objective reality
of the conception), he confounded with our synthesis
of objects in actual experience, which is always, of

course, empirical" (p. 466). But, unfortunately for Kant, Hume takes the very distinction which Kant charges him with having overlooked. " These two propositions " " are far from being the same—*I have found* that such an object has always been attended with such an effect ; and *I foresee* that other objects which are in appearance similar will be attended with similar effects " (iv. 42). " As to *past experience*," he says, " it can be allowed to give direct and certain information of those precise objects only, and that precise period of time which fell under its cognizance ; but why this experience should be *extended to future times* and to other objects, which, for aught we know, may be only in appearance similar; this," he says, " is the main question on which I would insist" (iv. 42). This main question of Hume, it is evident was the question, which, according to Kant, constituted the grand problem of the Transcendental Philosophy—How are synthetic judgments à priori possible ? (pp. 12, 44.) " All our experimental conclusions," he says, "proceed upon the supposition that the future will be conformable to the past: to endeavour, therefore, the proof of this last supposition by probable arguments, or arguments regarding existence, must be evidentally going in a circle, and taking that for granted which is the very point in question" (iv. 44). This may be regarded as the *formula* of Hume, " To say the inference is experimental," he says, " is begging the question, for all inferences from experience suppose as their foundation that the future will resemble the past, and that similar powers will be conjoined with similar visible qualities" (iv. 46). " It is impossible," he repeats, " that any arguments from experience can prove this resemblance of the past to the future, since all these arguments are founded on the supposition of that resemblance" (*ibid.*). How then is the inference to be explained? It is not an *intuitive* principle, he says; for " it implies no contradiction that the course of nature may change" (iv. 43). Neither is it a *demonstrative* truth; for " there is required a medium which may enable the mind to draw such an inference." How then is it to be explained? No reading, no inquiry, he says, had been able to remove his difficulty, or give him satisfaction on a matter of such importance (iv. 47). His conclusion was a simple one, though, he confessed, pretty remote from the common theories of philosophy (iv. 56). It was that " as nature has taught us the use of our limbs without giving us the knowledge of the muscles and nerves by which they are actuated, so she has implanted in us an *instinct* which carries forward the thought in a corresponding course to that which she has established among external objects" (iv. 66); and that thus there is ' a kind of pre-established harmony between the course of nature and the succession of our ideas' (iv. 65)—the very conclusion at which, as we shall hereafter see, the great Transcendentalist himself arrived.

Hume's anticipation of Kant's theory of causation

might have been regarded as complete had it not
been for his unfortunate dogma—that reason can
supply us with no original idea, and that every idea
is the copy of an impression. This compelled him,
in considering the relation of cause and effect, whether as a philosophical or as a natural relation—
whether as a comparison of two ideas, or as an association between them (i. 225)—to confine himself to
the related ideas, and ignore the idea of relation.
Hence it is that he defines a *cause* to be ' an object
precedent and contiguous to another, and so united
with it that the idea of the one determines the mind
to form the idea of the other, and the impression of
the one to form a more lively idea of the other'
(*ibid.*). Hence it is that he regards ' the impression
which affords us the idea of *necessity*' as being the
' determination of the mind' when, ' upon the appearance of one of the objects, the mind is determined by custom to consider its usual attendant,
and to consider it in a stronger light upon account
of its relation to the first object' (i. 207). But his
dogma not only compels Hume to ignore the conception of causation, and to distort the conception
of necessity which accompanies it, but it compels
him to misrepresent the important operation of the
mind by which the conception is attended. According to Hume, flame is constantly conjoined
with heat, and snow is constantly conjoined with
cold; and if, after experience of this constant conjunction, says Hume, ' flame or snow be presented
anew to the senses, the mind is carried by custom

to expect heat or cold, and to believe that such a quality does exist, and will discover itself upon a nearer approach' (iv. 56). *Belief*, according to Hume, 'is more properly an act of the sensitive than of the cogitative part of our natures' (i. 240). Being thus referred to the sensitive portion of our nature, belief comes under the purview of the dogma. According to Hume, it does nothing but vary the manner in which we conceive an object, and can only bestow on our ideas additional vivacity and force; and accordingly 'belief,' he says, 'may be most accurately defined a lively idea related to or associated with a present impression' (i. 132).

It is evident that it would have been far wiser for Hume to have modified his dogma in order to explain these various ideas, rather than to have mutilated the ideas in order to retain the dogma. But even in the dogma there is an element of truth. As Hume truly remarks, 'it is impossible for us to *think* of anything which we have not antecedently *felt*, either by our external or internal senses' (iv. 73). This is the doctrine of the Kritik; but Kant goes further in his approach to Hume. Though he recognises the Categories as the great instrument of thinking, he admits that in themselves they are mere 'forms of thought' (p. 174)—'mere functions of the understanding' (p. 113)—mere rules for the anticipation of experience (p. 160)—mere abstractions which, without the aid of the process which he calls *schematism*, could never be represented as an image (p. 110)—mere conceptions of the understanding which, apart from intuitions of sense, are absolutely void (p. 46).

Whether Hume was consistent, in regarding *custom* as the chronological condition of the development of the idea of causation, may well be doubted. If, as he consistently holds, the idea of causation is presupposed in *all* our experimental conclusions, it must be presupposed in the *first* of such conclusions as much as in the last. It may be true, as Archer Butler remarks in his *Lectures on the History of Ancient Philosophy*, that though habit cannot originate the belief, it may confirm it, and that Hume's theory derives its plausibility from that fact (ii. 87). It may be true, as Bishop Butler remarks in his *Analogy*, that probable evidence is essentially distinguished from demonstrative by this, that it admits of degrees, and that though a man's having observed the ebb and flow of the tide to-day affords some sort of presumption that it may happen again to-morrow, yet it is only the long-continued experience of mankind which gives us full assurance that it will (pp. 1. 2). But in the consideration of Hume's philosophy this is a minor point. The main point is, that he refers the belief in the uniformity of nature not to experience but to instinct. " This instinct," he says, " it is true, arises from past observation and experience; but can anyone give the ultimate reason why past experience and observation produces such an effect, any more than why nature alone should produce it?" (i. 235).

It is evident from what precedes that, in his

position that all our experimental arguments are based on the anticipation of experience which is implied in the law of physical causation, and that therefore this law must be regarded as a determination of the mind itself, Hume not only recognized the existence of synthetic a priori judgments in all physical science, but showed how such synthetic a priori judgments were possible, by referring them to a determination of the mind.   But there is another class of synthetic a priori judgments which Hume recognized, though he did not explain their possibility by applying to our intuitions of space and time the reasoning which he had applied to our conception of causation.   He held that "the ideas of space and time are no separate or distinct ideas, but merely those of the manner or order in which objects exist" (i. 62); and that "as it is from the disposition of visible and tangible objects we receive the idea of space, so from the succession of ideas and impressions we form the idea of time" (i. 56). But Kant went utterly astray when he charged Locke and Hume with attempting to explain mathematical science by an 'empirical derivation' (p. 79). He did not observe that though Hume rejected Locke's theory of the origin of ideas, he accepted Locke's theory of knowledge; and he did not observe that Locke's theory of knowledge referred the first principles of mathematics to 'intuitive evidence' and 'reason,' just as his theory of ideas recognized the ideas of relation which were the creatures and inventions of the understanding.

As to Hume's opinion with reference to the
a priori character of mathematics, there can be no
intelligent diversity of opinion. " All the objects
of human reason or inquiry," he says, " may naturally be divided into two kinds—to wit, *Relations of
Ideas* and *Matters of Fact.* Of the first kind are the
sciences of geometry, algebra, and arithmetic; and,
in short, every affirmation which is either intuitively
or demonstratively certain. That the square of the
hypotenuse is equal to the square of the two sides
is a proposition which expresses a relation between
these figures. That three times five is equal to the
half of thirty expresses a relation between these
numbers. Propositions of this kind," he says, " are
discoverable by the mere operation of thought without dependence on what is anywhere existent in the
universe " (iv. 32). In his earlier work, Hume, it
is true, had made a distinction between geometry
on the one hand, and algebra and arithmetic upon
the other. Holding all the primary mathematical
relations to be ' discoverable at first sight,' and to
fall ' under the province of intuition' (i. 99), he
nevertheless had held that geometry never attained
perfect precision and exactness, and therefore could
scarcely be regarded as a perfect science (i. 100).
The objects of geometry, he had said, not only
never did, but never could, exist in nature; no one
could pretend to draw a line, or make a surface conformable to the definition (i. 66). The standard of
equality in geometry was, therefore, loose (i. 73),
and the mind only proceeds to imagine a standard

more correct, as a galley, put in motion by its oars, is carried on its course without a new impulsion (i. 258). But Hume, upon reconsideration, did not care to reaffirm the tenet of his youth. He abandoned the doctrine of the Treatise, and left it derelict, to be appropriated as a discovery in the logic of the sciences by his successors. In his Inquiry he holds with Locke and with Kant that, "though there never were a circle or triangle in nature, the truths demonstrated by Euclid would ever retain their certainty and evidence" (iv. 32), and maintains that all mathematical propositions alike are independent of experience, and that they are alike discoverable by the mere operation of thought.

Nor was Hume ignorant of the different characteristics which distinguish our synthetical a priori judgments in mathematics from our synthetical a priori judgments in experimental science. "All other inquiries of men," he says, " regard only *Matter of Fact and Existence;* and these are evidently incapable of demonstration," since ' the existence of any being can only be proved by arguments from its cause or its effect' (iv. 34). Nor are the physical sciences an exception to this general assertion; for though ' every part of mixed mathematics proceeds upon the supposition that certain laws are established by nature in her operations' still ' the discovery of the law itself is owing merely to experience' (iv. 39). ' The contrary of every matter of fact is still possible, because it can never imply a contradiction, and is conceived by the mind with the same facility and distinctness as if ever so conformable to reality,' and therefore the evidence of its truth, however great, is not of a like nature with the evidence of mathematics (iv. 33). And Hume proceeds to develop the difference between them. 'The component parts of quantity and number,' he says, 'are entirely *similar*,' whereas 'all other ideas are clearly distinct and *different* from each other' (iv. 190)—for 'in this kind of reasoning from causation we employ materials which are of a mixed or *heterogeneous* nature' (i. 117). Although *necessity* is always ascribed to causes and effects, yet 'we have no notice of any necessity of connexion' beyond 'the constant conjunction of similar objects and the consequent inference from one to the other' in the course of our experience (iv. 97 ; i. 206); for 'it is only *experience* which teaches us the nature and bounds of cause and effect, and enables us to infer the existence of one object from that of another' (iv. 191). But 'while we cannot give a satisfactory reason why we believe after a thousand experiments, that a stone will fall, or fire burn; can we ever satisfy ourselves concerning any determination which we may form with regard to the origin of worlds, and the situation of nature from and to eternity ?' (iv. 190). 'It seems to me,' then, says Hume, 'that the only objects of the abstract sciences, or of demonstration, are quality and number, and that all attempts to extend this more perfect species of knowledge beyond their bounds are mere sophistry and illusion' (iv. 191).

It must be clear to the student of the Kantian philosophy that Hume's Relations of Ideas and Matter of Fact correspond to the *Mathematical and Dynamical Principles* of the Understanding, as Kant explains them in the Kritik—the one relating to intuition alone, the other to the existence of phenomena (p. 121)—the one effecting a synthesis of the homogeneous, the other a synthesis of things which, although heterogeneous, are represented a priori as connected by the principles of causality and substance (p. 122); the one constitutive of the phenomena so as to determine their existence, the other regulative of the understanding, so as to render possible their apprehension (p. 135); the one characterized by an absolute necessity, the other only conditionally (p. 121), and hypothetically (p. 170) necessary; the one, in fine, supplying a basis for mathematics as an apodeictic science, the other supplying a basis for natural science within the limits of experience, but supplying no basis for a science of metaphysics, considered as a science of supersensible existence (p. 328).

And in showing that metaphysics, as contrasted with the physical sciences and mathematics, are mere sophistry and illusion, Hume again anticipates the method and the arguments of Kant. If Kant in his *Rational Psychology* declares that the mind has no intuition of itself, and that we can never ascertain by reasoning whether there exists any object to correspond to our conception of the soul as a substance, simple, identical, and distinct from body (pp. 239, 244)—Hume maintains that others 'may perceive something simple and continued which he calls *himself*': but he is certain that there is no such principle in *him* (i. 321); and the fact that we have no satisfactory notice of substance, whether mental or material, seems to him a sufficient reason for abandoning utterly that dispute concerning the materiality and immateriality of the soul and makes him absolutely condemn the very question (i. 299). In his *Transcendental Theology* Kant proclaims that the fallacy of every attempt of the speculative reason to establish the existence of a God by way of demonstration is shown by this—that "in whatever way the understanding may have attained to a conception, the existence of the object of the conception cannot be discovered in it by analysis, because the cognition of the existence of the object depends upon the object's being posited and given in itself apart from the conception" (p. 392). These are the very words of Hume. "In the proposition *God is*, or indeed any other which regards existence, the idea of existence is no distinct idea which we unite with that of the object, and which is capable of forming a compound idea by the union" (i. 132). The inference of an Intelligent Cause is uncertain ' because the subject lies entirely beyond the reach of human experience' (iv. 166); and 'it is only experience which teaches us the nature and bounds of cause and effect, and enables us to infer the existence of one object from that of another' (iv. 191).

But nowhere, according to Hume, is the so-phistry and illusion of the so-called metaphysical sciences more patent than in the attempts that have been made to establish a system of *Rational Cosmology*, and to demonstrate the existence of an external world of matter.   It was with regard to the Senses that his scepticism was most pronounced.   The trite topics which Cicero, as the representative of the Academic school, had adduced, when arguing with Lucullus, Hume did not insist on.   He proposed an argument more profound than that based upon the crooked appearance of the oar in water, or the shifting colours on the bosom of the dove (iv. 176). He acknowledged it to be evident that " men are carried by a natural instinct, or prepossession, to repose faith in their senses; and that, without any reasoning, or even almost before the use of rea-son, we always suppose an external universe which depends not on our perception, but would exist though we and every sensible creature were absent or annihilated " (iv. 177).   But, he said, " it seems also evident, that when men follow this blind and powerful instinct of nature, they always suppose the very images presented by their senses to be the external objects, and never entertain any suspicion that the one are nothing but representations of the other " (iv. 177).   " But this universal and primary opinion of all men," he says, " is soon destroyed by the slightest philosphy, which teaches us that no-thing can ever be present to the mind but an image or perception, and that the senses are only the inlets through which these images are conveyed, without being able to produce any immediate intercourse between the mind and the object" (iv. 177). " So far, then," he continues, " are we necessitated by reasoning to contradict, or depart from, the primary instincts of nature, and to embrace a new system with regard to the evidence of our senses" (iv. 178). " But here philosophy finds herself extremely embarrassed when she would justify this new system, and obviate the cavils and objections of the sceptics" (iv. 178). It is evident that ' it is a question of fact whether the perceptions of the senses be produced by external objects resembling them'; and this question of fact, like all other questions of fact, must be determined by *experience.* " But here," says Hume, " experience is and must be silent, for the mind has never anything present to it but the perceptions, and cannot possibly reach any experience of their connexion with objects' (iv. 179). Is the question then to be determined by *reason*? ' To justify the pretended philosophical system by a chain of clear and consistent argument exceeds the power of all human capacity' (iv. 178); "for by what argument," he asks, " can it be proved that the perceptions of the mind must be caused by external objects, entirely different from them, though resembling them, if that be possible, and could not arise either from the energy of the mind itself, or from the suggestion of some invisible or unknown spirit, or from some other cause still more unknown to us?" (iv. 178; i. 117). This, then, is the philosophical position. "Do you follow the instincts and propensities of nature in assenting to the veracity of sense ? But these lead you to believe that the very perception or sensible image is the external object. Do you disclaim this principle in order to embrace a more rational opinion that the perceptions are only representatives of something external ? You here depart from your natural propensities and more obvious sentiments, and yet are not able to satisfy your reason, which can never find any convincing argument from experience to prove that the perceptions are connected with any external objects" (iv. 179). This is Hume's *dilemma.* The opinion of external existence, he says, "if rested on natural instinct, is contrary to reason, and, if referred to reason, is contrary to natural instinct, and at the same time carries no rational evidence with it, to convince an impartial inquirer" (iv. 181).

In thus pointing out the sophistical and illusive character of the ordinary arguments by which metaphysicians propose to demonstrate the existence of the external world, Hume anticipated the philosophy of Reid. But he went further, and again anticipated the more profound philosophy of Kant. When men follow the blind and powerful instinct of nature, they always suppose the very images presented by the senses to be the external objects (iv. 177). This is the *Transcendental Realism* of the Kritik ; for 'the realist in the transcendental sense regards the modifications of our sensibility, its mere representations, as things subsisting by themselves' (p. 307). But this *Transcendental Illusion*, as Kant calls it, involves the human reason in a conflict with itself. Had the world a beginning, or had it not? Is matter infinitely divisible or not? Is a free causality necessary to originate the phenomena of the world or no? Is there, or is there not, a necessary being required to account for the existence of the world? On each of these questions the thesis and antithesis are alike sustainable by reason, and this conflict of reason with itself was the *Transcendental Antithetic.* Kant settles the dispute by proclaiming that the combatants are fighting about nothing, and that it is no transcendental reality that is presented to us, but *phenomena* only (p. 315). Again, this is the philosophy of Hume. He, too, contemplated this conflict of reason, and perceived the true solution (i. 78). " As long as we confine our speculations to the *appearances* of objects to our senses," he says in the Treatise, "without entering into disquisitions concerning their real nature and operations, we are safe from all difficulties, and can never be embarrassed by any question " (i. 92, 93). " It seems to me not impossible to avoid these absurdities and contradictions," he says in the Inquiry, " if it be admitted that there is no such thing as abstract, or general ideas, properly speaking," and " that all the ideas of quantity, upon which mathematicians reason, are nothing but particular, and such as are suggested by the senses and imagination, and consequently cannot be infinitely divisible " (iv. 184). " It is

sufficient to have dropped this hint," he says, "without prosecuting it any further " (*ibid.*). The further
prosecution was reserved for Kant; and the hint
dropped by Hume was elevated by his successor
into the Critical Solution of the Cosmologic Problem (p. 310).

But while Hume, like Kant, pronounces metaphysics to be mere sophistry and illusion, he at the
same time, like Kant, pronounces it to be mere
sophistry and illusion when considered in the light
of *demonstration.* " We may well ask," he says,
" what causes induce us to believe in the existence
of body ?   But it is vain to ask, whether there be
body or not—that is a point which we must take
for granted in all our reasonings " (i. 245).   Though
no ' logic ' or ' process of argument ' can secure us
from the supposition that the course of nature may
change, yet as ' agents ' we are ' quite satisfied in
the point ' (iv. 47).   And in the same manner,
though Hume contends that we cannot demonstrate
the existence of a Deity in mathematical form, yet
he admits that ' the whole frame of nature bespeaks
an Intelligent Author,' and that ' no rational inquirer can, after serious reflection, suspend his *belief*
a moment with regard to the primary principles of
genuine theism and religion ' (iv. 435).   In fact,
the whole scope of his argument is shown in the
sentences with which he concludes his discussion
as to the materiality or immateriality of the soul—
sentences so thoroughly imbued with the spirit of
Kant that they read like an extract from the

Kritik : — "In both cases the *metaphysical* arguments for the immortality of the soul are equally inconclusive; and in both cases the *moral* arguments, and those derived from the analogy of nature, are equally convincing. If my philosophy, therefore, makes no addition to the arguments for religion, I have, at least, the satisfaction to think it takes nothing from them, but that everything remains precisely as before" (i. 319).

This contrast between the speculative demands and the practical necessities of human nature is constantly insisted on by Kant. Indeed, he professes to have abolished knowledge in the domain of metaphysics for no other purpose than to make way for belief (p. xxxv). "If anyone could free himself entirely from all considerations of interest," he says, "and weigh without partiality the assertions of *reason*, attending only to their content, irrespective of the consequences which follow from them, such a person, on the supposition that he knew no other way out of the confusion than to settle the truth of one or other of the conflicting doctrines, would live in a state of continued hesitation." "But," continues Kant, "if he were called to *action*, the play of the mere speculative reason would disappear like the shapes of a dream, and practical interest would dictate his choice of principles" (p. 298). This passage, again, might pass for a paraphrase of a dozen passages to be found in Hume. "Though a Pyrrhonian," he says, "may throw himself or others into a momentary

amazement and confusion by his profound reasonings, the first and most trivial event in life will put
to flight all his doubts and scruples"; and, " when
he wakes from his dream, he will be the first to
join in the laugh against himself, and to confess
that all his objections are mere amusement, and can
have no other tendency than to show the whimsical
condition of mankind, who must act, and reason,
and believe, though they are not able by the most
diligent inquiry to satisfy themselves concerning
the foundation of these operations, or to remove
the objections which may be raised against them"
(iv. 187). " These principles," he says, " may flou-
rish and triumph in the schools, where it is indeed
difficult, if not impossible, to refute them.   But as
soon as they leave the schools, and by the presence
of the real objects which actuate our passions and
sentiments, are put in opposition to the more powerful principles of our nature, they vanish like smoke,
and leave the most determined sceptic in the same
condition as other mortals" (iv. 185).

Such being the condition of human nature, the
advice which Hume gives to the philosopher has
been strangely overlooked. 'Be a philosopher,' he
says, ' but, amidst all your philosophy, be still a
man' (iv. 7). And it is the manly character of
Hume's philosophy that constitutes one of its best
titles to our respect. In point of fact, he was
neither a Dogmatist nor a Sceptic—he was the
Sapient of the Academics. Like Carneades, he
abolished perception to make way for assent. Like

Kant, he abolished knowledge to make way for belief. He saw, in fact, that the dispute between the Dogmatist and Sceptic was little better than a dispute about words—a dispute as to whether it was the convex or the concave side of the circumference that formed the circle—a dispute as to whether the suspended shield of the errant knights was made of silver or was made of gold. In his posthumous Dialogues concerning Natural Religion, which he modelled on the form of Cicero's Discourses concerning the Nature of the Gods, and which, in elevation of tone, in eloquence of language, and in comprehensiveness of thought, is worthy of its original, Hume thus describes the nature of the controversy which distracts the rival schools, and effects a compromise between them :—
" It seems evident," he says, " that the dispute between the Sceptics and Dogmatists is entirely verbal, or at least regards only the degrees of doubt and assurance which we ought to indulge with regard to all reasoning ; and such disputes are commonly at the bottom verbal, and admit not of any precise determination. No philosophical Dogmatist denies that there are difficulties both with regard to the senses and to all science, and that these difficulties are, in a regular logical method, absolutely insolvable. No Sceptic denies that we lie under an absolute necessity, notwithstanding these difficulties, of thinking and believing and reasoning with regard to all kinds of subjects, and even of frequently assenting with confidence and security. The only

difference, then, between these sects, if they merit
that name, is, that the Sceptic, from habit, caprice,
or inclination, insists most on the difficulties, the
Dogmatist, for like reasons, on the necessity ''
(ii. 537).

The criticism which Kant passed upon the philosopher who awoke him from his dogmatic slumber
is well known. Hume, he says, stopped short at
the synthetical proposition of the connexion of an
effect with its cause, and insisted that such a proposition a priori was impossible (p. 12). He adopted the
empirical derivation of Locke, and therefore could
not explain how it was possible that conceptions
which are not connected with one another in the
understanding must nevertheless be thought as
necessarily connected in the object (p. 78). He
never clearly developed the notion that we proceed
in judgments of a certain class beyond our conception of the object (p. 464). He confounded the
passing beyond the conception of a thing to possible experience with our synthesis of objects in
actual experience, which is, of course, empiric
(p. 466). He made no distinction between the
well-grounded claims of the understanding and the
dialectical pretensions of the reason (*ibid.*). He
merely declared the understanding to be limited,
instead of showing what its limits were; and he
created a general mistrust in the power of our
faculties, without giving us any determinate knowledge of the bounds of our necessary and unavoidable ignorance (*ibid.*).

The injustice of this criticism is obvious from what precedes. In proposing the question, why experience should be extended to future times and other objects, Hume suggested the *Transcendental Problem* of the Reason. In arguing that the conception of causation could not be derived from experience because all our experimental conclusions are based on the conception of causation, Hume employed the *Transcendental Method*. In holding that nothing can be present to the mind but an image or perception, and in denying that the images presented to the senses are external objects, or things subsisting by themselves, he enounced the conclusion which the *Transcendental Æsthetic* professed to have established (*Kritik*, 307). In holding that the existence of any being can only be proved by arguments from its cause or its effect, and that it is only experience which teaches us the nature and bounds of cause and effect, and enables us to infer the existence of one object from that of another, he, in effect, held that the understanding is competent to effect nothing a priori except the anticipation of the form of a possible expression, and reached the result at which the *Transcendental Analytic* afterwards arrived (*Kritik*, 183). And finally, his position, ' that the only objects of the abstract sciences or of demonstration, are quantity and number, and that all attempts to extend this more perfect species of knowledge beyond these bounds are mere sophistry and illusion,' is the very conclusion of the *Transcendental Dialectic*—the conclusion to the ultimate establishment of which the whole of the Kritik was directed (*Kritik*, 429).

If it should be asked how these resemblances between the conclusions of the two greatest of the philosophers of modern Europe have been over-looked, the answer is obvious. It is the result of the confusion of tongues in which the Babel of Philosophy is involved. The one of the great thinkers spoke English, and the other Greek. Hume saw as clearly as Kant that men will never be induced to abandon the airy sciences from disappointment; that the only method of freeing learning from those abstruse inquiries was to make an exact analysis of the powers and capacities of the human understanding; and that we must submit to this fatigue in order to live at ease for ever after (iv. 10); but, unfortunately, he did not style his analysis a *Propædeutic* or a *Kritik*. He saw that the mind in all its experimental conclusions anticipates its experience without seeing this was a *Synthetic a priori Judgment*; and when he saw that such judgments could not be formed without a determination of the mind, he failed to see that this was the solution of the grand *Transcendental Problem* of Pure Reason. He said that the law of causation could not be founded on arguments from experience, because all arguments from experience are founded on the law of causation (iv. 46, 7); but he had no suspicion that this should be called the *Transcendental Method*. He said the mind was a centre of perceptions; but he did not baptize it the *Transcendental*

Unity of Consciousness. He held that objects are nothing but a collection of simple ideas that are united by the imagination into one (i. 33); but he did not confer upon the collection the title of the *Transcendental Synthesis of the Imagination.* He saw that the philosophical relations which the understanding framed might be classified under seven different heads; but he did not dub them *Categories of the Understanding.* He divided philosophical relations into two classes (i. 98), and the objects of human inquiry into two kinds (iv. 32); but he never dreamt that his relations of ideas and matters of existence were to be elevated to the rank of the *Mathematical and Dynamical Synthesis* of Thought. He saw that when men follow the instincts of their nature they suppose the images presented by the senses to be the external objects (iv. 177); but he did not dream that this was *Transcendental Realism.* He dropped the hint that all our ideas of quantity are nothing but particular, and such as are suggested by the senses (iv. 184); but he had no notion that this hint would ever be developed into the *Critical Solution of the Cosmologic Problem.* He saw that the mind was involved in absurdities and contradictions in its ideas of the world, and that its conclusions as to the nature and essence of the soul were inconclusive; but words of such pretence as the *Antinomies of Cosmology,* or the *Paralogisms of Psychology,* were foreign to his simple tastes. He saw, in fine, that the mind, in straining after the infinite and absolute, was constrained to form the last and most ennobling of ideas;

but he never thought of *Prototypon Transcendentale* as a name for God.

The fact is that Hume employed the simple language of ordinary men, while Kant invented an artificial language for the schools. And the effect of this diversity has been decisive. The two philosophers have spoken a different language, and they have been regarded as holding hostile views. Hence, too, the reputation of the transcendentalist has been exalted, while that of the sceptic has been depressed. In the system of the one there was nothing to impede the progress, and the treacherous facility betrayed the reader into the belief that he was learning nothing; in the system of the other there was a language to be mastered, and the difficulty of mastering it inspired the student with a respect for the thinker who imposed upon him such laborious toil. Nor did the effect terminate in this. The Kantian student is apt to mistake the mastery of a language for the acquisition of a science. Conscious of the possession of a recondite learning, he is inspired with the conceit of a superior knowledge. The vulgar, too, are apt to look with mysterious awe upon what they cannot understand, because they cannot understand it; and hence the different estimation in which the two great philosophers of modern Europe have been held. In the one, the stream of speculation has appeared to be shallow because it was so clear; in the other, it has been regarded as a dark profound, and has been deemed to be the deeper because it was so dark.

The moral deduced from the paralysis of the
speculative reason by the transcendentalist and the
sceptic was the same. Each, while he surrendered
the power of cognising, reserved the power of cogi-
tating, the supersensible. Each, while he abolished
knowledge, made room for belief. Each left the
space which had been left vacant by speculation to
be filled by the principles of action. According to
both, the weakness of our intelligence should induce
us to moderate the strength of our assertions. According to both, the fallaciousness of sense, and the
incompetence of reason, should teach us modesty
and mutual toleration and reserve. According to
both, the result of the most profound philosophy
was the limitation of our inquiries to such subjects
as are best adapted to the narrow capacity of human understanding. The lesson taught by both, in
fine, was that which was taught centuries before by
Socrates, and which generations before Socrates had
been inculcated by that first and saddest of books,
the inspired idyll, in which the Idumean patriarch
bewailed the weakness and the ignorance of man.

What then is the attitude assumed by Hume
with regard to the great mystery of sense, the
problem of the world? By anticipation he rejects
the Natural Realism, or, as it might be better
named, the *Cataleptic Idealism* of Hamilton; for he
denies that there can be any immediate intercourse
between the mind and the object (iv. 177), and
maintains that in perception 'the mind has never
anything present to it but the perceptions, and can-

not possibly reach any experience of their connexion with objects' (iv. 179). In like manner he
repudiates the *Cosmothetical Idealism* of Reid; for he
agrees with Berkeley that the primary qualities of
the objects of sense stand on the same footing as
the secondary, and that the secondary qualities are
'perceptions of the mind without any external arche-
type or model which they represent' (iv. 180). In
holding that the mind is nothing but a collection
of different perceptions which succeed each other
with an inconceivable rapidity, and are in a perpetual flux and movement (i. 321)—above all, in
holding that ' the idea of existence is the very same
with the idea of what we conceive to be existent'
(i. 96)—he seems to accept the *Psychological Idealism*
of Mill. But though in his psychology he refuses
to recognize either the conceptions or the principles
of efficient causation and essential substance, yet in
his metaphysics he finds himself compelled to admit
that our impressions have a cause, and thus to recognize with Kant the existence of a non-sensuous
cause of our sensations. This cause, however, he
regards as essentially unknown, and accordingly he
refuses to identify it with God, and rejects the
Theistic Idealism of Berkeley. For the same reason
he refuses to identify it with the soul, and rejects
the *Egoistical Idealism* of Fichte. "As to those
impressions which arise from the senses," he says
in the Treatise, "their ultimate cause is, in my
opinion, perfectly inexplicable by human reason,
and it will always be impossible to decide with cer-

tainty whether they arise immediately from the object, or are produced by the creative power of the mind, or are derived from the Author of our being" (i. 117). " By what argument can it be proved," he asks in the Inquiry, " that the perceptions of the mind must be caused by external objects, entirely different from them, though resembling them (if that be possible), and could not arise from the energy of the mind itself, or from the suggestion of some invisible and unknown spirit, or from some other cause still more unknown to us ?" (iv. 178). In short, Hume agrees with Kant when he says that the non-sensuous cause of our sensations is "an object of which we are quite unable to say whether it can be met with in ourselves or out of us, whether it would be annihilated together with sensibility, or, if this were taken away, would continue to exist " (p. 206). But although Hume thus agrees with Kant, he formed no conception of the *Transcendental Idealism* of the Kritik. He held that ' the ideas of space and time are no separate and distinct ideas, but merely those of the manner or order in which objects exist ' (i. 62) ; and he seems never to have thought of applying the formula by which he had determined the nature of our conception of causation to the determination of the nature of our ideas of time and space. Indeed, so far is Hume from dogmatically denying the existence of an external world in external space that he systematically assumes it (i. 245). He admits that the arguments against the existence of material things produce

no conviction, though they admit of no answer
(iv. 181). His idealism was merely a *Problematical
Idealism.* He proposed to philosophy a problem,
and he confronted it with a dilemma. His problem was, the ground of the opinion of external
existence; and his dilemma was, that " the opinion of external existence, if rested on natural
instinct, is contrary to reason, and if referred to
reason, is contrary to natural instinct, and at the
same time carries no rational evidence with it to
convince an impartial inquirer" (iv. 181).

This then was the position of the problem as to
the external world when Hume transmitted it to
Reid. Hume had professed to show the whimsical
condition of mankind, who must act, and reason, and
believe, though they are not able, by their most diligent inquiry, to satisfy themselves concerning the
foundation of these operations, or to remove the objections which may be brought against them" (iv. 187).
Let us see how Reid satisfied himself concerning
the foundation of the operations in question, and
how he proposed to remove the various objections
which had been advanced by Hume.

COSMOTHETICAL IDEALISM:

OR

REID.

COSMOTHETICAL IDEALISM:

OR

REID.

Rerum ignarus Imagine gaudet.—VIRG.

THE influence exerted by Reid on the development of European thought has been neither slight nor transitory. Though Hutcheson is regarded as the founder of the Scottish school, it was Reid who gave it character, and consistency, and strength. Stewart avowedly regarded him as his master; and if Brown disputed his authority, the influence of Reid's speculations is everywhere visible in the writings of that brilliant thinker. Attracted by the masculine simplicity and sober common sense of the Scottish sage, men of a far higher order of metaphysical ability, have devoted themselves to the diffusion and elucidation of his writings. The philosophy of the chief of the Scottish school was taught by Royer-Collard, and his complete works were translated for the benefit of continental readers by Jouffroy. The most learned of the philosophers of modern times devoted himself to the development of his doctrine; and Sir William Hamilton's edition of the works of Reid, defective as it may be in point of consistency and form, contains the richest deposit of materials for metaphysical speculation that the literature of philosophy can furnish.

The position of Reid as a philosopher was a peculiar one. He had himself been an idealist (*Works*, p. 88). He had not only been an idealist, but he had been a Berkeleian (p. 283). He had been a Berkeleian though he believed that Berkeley, while rejecting the world of material things, had accepted a world of material ideas (p. 263). Nay, he had been a Berkeleian although he professed himself unable to understand Berkeley's theory of notions, and regarded all his ideas as resolvable into ideas of sensation (p. 289). But the idealism of Hume aroused him from his ideal dreams. He was shocked at the discovery that the mind in which he had supposed the world of ideas to exist was destitute of substance. He found that in descending the winding pathway of ideas he had been conducted, unaware, to the abyss—

> Hic specus horrendum, saevi spiracula Ditis
> Monstrantur; ruptoque ingens Acheronte vorago
> Pestiferas aperit fauces.

Descartes and Locke, he said, had taken the same road, but they did not see the end. Berkeley saw the danger, and endeavoured to avoid it. But the

author of the Treatise of Human Nature was more
daring—he turned neither to the right hand nor to
the left, and like Virgil's Alecto shot boldly and directly into the yawning gulf (pp. 207–8).

When Reid thus fancied that Acheron had burst
its borders, in the first paroxysm of terror, he seems
to have reproached philosophy with the pernicious
and malignant ray which it supplied, and to have
declared his determination to renounce its guidance,
and to allow his soul to dwell with common sense
(p. 101). He railed at philosophy like the old fellow in one of Goldsmith's plays. This same philosophy, said Jarvis, is a good horse in the stable,
but an arrant jade upon a journey. Philosophy,
said Reid, is a hobby-horse, which a sick man
might mount in his closet but could not ride to
the exchange (p. 110). Scepticism was the lunacy
of metaphysics (p. 209). If the sceptic were sin-
cere, he should run his head against the post, he
should step into the kennel, he should walk over the
precipice, and the only way to save him would be
to clap him into a lunatic asylum (p. 184). Sometimes, indeed, Reid takes a loftier tone. The philosophers, he said, had carried on an unequal
contest with common sense. They had engaged in
an attempt no less audacious and abortive than the
attempt of the giants to dethrone great Jove (p. 101).
The principles of common sense were the inspiration of the Almighty, and those who disowned their
authority proclaimed God himself to be a mere de-
ceiver (pp. 130, 329).

So far Reid would seem to be the mere dema-
gogue of philosophy, appealing to the populace
against the aristocracy of thought, and Hume might
have addressed him as Cicero addressed Lucullus:—
quid me in invidiam, et tanquam in concionem,
vocas, et quidem, ut seditiosi tribuni solent, occludi
tabernas jubes ? (*Acad.* ii. 47). But Reid, in his own
opinion, was no seditious tribune of the people.
He considered himself the Cincinnatus, not the
Clodius, of philosophy. He was the sober dictator,
summoned, as it were, from the plough, to repel the
inroads of the sceptics, and to regulate and har-
monize the state. He was the inventor of a new
method. He regarded himself as the new Bacon.
His principles were a novum organum for the science
of the mind ; and, like the Baconian induction, his
method was the birth of time.

"The merit of what you are pleased to call my
philosophy," he says to one of his correspondents,
"lies, I think, chiefly in having called in question
the common theory of ideas or images of things in
the mind, being the only objects of thought ; a
theory founded on natural prejudices, and so universally received as to be interwoven with the
structure of the language" (p. 88). He himself,
he said, had long held this theory, and regarded
it a self-evident and unquestionable truth. It was
the unsuspected consequences to which it led that
occasioned his misgivings. 'The discovery,' he said,
'was the birth of time, and Berkeley and Hume did
more to bring it to light than the man that hit on

it' (*ibid.*).   In the chapter of his Essays in which he
gives an historical sketch of the sentiments of philosophers about the perception of external objects,
he tells us what this capital discovery was.   "All
philosophers, from Plato to Mr. Hume," he says,
"agree in this—that we do not perceive external
objects immediately, and that the immediate object
of perception must be some image present to the
mind" (p. 263).   It was in the detection of this
prejudice that Reid himself rested his reputation
as a thinker, and it was on its refutation that
his fame is rested by the most eminent of his disciples.

That we do not perceive external objects immediately is, undoubtedly, the accredited doctrine of
philosophy.   The predominant opinion cannot be
better expressed than in the language of the Cy-
renaic philosophers :—Negant esse quidquam quod
percipi possit extrinsecus ; ea se sola percipere quae
tactu intimo sentiant, ut dolorem, ut voluptatem;
neque se, quo quid colore, aut quo sono, sit scire, sed
tantum sentire, adfici se quodam modo (*Acad.* ii. 24).
The great majority of philosophers have agreed
with Descartes that all our knowledge, whatever its
extent, is essentially subjective.   They have agreed
with Locke, that though the mind of man may take
its flight beyond the stars, and make incursions into
the incomprehensible inane, it never goes beyond
its own ideas (II. vii. 10).   They have agreed with
Berkeley, that all the choir of heaven and all the
furniture of earth, so far as they are objects of con-

sciousness, or immediate intuition, have no existence but in mind (*Prin.* vi).   They have agreed
with Hume, that if we chase our imagination to the
heavens, or to the utmost limits of the universe, we
never really advance a step beyond ourselves (i. 97).
They have agreed with Condillac, that whether we
ascend to the heavens, or descend to the abyss, we
never issue from ourselves, or perceive anything
beyond our own perceptions.   They hold with Kant
that in whatever way our knowledge may relate to
objects, the only manner in which it immediately
relates to them is by means of intuitions (p. 21).
They hold with Cousin that neither the outward
world, nor God, nor the soul itself, as substance,
are objects of consciousness, and that the only
objects of consciousness are the operations of the
mind—its ideas, conceptions, and beliefs (*Psych.*
p. 101).

But this was not the doctrine of the philosophers
which Reid selected for attack.   He conceived that
all the philosophers before him held our sensible
ideas to be ' self-existent and independent ' entities
(p. 109).   He conceived them to hold that the ideas
furnished through the senses are ' objects that are
present in the mind or in the brain,' on which ' the
operations of the mind, like the tools of an artificer,'
are employed (p. 277).   The ideas of the existence
of which he required a proof were ' not the operations of the mind, but the supposed objects of those
operations' (p. 298).   They were ideas distinguished
at once from the external object and from the per-

cipient sense. In the words of his editor, commentator, and disciple, he always 'understands by idea, image, phantasm, species, etc., a *tertium quid*, numerically different both from the object existing and from the subject knowing' (*Psych.* p. 106)—he 'understands always certain representative entities distinct from the knowing mind' (p. 326). These ideas, says Reid, were first introduced into philosophy in the humble character of representatives of things; but by degrees they supplanted their constituents (p. 109). They had led to the negation of material things by Berkeley, and to the negation of all substantial reality by Hume (*ibid.*). These ' self-existent and independent ideas,' he said, were thus ' left alone in the universe' (*ibid.*)—'free and independent as the birds of the air,' or as the atoms of Epicurus 'when they pursued their journey in the vast inane' (p. 109). According to Reid, the shadows of the subterranean cave of Plato, and the pictures in the darkened room of Locke might be applied to all the systems of perception that had been invented (p. 263). All philosophers, from Plato to Hume, he said, were agreed that these representative entities were the sole object of perception (*ibid.*).

Whether the philosophers, in reality, held this imputed doctrine, has been made the subject of a most acrimonious dispute. The dispute was commenced by Priestley, and was taken up by Brown. Brown contends that, with the exception of Malebranche and Berkeley, who, he says, entertained peculiar notions on the subject, the philosophers whom Reid considered himself as opposing would all, if they had been questioned by him, have ad-mitted, before they heard a single argument on his part, that their opinions with respect to ideas were precisely the same as his (*Lect.* xxvii). Hamilton, on the other hand, maintains that "the attempt to show that Reid in his refutation of the previous theory of perception was only fighting with a sha-dow—was only combating philosophers who, on the point in question, really coincided with himself—would, if successful, prove not merely that the philosophical reputation of Reid is based upon a blunder, but would, in fact, leave us no rational conclusion, short not of idealism only, but of abso-lute scepticism" (*Lect.* ii. 44). But this controversy must be decided in favour of the views of Brown. It is true that the followers of Democritus held, in the language of their laureate, that our sensible ideas are the effigies and spectral forms of things —simulacra stripped from the surface of the object —films flitting in every direction through the air. But seventeen centuries before Reid this theory of entity images had been overwhelmed with ridicule. What are these images of yours, said Cicero to Velleius, and whence are they derived ? How is it that one image comes into my mind, and another into yours ? How do you explain the image of a scylla, a chimæra, or a hippo-centaur? How do you stamp the image not only on the eye but on the mind ? Such, in effect, was Cicero's polemic against

the Epicurean doctrine in the Tusculan Questions,
and the Discourses on the Nature of the Gods.   As
to the great mass of ancient and modern philosophers, it would be a vain affectation to turn against
Hamilton the learning derived from Hamilton himself.   For Hamilton sings a palinode in his edition
of the works of Reid.   In that admirable production
he shows that the doctrine of membranes, and
images, and films, received no countenance from
Plato (p. 262).   He shows that the doctrine of intentional species can only be attributed to Aristotle
on the ground of vague and metaphorical expressions, and is inconsistent with the whole spirit of
his philosophy (p. 827).   He shows that the Schoolmen distinguished the physical impression from the
mental act (p. 267).   He shows that Descartes and
Leibnitz identified idea with perception, and only
admitted a logical difference between them (p. 877).
He expressly says, " that from the period of Descartes we may confidently affirm that the hypothesis
of a representative perception, where the immediate
object was something different from the mind, had
been almost universally superseded by the representative hypothesis, in which the vicarious object was
held only for a modification of the mind itself "
(p. 957).   The case, he says, is different with
Malebranche and Berkeley (p. 207).   But even
Malebranche held, as already has been shown, that
ideas were modifications, not of the mental essence,
but the mental action ; and it is the cardinal point of
Berkeley's system that ideas are mere affections of

the mind. Hamilton, it is true, stigmatizes the generality of the English psychologists as mechanical, and maintains that the theory of entity ideas was held by Hobbes, and Locke, and Hume; by Newton, and by Norris, and by Clarke, to say nothing of Willis, and Porterfield, and Hook (*Disc.* 80, 85). But the great English psychologists are precisely those whom Hamilton would seem never to have studied. Hobbes ridicules the visible and audible species of the philosophy schools (*Works,* iii. 3), and defines a phantasm to be the act of sense (i. 392). Locke speaks with scorn of the intentional species of the Schoolmen (III. x. 14), and declares that our ideas are nothing but actual perceptions in the mind (II. x. 2). Hume takes the trouble to explain that by the term impression he would not be understood to express the manner in which our lively perceptions are produced in the soul, but merely the perceptions themselves (i. 16). Cudworth, in his Immutable Morality, tells us that sensations, formally considered, are certain passions or affections of the soul, fatally connected with some local motions in the body (p. 82). Clarke, in his Discourse on the Being and Attributes of God, declares that our sensible ideas are plainly thoughts or modifications of the mind itself, which is an intelligent being, and are not properly caused, but only occasioned by the impressions of figure and motion (p. 54). Even Norris, in his Theory of the Ideal World, repudiates the ideal theory with as much scorn, and in much the same style of language as Reid himself (pp. 184, 5). He sneers at this pretty metaphysical furniture, as he styles it. He inquires how the action of external bodies could make such fine engravings and artificial images of things upon the fluid brain. He laughs at the notion that the head of a man should be like a gallery hung round with pictures. He wants to be informed, in fine, how a corporeal image, consisting of material lineaments, should be the immediate object of thought, or be any way, by itself, intelligible to the mind, or how body should be enabled to enlighten spirit.

What, then, becomes of the great discovery of Reid? It is clear that the entity-idea which he fancied he saw in the systems of the philosophers had no existence there. His whole philosophy in this respect was nothing but a blunder, and the philosopher was in the predicament of the astronomer who, with the dead fly on the glass of his telescope, imagined he had discovered a monster in the moon.

The causes which could have seduced so sage and sensible a writer into such a marvellous series of misconceptions may well be made the subject of inquiry, the more so as these causes still continue to operate insensibly upon the minds of both philosophers and critics, and, till detected and exposed, will never cease their operation. In the first place, then, there is always a something which, though unknown to consciousness, is intermediate between the perception and the things perceived—the *physical antecedent* of

sensation.   Unless the ray alights upon the eye,
unless the pulsation strikes upon the ear, there is
neither sight nor sound.   Hence the language of
emission and impulse and impression; hence the
supposition of vibrations and vibratiuncles in the
nerves, of traces and motions in the brain.   All
these physical facts have abusively been named
ideas, and it required the learning and the power of
subtle distinction of Hamilton to show that the
philosophers had distinguished between the cognitive reason within and the motion or image from
without; between the species expressa of perception
and the species impressa from the object; between
the idea in the mind, of which we are conscious, and
the idea in the brain, of which we have no consciousness whatever; between the idea which is an
intellectual notion and the corporeal species which
is the mere affection of the organ; between the sensible idea, which is properly styled an idea, and the
material idea, which is a mere abuse of language.

But a still subtler cause of confusion is to be
found in the language in which the psychological
phenomenon itself, the idea proper, is expressed.
Granting that the idea is nothing but a condition or
an act of mind, the condition or the act of mind
exists, and therefore may be denominated an *existence*.   The ideas of the mind, accordingly, have
been styled beings, existences, and things.   They
have been so denominated, for instance, by Malebranche, by Berkeley, and by Cudworth; they
have occasionally been so denominated by Locke

and Hume. But, as Mill remarks, whenever we speak of an existence, we are apt to regard it as a separate existence; whenever we speak of a thing we are apt to regard it as a separate thing, and presume it to denote a substance. The operation of this principle is obvious in the case of Cudworth. An avowed disciple of Plato, he reproduces the theory of the Platonic ideas. He invests these ideas with certain immutable natures of their own. He attributes to them not only an eternal but a necessary existence. He confers upon them a constant and never-failing entity. He tells us that they always are, whether our particular minds think of them or not. He endows them with a constant being, and denominates them things. But what are the explanations of Cudworth—explanations which, doubtless, would have been those of Plato also? "The rationes or essences of things," he says, "are not dead things, like so many statues, images, or pictures, hung up somewhere by themselves alone in a world; neither are truths mere sentences and propositions written down with ink upon a book; but they are living things, and nothing but modifications of intellect or mind."

It is true that in the opinion of many philosophers the ideas of the mind which we style perceptions, though not conceived as having a separate, may still be conceived as having a *substantial* existence. They may be considered not as modifications of thought, but as modifications of mind; not as modifications of the mental action,

but as modifications of the mental substance. It
was owing to this ambiguity of the word modification that Malebranche was misunderstood by Locke
and Berkeley.   It was owing to the same ambiguity
that Locke himself was misunderstood by Hamilton.
And though Reid does not seem to have distinctly
considered this form of the ideal theory—though
the idea he assailed was regarded by him as a
separate entity, not as a substantial modification of
the mind itself—there can be no doubt that the
error operated insensibly on his judgment, and
prevented him from seeing that the idea of the
philosophers, like his own, was nothing but the
mental act.

But what seems in a peculiar manner to have
misled the mind of Reid was the philosophical employment of the words *object* and *objective*.   Granting ideas to be mere states or acts of mind, the
mind can turn inwards on itself, reflect on its own
operations, and make those operations the object of
reflective thought.   As an object of thought, accordingly, philosophers denominated perception an
idea ; as a primary act of thought they left it the
title of perception.   But Reid, forgetting that in
the philosophy of Locke the mind takes notice of
its own operations, and that these operations are
the appropriate objects of reflection—forgetting
that Arnauld employed the word objective to denote the mental presence of a thought, as distinguished from the local presence of a thing (p. 296)—
forgetting all this, Reid strangely imagined that the

philosophers, when they spoke of ideas as objects, necessarily regarded them as objects endowed with a separate existence, and that, accordingly, they maintained that the operations of the mind, like the tools of an artificer, could only be employed on objects which are present in the mind, or in the brain, where the mind is supposed to be residing (p. 277).

The sources of error already indicated have a tendency to vitiate our conceptions when we consider even the ideal systems of philosophy. But if it be held that the mind is conscious only of its own ideas, and if it be held at the same time that these ideas must nevertheless be regarded as *representative* of realities without the mind, then a new source of error and illusion rises. Cousin, who on this subject reproduces and systematizes all the misconceptions of all the preceding and succeeding critics, reduces the matter to a species of sorites. The recognition of ideas, he says in effect, supposes representation ; all representation implies resemblance ; all resemblance involves an image ; every image comprises figure ; figure is one of the qualities of matter ; and therefore the ideas of the idealists are material idea-images. The same misconception operated on the mind of Stewart. From the word representation employed by Buffier, he says, "it would appear that even he conceived the idea or notion of the mind to bear a resemblance to the external corresponding object (*Works*, ii. 167). In the same manner he charges Leibnitz as holding the ideal theory, because he held every human mind to be a living mirror of the universe (*Works*, i. 459). Nay, on the same ground he charges even Kant and the German school with holding the theory assailed by Reid. But the solution of this difficulty was obvious enough to the practised intellect of Hamilton. "If," he says, "we modify the obnoxious language of Descartes and Locke, and instead of saying that the ideas or notions of the primary qualities resemble, merely assert that they truly represent, their objects, that is, afford us such a knowledge of their nature as we should have, were an immediate intuition of the extended reality in itself competent to man—and this is certainly all that one, probably all that either philosopher intended—Reid's doctrine and theirs would be found in perfect unison " (*Reid*, p. 842).

The remaining cause of misconception in the mind of Reid was peculiar to himself. The sage of common sense was an unimaginative man. The great philosophers who had preceded him were not only profound thinkers, but they were men of deep feeling and poetic fancy. They delighted in comparing our ideas to the shadows flying over fields of corn. They dwelt on the pictures which were laid in fading colours on the mind. They described the flames of fever as calcining into dust the images which seemed as lasting as inscriptions graved on marble. With touching pathos they mourned over the ideas which die before us, like the children of our youth. They described our minds as representing the tombs to which we are hastening, where, though the brass and the marble may remain, yet the imagery moulders and the inscriptions are effaced by time. But the language of high poetry Reid took for sober prose. He mistook the play of the imagination for a form of spurious science. He converted a metaphor into a theory. He realised, in short, the fable of the fairy gifts—he received the fine gold of fancy and imagination and found it transmuted in his hands to lead.

It is difficult to conceive how Reid could, by any possibility, have imagined that, by a refutation of the theory of entity ideas, he was refuting idealism. So far indeed is the confutation of the ideal hypothesis from being a confutation of the sceptical argument that, as Brown observes, we have only to change the word *ideas* into the synonymous phrase *affections of the mind,* and the scepticism, if not stronger, is at least in strength exactly what it was before (*Lect.* xxviii). To attempt to confute the idealism of one who founds his argument on consciousness merely, and professes to have no knowledge of anything beyond it, would be as idle, to use the words of Brown, as it would have been for a Cartesian to attempt to confute the Newtonian system of attraction by a denial of the Ptolemaic spheres. But these considerations seem never to have occurred to Reid. The theory of ideas, he said, was the Trojan horse, which the philosophers had admitted within their walls, though it carried in it death and destruction to science and to common

sense (p. 132). It originated in a vain attempt to
account for what is unaccountable (p. 326); it led
to a demand for proof in the case of those elemen-
tary truths which could not possibly be proved
(p. 306); and it ended in the denial of what could
not rationally be denied (p. 109).

But this was not the only point of view from
which Reid looked upon the question. Disbelief in
the existence of a material world, he said, was not
only an *error personae* which supposes a world made
up of ideas, but it was also an *error juris*, inasmuch
as it presupposed that we have no ideas but those of
sensation and reflection (p. 128). If the senses furnished us with no materials of thought but sensations, he said, the conclusions of Berkeley must be
just; for no sensation can give us the conception
of material things (p. 313). Hume, he said, adopts
Locke's account of the origin of ideas, and from
that principle infers that we have no idea of substance, corporeal or spiritual, no idea of power, no
other idea of a cause but that it is antecedent, and
constantly conjoined to that which we call the effect
(p. 294). To refute these paradoxes, he conceived
it sufficient to show that there were ' certain principles which the constitution of our nature leads us to
believe, and which we are under a necessity to take
for granted in the common concerns of life' (p. 108).
These were the principles of common sense, the
foundation of which is laid in a class of natural
signs which on the presence of a mere sensation
suggest the conception of an object, and create a

belief in its existence (p. 122). This was a part
of human nature which had never been explained
(p. 122). This was a department of the mind which
did not tally with any system of the human faculties
which had ever been advanced (p. 126).

In thus virtually attributing the sensualistic doctrine to the great mass of the philosophers who
preceded him, Reid was betrayed into a grave misconception, and into an injustice still more grave.
Under a different name the conceptions which he
regarded as the natural suggestions of the reason,
and their concomitant beliefs, which he dignified
with the name of the principles of common sense,
had been recognised by the most eminent of his
predecessors. The ἰδέαι of Plato, the νοῦς of Aristotle, the ἔννοιαι of the Stoics, the *lumen naturale* of
the Schoolmen, the innate ideas of Descartes, the
relative ideas of Locke, the rational ideas of Cum-
berland and Cudworth, and the notions of Berkeley,
were in reality the same as Reid's conceptions.

But it is with reference to his three immediate
predecessors that Reid's criticism is the most conspicuously unjust. As far as Locke is concerned,
it is difficult to believe that Reid could ever have
consecutively studied the Essay concerning Human
Understanding. Like the other critics of Locke's
philosophy, he would seem to have neglected to
read the fourth book of the Essay in conjunction
with the second; and in reading the second he
would seem to have read no further than the opening chapter, which declares that ' all the *materials*

of reason and knowledge' are derived from experience, and that the only forms which human experience assumes are sensation and reflection. He
seems to have had no notion of what Locke meant
by 'simple ideas,' or by 'the origin of ideas,' or
by 'ideas of relation,' or by 'knowledge' itself, as
distinguished from its 'materials.' He seems, in
short, to have had no glimpse of the fact that Locke
regarded the conceptions of cause and substance as
' creatures and inventions of the understanding,'
and that he attributed all our 'certain and universal
knowledge' not to 'experience,' but to 'reason.'

Misunderstanding the philosophy of Locke, it is
no wonder that Reid misunderstood the philosophies
of Berkeley and Hume, and the relation in which
they stood to Locke and to each other. He confesses that he found it difficult to understand what
Berkeley meant by notions as distinguished from
ideas (p. 289) ; and never dreaming that Berkeley's
' notion' was in reality his own 'conception,' he
reduced it to a mere idea of imagination (p. 290).
His misconception of Hume's psychology is more
curious still. He never saw that Hume accepted
Locke's theory of knowledge, though he rejected
his theory of ideas; and he never saw that Hume
accepted the principles of common sense as principles of action, though he refused to rely upon
them as principles of speculative science.

The characteristic feature of Reid's philosophy
is its attempt to convert the principles of common
sense into an organon of the speculative reason.

And this opens before us a new vista for investigation. We have considered the critical portion of Reid's philosophy; let us now examine its constructive aspect. Did Reid admit the fundamental position of idealism, that the mind is conscious only of its own ideas? According to Brown, he did; according to Hamilton, he did not. Hamilton is 'decidedly of opinion that, as the great end, the governing principle, of Reid's doctrine was to reconcile philosophy with the necessary convictions of mankind, he intended a doctrine of natural, consequently a doctrine of presentative, realism; and that he would at once have surrendered every statement which was found at variance with such a doctrine' (*Reid*, 820). But the question is not what he would have surrendered, but what he actually held; and he systematically held that we have no presentative, no objective, knowledge of external objects. In fact, if he had surrendered this position, he would have abandoned the whole of his philosophy; so that here again the palm is carried off by Brown.

Reid, it must be conceded, in a variety of passages, asserts our knowledge of the external world to be *immediate*. But by the word immediate he does not mean, as Hamilton supposes, the negation of the intermediation of any third thing between the reality perceived and the percipient mind (*Reid*, 296); he merely means, as he himself tells us, that perception is 'the immediate effect of our constitution' (pp. 183, 332), and that 'it is not by a train of reasoning that we come to be convinced of the

L

existence of what we perceive' (pp. 259, 183). He
expressly denies that there is any necessity for an
' immediate intercourse' between the percipient
mind and the object of perception (pp. 302, 368).
He expressly asserts that there are certain means
and instruments, a certain train of machinery, that
must *intervene* between perception and its object
(pp. 186, 248). He repudiates, in fine, the theory
which represents all our senses to be different modifications of *touch*, and describes it as 'a theory which
serves only to confound things that are different,
and to perplex and darken things that are clear'
(p. 305).

In Reid's philosophy, in fact, touch itself is
regarded as essentially subjective; for he holds that
touch merely supplies us with ' certain sensations,'
and that 'extension, solidity and motion,' are merely
' conceptions' which these sensations, by the constitution of the mind, ' suggest' (p. 111). And it
is on this theory of *Natural Suggestion* that Reid's
whole theory of perception rests. Hamilton, it is
true, asserts that the theory of suggestion and natural signs, so explicitly maintained in the Inquiry, is
not repeated in the Essays (*Reid*, 821). But this is
not correct. Even in the Essays he holds that ' in
perception, whether original or acquired, there is
something which may be called the *sign*, and something which is signified to us, or brought to our
knowledge, by that sign'; and that ' in original
perception the signs are the various sensations,
which are produced by the impressions made upon

our organs' (p. 332). In point of fact, Reid's theory
of perception is identically the same in his earlier
and in his later work. In both he holds that the
presence of the object is *followed* by an impression
on the organ, and that the impression on the organ
is followed by a sensation, and that the sensation is
followed by a perception, and that this perception
is nothing but the conception of the object and a
belief in its existence (pp. 186, 248). In both he
holds that rays of light, vibrations of air, and effluvia of scent, must pass from the object to the organ
before the impression is produced. In both he holds
that the impression on the organ must be transmitted to the brain in order to produce sensation.
In both he holds that there is not any necessary
connexion between the sensation and the perception.
In both he holds that ' we are *inspired* with the
sensation, and we are inspired with the corresponding perception, by means unknown ' (pp. 188, 329).
In both he builds his philosophy on a system of
natural signs, 'which, though we never before had
any notion or conception of the thing signified, do
suggest it, or conjure it up, as it were, by a natural
kind of *magic*, and at once give us a conception
and create a belief ' in its existence (pp. 122, 332).
In both he officially defines perception to be
nothing but conception and belief (pp. 183, 318).

It appears, then, that Reid professes to have
accomplished two results by his philosophy—first,
to have superseded the ideas of the philosophers by
conceptions; and, secondly, to have vivified these

conceptions by the beliefs of common sense. But, in thus resolving our knowledge of material things into mere conception and belief, Reid, it is evident, adopts the principle of the ideal theory which he rejects, and practically admits that in perception the mind is conscious of nothing but its own ideas. And this determines his philosophical position. On the basis of his idea he posits a cosmos; and is therefore what Sir William has termed, a *Cosmothetical Idealist.* But the difficulty in the way of every system of cosmothetical idealism is the same. How can we know that the idea truly represents the cosmos? How can we know that the picture is a portrait? How can we know that there is any original beyond the picture? Sir William Hamilton puts the difficulty with his usual point—' How can we deny to the mind all immediate cognisance of matter, and yet confer upon it the inconceivable power of truly representing to itself the external world, which, ex hypothesi, it does not know?' (*Reid,* 755; *Disc.* 66.) This is a crucial question for the philosophy of Reid—let us see how he attempts to meet it.

Reid's immediate perception, as we have seen, is nothing but an immediate inspiration, and his natural realism is nothing but a natural magic. Let us consider his theory of perception, then, in its theological aspect as a *Divine Inspiration* (p. 329). His system compelled him to adopt the Cartesian theory of Divine Assistance; for he holds that our impressions are not the efficient cause of our perceptions—that there is no necessary connexion between them—and that 'we perceive because God has given us the power of perceiving, and not because we have impressions from objects' (p. 257). And as he adopted the principal hypothesis of the Cartesians, so he adopted the subsidiary hypothesis by which they endeavoured to support it. He supplemented the theory of Divine Assistance by an appeal to the Divine Veracity to establish the veracity of the senses. If we are deceived in the evidence of the senses, he said, we are deceived by Him that made us (pp. 130, 329). But to have recourse to the veracity of the Supreme Being in order to prove the veracity of the senses, as Hume observes, is to make an unexpected circuit (*Works*, iv. 179). The existence of God is not clearer than the existence of the world; and if the divine veracity were concerned in the matter our senses would be infallible on every point. But the divine veracity is not concerned. The informations of sense are sufficient for all the purposes of life and action, but the Deity has given us no reason to believe that they are sufficient for any other purpose. For the purpose of discipline He has left us liable to error; and we have no reason to believe that we are any more exempt from error here than in any other department of human speculation. If we draw erroneous conclusions from the evidence of sense the fault is not in the evidence but in the conclusions which we draw. Poets may sing that 'the voice of nature is the voice of God,' just as politicians may profess to hear the voice of God in the voices of the people. But philosophers should leave such platitudes to the politicians and the poets. The theory which Reid adopts from the Cartesians is only an instance of that unwholesome admixture of things, human and divine, which Bacon describes as the apotheosis of error, and which, he says, produces not only fantastic philosophy but heretical religion.

As the religious aspect of Reid's theory of perception is displayed in his theory of Divine Assistance, so its fantastic aspect is displayed in his theory of *Natural Magic.* There is a story in the Turkish Tales, which is told by Addison in one of the earlier numbers of the Spectator, which may illustrate the point in question. An unbelieving Sultan had ridiculed the famous passage in the Koran which records how the Angel Gabriel, having taken Mahomet out of his bed one morning, gave the Prophet a full view of hell, conducted him through the seven heavens of paradise, enabled him to hold ninety thousand conferences with God, and brought him back again to his bed before the bed was cold, and before the pitcher, which was capsized at the moment the Angel carried him away, was emptied. A doctor in the law, who had the gift of working miracles, undertook to convince the Sultan of the truth of this passage in the history of the Prophet. The holy man bade him plunge his head into a tub of water. The Sultan did as he was bid, and found himself

alone at the foot of a solitary mountain by the sea.
He made for a forest which he saw in the distance,
and met some woodcutters who conducted him
to a neighbouring town. He married a lady of the
land by whom he had seven sons and seven daughters. He was afterwards reduced to abject poverty,
and was compelled to ply as a porter for his living.
Walking one day by the seashore he was seized
with a fit of devotion, and threw off his clothes
with the design of performing his ablutions after
the manner of the followers of the Prophet. He
plunged headforemost into the water, rose to the
surface, when, lo and behold, he found himself still
standing by the tub, with the great men of his court
around him, and the holy man, who had performed
the miracle, beside him. He had not stirred from
the place where he originally stood. He had been
leading a magical existence—he had been enchanted.
Told by Addison, to illustrate the doctrine of Malebranche and Locke as to the relativity of time, the
story admirably illustrates Reid's doctrine of the
natural magic of perception. By a stroke of magic
the enchanted Sultan perceived the mountain and
the sea. He perceived the forest and the sun. He
conversed with the woodcutters, married his wife,
and begat his sons and daughters. He had a vivid
conception of all these various objects, and an unwavering belief in their existence. Everything was
intensely real, and yet everything was mere illusion.
He was the fool of a false conception and belief.

But leaving these fanciful speculations of Natural

Magic and Divine Assistance, let us direct our attention to the *Constitution of our Nature.* In the case of the belief in the existence of material things, as in the belief in the continuance of the course of nature, the belief, according to Reid, ' is not the effect of reasoning, nor does it arise from intuitive evidence in the thing believed ; it is,' as he apprehends, 'the immediate effect of our constitution ' (pp. 332, 209). Let us see what is the result of Reid's theory of perception regarded in this aspect of the question. ' It seems to be admitted as a first principle by the learned and unlearned,' he says, 'that what is really perceived must exist, and that to perceive what does not exist is impossible ' (p. 274). But the possibility of perceiving what does not exist, in Reid's sense of perception, may be submitted to a crucial test. Astronomers tell us that there are fixed stars at such an immeasurable distance from the earth, that their light, with all its inconceivable velocity, takes a period of years to reach us. They tell us, also, that stars are extinguished and disappear for ever from the wilderness of worlds. Suppose, then, the case of an extinguished star. Suppose the rays which it emitted during the period immediately preceding its extinction to reach the earth. The ray would strike upon the organ, the impression would be followed by the sensation, and the sensation would be followed by the conception and belief which constitute perception. For years we should be forced by the constitution of our nature to form a conception of the non-existent star, and a belief in its existence.

According to Reid's theory we should perceive the non-existent star; and the non-existent star, because we perceived it, would exist.

Let us next consider the constitution of our nature, with reference to ' the more profound philosophy' of Hume (*Works*, iv. 176). Hume concedes to Reid that men are carried by a natural instinct or prepossession to repose faith in their senses, and without any reasoning to suppose the existence of an external world which has no dependence on perception (p. 177). But this prepossession involves something more than a belief that the external world exists. " When men follow this blind and powerful instinct of nature," as Hume observes, " they always suppose the very images presented by the senses to be the external objects, and never entertain any suspicion that one are nothing but representations of the other " (*ibid.*). The fact that such a supposition is made is attested by consciousness, and cannot for a moment be denied. If authority be required for the establishment of a fact so patent, take the authorities adduced by Hamilton (*Reid*, pp. 747–8). As Descartes remarks, we believe we see the torch and hear the bell. As Berkeley contends, the vulgar are of opinion that the things which they immediately perceive (that is, their perceptions) are the real things. As Schelling says, the man of common sense believes, and will not but believe, that the object he is conscious of perceiving is the real one. As Stiedenroth asserts, it appears as if the sense actually apprehended things out of itself and in their proper place. Reid himself admits the fact as readily as Hume or Berkeley, as Stiedenroth or Schelling. "The vulgar," he says, "undoubtedly believe that it is the external objects which we immediately perceive, and not a representative image of it only" (p. 274). But this natural and irresistible belief is false. Hamilton admits it to be false, for he says we do not see the *sun,* 'but only certain rays in connexion with the eye' (*Reid,* 303). Reid admits it to be false, for, holding that we merely form a conception of the sun, and entertain a belief of its existence, he says, "that the object perceived is one thing, and the perception of that object another, I am as certain as I can be of anything" (p. 292). But everyone may be as certain as anyone can be of anything, that common sense and natural instinct confound the two. Men believe, and irresistibly believe, the conception of the thing to be the thing conceived. But this belief is confessedly erroneous. As Hume remarks, this universal and primary opinion of all men is destroyed by the slightest philosophy. Here, then, Reid is confronted with the dilemma of the sceptic. The opinion of external existence, if rested on natural instinct, is contrary to reason; and, if referred to reason, is contrary to natural instinct (iv. 181).

But we may test the constitution of the human mind, not only by the application of Hume's dilemma, but by reference to one of the 'repugnancies' of Berkeley. This is the second topic of 'the more profound philosophy' on which Hume insists; and

which he avowedly adopts from his immediate predecessor' (iv. 180). Reid, with the vulgar, considers it lunacy to question the existence of external
objects (p. 274). But what is the external object
of the vulgar? If the vulgar regard it as supremely
ridiculous to prove by metaphysical arguments the
existence of the earth, and sea, and sky (p. 306);
they regard it as equally ridiculous to question whether the sky and the sea are blue, and whether the
earth is decorated with all its tints, and shades, and
harmonies of colour. Reid saw the difficulty, and
endeavoured to evade it. "When philosophers,"
he says, " affirm that colour is not in bodies, but in
the mind, and the vulgar affirm that colour is not
in the mind, but is a quality of bodies, there is no
difference between them about things, but only
about the meaning of a word" (p. 139). The word
colour, he says in effect, is both a quality in bodies
and an appearance in the mind. But this is scarcely
a fair statement of the case. The question at issue
relates, not to the *cause* of colour, of which the
vulgar never think, but to the *appearance* of colour,
which can exist only in the mind, though the vulgar
regard it as existing in the external object. What
then, once more, is the external object? To the
eyes of the vulgar it is something coloured and
extended. To vulgar apprehension the colour is
inseparable from the extension, and the extension is
inseparable from the colour. No man of common
sense will admit that the extended colour is within,
and that the coloured extension is without. Accord-

ingly Berkeley contended that both colour and extension are within. What has Reid, the quondam
Berkeleian, to reply? Again he is involved in a
dilemma. He cannot assert that the total thing perceived exists *without*, for that would be an outrage
upon reason; he cannot assert that the total thing
perceived exists *within*, for that would be an outrage
upon common sense. Again reason and natural instinct are at issue. In this division of the house
against itself Reid, in the first instance, takes the
side of reason; for he is as certain that our sensations are not like any quality of body as that the
toothache has no resemblance to a triangle (p. 131).
But as a set-off he again shifts to common sense;
for he is as certain that the material world exists
as he is that no quality of body can resemble our
sensations. But what is gained by a compromise
such as this? Suppose the existence of an external world of matter to be admitted on the authority of natural belief, what is the condition to which
it is reduced by reason? Reid's compromise leaves
it uncoloured, if not unextended. He degrades it
to an unknown something, which is destitute of
causal energy and force. He unconsciously identifies it with the *materia prima* of the Schoolmen.
Again he falls into the hands of Hume. If
you " bereave matter of all its intelligible qualities, both primary and secondary," says Hume,
" you in a manner annihilate it, and leave only
a certain unknown, inexplicable *something* as the
cause of our perceptions—a notion so imperfect

that no sceptic will think it worth while to contend against it" (iv. 181).

What, then, is the position in which Reid's
philosophy is placed by its appeal to *Common Sense*
against the conclusions of the sceptic? On the
question of the external world he is involved in
vacillations as ridiculous as those in which Panurge
was involved on the question of his marriage.
Perplexed with the dilemmas with which he was
posed ʝy Hume, Reid resolved to take counsel
of the common man, just as Panurge, when perplexed with the contradictions of the Ephectic and
Pyrrhonian Philosopher, resolved to take counsel of the fool. But as the Pantagruelist found
no more comfort from the fool than from the
philosopher, so the sage of common sense found as
little satisfaction in his morosoph as he did in the
metaphysician whom he acknowledged as his master. His philosophy, in fact, was a constant see-saw
between what common men call sense and what
common men call nonsense. The vulgar, he says
in reply to Hume, believe that we immediately perceive external objects; and in this division, to my
great humiliation, I find myself ranked among the
vulgar (p. 302). He turns the matter in his mind,
and comes to the conclusion that perception is
different from the thing perceived; and he aban-
dons the vulgar, and ranks himself with the philosophers whom he had derided. The vulgar protest that
the earth is green and that the sky is blue, and that
the sea is the same colour as the sky, and Reid

is again found shifting to the vulgar (p. 138). The philosophers maintain that colour as perceived is nothing but a mere appearance in the mind; and Reid acknowledges that a sensation is no more like a quality of body than a toothache is like a triangle, and finds himself a philosopher once more. He makes a last desperate attempt to reconcile philosophy and common sense, and distinguishes between colour as a perceived appearance in the mind and as an unperceived quality in body; but both philosopher and vulgar repudiate the compromise, and the conflict between the reason of speculation and the common sense of practice is left as irreconcilable as ever.

While Reid was thus oscillating between reason and common sense, it is plain that, so far as he consulted reason, he was still almost, if not altogether, a Berkeleian. He agreed with Berkeley that we have no presentative or objective knowledge of the material world. He agreed with him that the object is not the efficient cause of the impression, and that the impression has no necessary connexion with the sensation by which it was immediately followed (p. 257). He admitted that our sensations, whether agreeable or disagreeable, are the same on Berkeley's system as upon any other (p. 285). He admitted that if sensation be produced the corresponding perception follows even where there is no object (p. 320). He admitted that 'we are inspired with the sensation, and that we are inspired with the corresponding perception'

(p. 188); and that our 'original and natural judgments,' as well as our 'notions or simple apprehensions,' are 'the inspirations of the Almighty'
(pp. 209, 329). It is true he resolved perception
into conception and belief, and on the authority of
the belief which accompanies the conception of external things, seceded from his master. Yet even
in insisting on the authority of belief, he was
obliged to admit with Berkeley that belief may be
erroneous (p. 320), and was fain to fortify it by
an appeal to the veracity of God.

But as Reid, when he listened to reason, was
a follower of Berkeley, so when he became a man
of common sense he was merely a follower of
Hume. In holding that the mind in perception is
conscious of nothing but conception and belief,
Reid conceded Hume's fundamental position that
nothing can ever be present to the mind but an
image or perception. In holding that there is no
necessary connexion between our perceptions and
material things, he conceded to Hume that the
mind cannot attain to any *experience* of the connexion of material things with our perceptions.
In holding, as he systematically held, that it is not
by a train of reasoning and argumentation that we
come to be convinced of the existence of what we
perceive (pp. 183, 259), he in like manner conceded
Hume's position that by no possible argument could
it be *proved* that the perceptions of the mind must
be caused by external and resembling objects. But
as Reid conceded to Hume that the existence of the

external world cannot be established by argument,
so Hume in his turn conceded to Reid that the
existence of the external world is suggested by
natural belief.   He conceded in the amplest manner that men are carried by a natural instinct or
prepossession to repose faith in their senses, and
to believe in the existence of an external universe,
which has no dependence on perception. But Hume
insisted that this natural belief, though sufficient for
the purposes of life and action, was insufficient for
the purposes of science.   He showed that it confounded perception with the thing perceived.   He
showed that it transferred to the thing perceived
what was confessedly mere perception.   He confronted it with its inconsistencies and its errors.
He formulated his objections in his dilemma and
his contradiction ; and he called upon it to vindi-
cate its character, and to substantiate its claims
to be regarded as the oracle of truth.   But, again,
Reid virtually admitted everything for which Hume
contended.   He admitted that the process of perception could not possibly be explained (p. 326).
He admitted that the mystery of sense was involved in impenetrable darkness.   All he had to
say was, what was virtually said by Hume, that
in spite of all the contradictions and inconsistencies of sense, the statesman continues to scheme,
the soldier to fight, and the merchant to buy
and sell, without being affected by the reasonings of philosophy ; and that a man might as well
attempt to draw the moon from its orbit as to

destroy our belief in the existence of external things (p. 329).

It is evident, therefore, that Brown's opinion as to the relation in which Reid stood to Hume is critically correct. The sceptic and the orthodox philosopher arrive at precisely the same conclusion. " The creed of each," says Brown, " is composed of two propositions, and of the same two propositions— the first of which is, that the existence of a system of things, such as we understand when we speak of an external world, cannot be proved by argument ; and the second, that the belief of it is of a force which is paramount to that of argument, and abso- lutely irresistible " (*Lect.* xxviii.). Brown proceeds to state the difference between the two philosophers in his Lectures ; but he stated it far more pointedly in conversation. When talking on the subject with Mackintosh, he agreed that the difference between Reid and Hume was more in words than in opinion. Hume, he said, shouted, we can give no reason for our belief in an external world, but whispered, we cannot help believing ; Reid, on the other hand, shouted, we cannot help believing in an external world, but whispered, we can give no reason in support of our belief. This was the very distinc- tion which Hume himself took when he said that the dispute between the sceptic and the dogmatist was verbal (ii. 537). Reid did not deny that there are insolvable difficulties with regard to the senses, though he maintained the absolute necessity of thinking and believing. Hume did not deny the

M

absolute necessity of thinking and believing, though he maintained that the difficulties with regard to the senses were incapable of a solution. The only difference between them was that Hume from habit, inclination or caprice, insisted on the difficulties, while Reid, for the like reasons, insisted on the necessity of our belief.

According to Kant, 'however harmless idealism may be considered—although in reality it is not harmless—it must still remain a scandal to philosophy to be obliged to assume, as an article of mere belief, the existence of things external to ourselves, and not to be able to oppose a satisfactory proof to anyone who may call it into question' (p. xl.). To this scandal Reid left philosophy exposed. Let us see how Kant proposed to obviate the scandal.

TRANSCENDENTAL IDEALISM:

OR

KANT.

TRANSCENDENTAL IDEALISM:

KANT

———◆———

Visae correptus imagine Formae
Rem sine corpore amat.

OVID.

THE opinion which Kant entertained of his own
philosophical position is reflected in a passage from
the preface to the Instauratio Magna which he pre-
fixed to his own great work. He compared his
Kritik to the Novum Organum of Bacon. Like
Bacon, he claimed to have opened a new road to
the human mind, and to have supplied it with fresh
aids to knowledge. He demanded that men should
regard his method, as not a mere opinion, but an
opus. Let them know, he said, that we are not
founding a sect, or system, but are laying the foundations of the happiness and dignity of man. Let
them adopt the method, he said, and share the toil.
Let them be of good cheer, and let them not con-

sider the task to be something endless, and beyond mortal reach, for in reality it is the end of an endless error, and its appointed term.

While Kant thus claimed to be the Bacon of the eighteenth century, he reproduced, in his own person, many of the characteristics of the great original whom he thought to rival. Like him he was animated by an intense egotism of genius. To read the works of Bacon, no one would suspect that he had been preceded by Telesio and Campanella, or that anything had been done by Galileo or Gilbert. To read the works of Kant, the reader would imagine that Descartes and Leibnitz were children in philosophy, that Locke had done nothing for the human understanding, and that Berkeley and Hume were honest, well-intentioned men who had mistaken their vocation. And it is this intellectual arrogance which is one of the secrets of his fame. His precise nomenclature, his systematic exposition, his philosophical epigrams, his bursts of eloquence, his flights of elevated thought, and, above all, his profound mastery of his subject—these constitute his real claims to the consideration of posterity. But a man of ability is generally taken for what he claims to be. Assumption is a source of authority. To speak confidently begets confidence; and the dogmatism of Kant, like the dogmatism of Hobbes, is one of the causes of the intellectual predominance which he has achieved.

But there are points of contact between the philosopher of Kœnigsberg and the great English Chancellor, which are far deeper and more significant than the points of resemblance to which we have alluded. When Bacon had set forth his method in the preface, from which Kant selected his motto, he sums up the matter in these weighty words:—Atque hoc modo, inter empiricam et rationalem facultatem (quarum morosa et inauspicata divortia et repudia, omnia in humana familia turbavere) conjugium verum et legitimum, in perpetuum nos firmâsse existimamus. In this passage Bacon states the whole aim of the inductive philosophy; and it might well have been selected as a motto for the philosophy of Kant. The transcendental philosophy, like the inductive, aims to effect a union between the rational and the empiric faculties. It refers all the disputes which had agitated philosophy to their estrangement; it sees the only hope of progress and improvement in their reconciliation; and the Kritik of the Reason, like the Instauratio Magna, to use the phrase of Bacon, is a mere epithalamium to celebrate their marriage.

The Novum Organum is an instrument for the advancement of physical science; but even in physical investigations Bacon, so strangely considered as the leader of the empiric school, is constantly insisting on the necessity of the initiative of the mind. Whether in the conduct of our experience, or in the process of induction—whether in interrogating nature in order to ascertain the fact, or in interpreting the answers of nature in order to ascertain the form—the mind, according to Bacon, must invariably assume the lead with nature. In the interrogation of nature he accepted the maxim of Plato—qui aliquid quaerit id ipsum, quod quaerit, generali quâdam notione comprehendit; aliter, qui fieri potest, ut illud, cum fuerit inventum, agnoscat? In the interpretation of the evidence of nature, it was by the *anticipatio mentis* that the physical philosopher first caught sight of the differentia vera, the natura naturans, the fons emanationis, which the moderns style laws of nature, and which Bacon, in his determination to follow antiquity to the very altar, denominated forms.

But we must dig still deeper, and beneath the very foundations of the Baconian philosophy, before we discover the real point of contact between Kant and Bacon. Below the Baconian anticipatio mentis there is another and more latent anticipation. With his rapid philosophical insight, which seemed akin to inspiration, Bacon sketched the outlines of a universal science which he designated *Philosophia Prima*, and described as the mother of the rest. The different sciences, he said, are not lines springing from an angle, but they are branches shooting from a trunk which had its roots in nature. There are certain common notions and common principles which all the sciences involve. These common principles he called the *axioms* of philosophy; these common notions he named *transcendents;* and the First Philosophy was the repository, the receptacle, of these. A more remarkable anticipation of the language of the Kritik of the Reason can scarcely be imagined. But it was also an anticipation of its aim. The transcendents which he enumerates in the fifth book of the De Augmentis are majus, minus; multum, paucum; prius, posterius; idem, diversum; potentia, actus; habitus, privatio; totum, partes; agens, patiens; motus, quies; ens, non-ens; et similia (c. iv). These evidently were the *categories* in their embryo state. Bacon, it is true, was infelicitous in the instances which he selected to illustrate his thought, and it is not without reason that Macaulay ridicules his illustrations. But Macaulay failed to see the true scope and comprehension of this remarkable First Philosophy of Bacon, which in reality was a foreshadowing of the Transcendental Philosophy of Kant.

The *Transcendental Philosophy*, as Kant described it, is the idea of a science which should contain a complete exposition of all the analytic and synthetic judgments, which, prior to experience, are presupposed in all our physical investigations. It is conceived as a system of all the principles of pure reason employed by the mind in acquiring a knowledge of the phenomena of nature (*Kritik*, 16, 17). Its relationship to the Baconian philosophy is recognized by Kant himself. The wise Bacon, he says, gave a new direction to physical studies. When Galileo experimented with balls of a definite weight on the inclined plane—when Torricelli caused the air to sustain a weight which he had calculated beforehand to be equal to that of a definite column of water—when Stahl, at a later period, converted

metals into lime and reconverted lime into metals
by the addition and subtraction of certain elements
—they recognized the importance of the truth which
had been taught by Bacon, that reason only perceives that which it produces after its own design;
and that it must not be content to follow, as it were,
the leading strings of nature, but must proceed in
advance with principles of judgment according to
unvarying laws, and compel nature to give an
answer to its questions (p. xxvii.).

In all the physical sciences, in fact, there are
certain principles, certain unvarying laws, which
must be *presupposed*. Every minister and interpre-
ter of nature assumes that all the changes which
he observes take place in accordance with a law of
succession and connexion, and that the law elicited
from a mass of existing facts will continue to be the
law of similar combinations whenever they recur.
The illustrious chemists who tracked matter through
its Protean transformations, and weighed the atmosphere, and detected the latent laws of light,
and electricity, and heat, all of them assumed as
the very basis of their speculations that the quantity
of matter in the world is constant. The great geo-
meters who observed the facts and ascertained the
laws of the heavenly motions, and thus augmented
the number of those mixed mathematics which
Bacon with his prophetic vision had foreseen, all of
them assumed that, even in the most inaccessible
recesses of the universe, phenomena are subjected
to the laws of time and space, and quantity and

number. Take the simplest objects of physical inquiry. What is the weight of smoke? We assume the quantity of matter in the world to be constant, and the answer is, subtract from the weight of the burnt wood the weight of the remaining ashes and you will have the weight of smoke (p. 139). What is the cause of the melting of a piece of wax? We assume that phenomena, as objects of experience, succeed each other in a settled order, and that they do not drift at random down the stream of time (p. 144); and the answer to the question is, that we know a priori that there must have been something—the sun's heat—preceding, which the effect follows according to a fixed law (p. 465). In short, as Kant observes, we have only to look at the different propositions which are commonly stated at the commencement of every treatise on physical science—those, for example, relating to the continuance of the laws of nature, the permanence of the quantity of matter, the vis inertiae, the equality of action and reaction, and the like—to be convinced that they form a science of pure physics which, whatever its extent, deserves to be separately expounded (p. 13).

The question of the origin of these transcendental principles was one which fell within the peculiar province of the Essay concerning Human Understanding. But though Locke's treatment of the subject is defective, he did not merit the reproach of Kant by attempting a *physiological* derivation or deduction (p. 73). While he held that our simple

ideas, the equivalent of Kant's intuitions, are derived from sensation and reflection, he held that
our ideas of relation, which correspond with Kant's
conceptions, are the creatures and inventions of the
understanding.   While he held that 'all the materials of reason and knowledge' are derived from
' experience' (II. i. 2), he held that ' our highest degree of knowledge' is that supplied by immediate
intuition (IV. ii. 1 ; xvii. 14).   He anticipated the
division of our intuitive judgments into analytic
and synthetic (IV. viii. 8), and furnished an 'infallible rule' by which the one might be distinguished
from the other (IV. viii. 13).   He anticipated the
distinction of our synthetic judgments into judgments a priori, such as those of mathematics; and
judgments a posteriori, such as those of experimental science (IV. iii. 29), and signalized their contrast
by attributing the one to 'reason,' and the other to
'experience' (IV. xii, 9).   He even anticipated Kant
in enunciating the criterion by which rational and
empiric knowledge are to be distinguished—the
' necessary connexion' and 'necessity' which are
absent from all mere ' experimental knowledge'
(IV. xii. 9), and the 'universality' which cannot be
known 'from experience,' but is to be discovered
only ' in our minds' (IV. iii. 31).   Nor did Locke
fail to see that even in our experimental knowledge
there is an element which is not experimental.
Having stated that 'in some of our ideas there are
certain relations, habitudes, and connexions, so visibly included in the nature of the ideas themselves,

that we cannot conceive them separable from them by any power whatsoever,' he goes on to say that ' the things which, as far as our observation reaches, we constantly find to proceed regularly, *we may con-clude* do act by a law set them, but yet by a law we know not, whereby, though causes work steadily, and effects constantly flow from them, yet, their connexions and dependencies being not discover-able in our ideas, we can have but an experimental knowledge of them' (IV. iii. 29). But Locke did not ask himself what right have we to ' conclude ' that causes work ' steadily,' and that effects ' con-stantly ' flow from them. He saw that this was a synthetic a priori judgment; but he did not ask himself how is such a judgment possible—he did not recognize the importance of the question.

Hume in this respect evinced a more inquiring spirit and a more penetrating genius than had been evinced by Locke. As Locke fastened on the con-ception of substance, so Hume fastened on the con-ception of causation; and as Locke had resolved substance into a collection of attributes, together with a supposition of something we know not what, so Hume resolved causation into a succession of phe-nomena, together with an anticipation of something we know not why. What is the origin of that antici-pation? On this point, Hume, as we have seen, pro-fessed to have discovered no light in anything that he had read. "I have *found* that such an object has always been attended with such an effect, and I *fore-see* that other objects, which are in appearance simi-

lar, will be attended with similar effects "—these two
propositions, he said, are far from being the same
(*Works*, iv. 42). The latter, in fact, was a synthetic
a priori judgment. "Why past experience should
be extended to future times, and to other objects,
which, for aught we know, may be only in appearance similar—this," says Hume, " is the main question on which I would insist" (iv. 42). This
question, it is evident, is identical with the question which Kant regards as 'the grand problem of
transcendental philosophy' (p. 44)—'how are synthetical propositions a priori possible?' (*ibid.*). But
Hume not only anticipated the problem—he anticipated the method to be pursued for its solution.
The conception of causation cannot be educed from
experience, he said, for experience only reveals the
' constant conjunction' of two objects in the past,
whereas the conception of cause and effect involves
the idea of their 'necessary connexion' in all time
past, present, and to come. 'It is impossible,' he
says, ' that any arguments from experience can
prove this resemblance of the past to the future,
since all these arguments are founded on the supposition of that resemblance' (iv. 46). Hume
accordingly, as we have seen, arrives at the conclusion that ' the efficacy of causes lies in the determination of the mind,' as distinguished from a
determination of the object (i. 222); and holds that
when we draw an inference from one object to
another, after the discovery of their constant conjunction, 'the necessary connexion depends upon

the inference, instead of the inference's depending on the necessary connexion' (i. 123).

The Kritik of Kant is nothing but a generalisation of this idea; and the full scope and significance of Hume's reasoning on the subject of causation cannot be more clearly brought into evidence than by reference to the reasoning of the Kritik. 'It has hitherto been assumed that our cognition must conform to the objects,' says Kant in his Second Preface; ' but all attempts to ascertain anything about these objects a priori, by means of conceptions, and thus to extend the range of our knowledge, have been rendered abortive by this assumption. Let us then make the experiment whether we may not be more successful in metaphysics if we assume that the objects must conform to our cognition' (p. xxviii.). 'Here,' says Kant, 'we propose to do just what Copernicus did in attempting to explain the celestial movements.* When he found that he could make no progress by assuming that all the heavenly bodies revolved around the spectator, he reversed the process, and tried the experi-

---

* The scope of Kant's astronomical illustration has been made the subject of dispute. ' It is with reference to this and the accounting for the a priori or necessary element in intuitions and concepts,' says Mr. Mahaffy in his Translation of Kuno Fischer's Commentary on the Kritik, 'that Kant in his Second Preface compares himself and his system to Copernicus, and to the *rotation of the earth* as discovered by him, not to the heliocentric hypothesis, as Cousin and Professor Webb suppose ' (p 36). But though either the earth's rotation on its axis or its revolution round the sun would equally have answered his purpose, Kant himself refers to the central laws of the movements of the heavenly bodies (p. xxx.). It is strange anyone should have thought that it refers to ' the supposed laws of being as being, the fixed stars of metaphysics,' as Mr. Mahaffy seems to think (p. 37).

ment of assuming that the spectator revolved while the stars remained at rest' (p. xxix.).

Hume's argument, that a given conception cannot be given by experience, because all conclusions from experience are based on the conception, may be regarded as the formula of the *Transcendental Method.* That method lays it down that whatever is presupposed by experience must be regarded as necessary to experience, and as prior to experience, and as transcending experience, and therefore as *transcendental* and a product of the mind. The difference between this mode of reasoning and the ordinary procedure of the a priori school is obvious. The transcendental method does not argue that certain principles must be regarded as a priori because experience is incompetent to explain them ; it argues that they must be regarded as a priori because they themselves are necessary to the explanation of experience. And this again shows the true character of the *Transcendental Criterion* (p. 21). The transcendental philosopher does not argue that certain principles cannot be educed from experience merely because they are necessary and universal ; he argues that they are necessary and universal, because they are essential to the conception of that experience from which they are said to be educed. All this is involved in Hume's position, that the mental inference in causation is not determined by any necessary connexion in the objects, but that the supposed necessary connexion in the objects is merely the result of the mental inference.

But if Hume was the Copernicus of the new method of investigating the phenomena of the mind, Kant must be regarded as its Newton. While Hume applied the method to determine the nature and origin of a single conception, the *Transcendental Kritik* proposes to ' lay before us a complete enumeration of all the radical conceptions which constitute pure knowledge' (p. 17); and if it ' does not assume the title of *Transcendental Philosophy*, it is only because, to be a complete system, it ought to contain a full analysis of all human knowledge a priori' (*ibid.*), whereas it pretermits the consideration of our analytical a priori knowledge, and confines itself to the consideration of our synthetical a priori knowledge only (p. 16). The *Transcendental Problem*, therefore, which the Kritik of the Reason undertakes to solve is embodied in the question—how are synthetical a priori judgments possible? (pp. 12, 44); and in answering this question Kant traverses the whole domain of speculation, and completes the work of Hume.

The general principles of Kant's psychology, allowing for variations of language, are identical with those of Locke's. Pure Reason is a perfect unity (p. xx). There are two sources of knowledge which perhaps spring from a common but unknown root, Sensibility and Understanding (p. 18)—the one being a receptivity for impressions, the other a spontaneity in the productions of conceptions (p. 45). Intuitions and conceptions, therefore, constitute the elements of knowledge (p. 45). But as sensibility

N

and understanding may spring from a common root,
so they can only operate in conjunction (p. 189).
Without the one no object would be given; without the other no object would be thought (p. 46).
Intuitions without conceptions would be blind ; conceptions without intuitions would be empty forms
(p. 46).   Sensibility manifests itself under the twofold form of the external senses and the internal
sense (pp. 23, 43) ; and understanding employs itself
with the twofold aim of anticipating experience by
means of its conceptions, in which case it retains
its name as understanding, and of attempting to
transcend the sphere of experience by means of its
ideas, in which case it assumes the name of reason
(p. 54).

The opening sentence of the Kritik contains the
substance of the polemic against innate ideas with
which Locke opens the Essay concerning Human
Understanding.   " That all our knowledge begins
with *experience* there can be no doubt," says Kant;
"for how is it possible that the faculty of cognition
should be awakened into exercise otherwise than
by means of objects which affect our senses, and
partly of themselves produce representations, partly
rouse our powers of understanding into activity,
to compare, to connect, or to separate these, and so
to convert the raw material of our sensuous impressions into a knowledge of objects which is called
experience" (p. 1).   But what, according to Kant,
are the objects the knowledge of which we are thus
supposed to be able to attain ?   " In whatsoever

mode, or by whatsoever means, our knowledge may relate to objects," says Kant, "it is at least quite clear, that the only manner in which it immediately relates to them is by means of *intuition*" (p. 21). Is Kant's intuition, then, objective? No. "Our mode of intuition," he says, "is not such as to give us the existence of its object"; for that is "a mode which, so far as we can judge, belongs only to the Creator" (p. 43). But though our mode of intuition does not give us the existence of the object, he holds that it is 'dependent on the existence of the object' for its manifestations, because it is 'possible only on condition that the representative faculty of the subject is affected by the object' (*ibid.*).

What, then, in the Transcendental Philosophy, is the object which affects the subject? and what is the subject which is affected by the object? Both are presupposed in Kant's conception of experience; and both, therefore, must be viewed as transcendental. Accordingly, throughout the Kritik of the Reason, Kant assumes the existence of a *Transcendental Object*, which he regards as the non-sensuous cause of our sensations (p. 309). It is true 'the transcendental ground of this unity of subjective and objective' constitutes 'the mystery of the origin and source of our faculty of sense'; and, therefore, he regards the transcendental object as a mere *nescio quid*, the nature of which we could not understand, though some one were found able to tell us what it is (p. 200). But it must be postulated by the understanding as 'the mental correlate of sensi-

bility' (p. 309). And hence it is that *phenomena*, or
the sensuous existences which are the sole objects of
our knowledge, present a double aspect—one turned
to the object as a thing in itself, and the other
turned to our own form of intuition (p. 33); so that
the name of phenomenon is given to that which is
not found in the object itself, but which is only
found in the relation of the object to the subject,
and forms our representation of it (p. 42). The
conception of a *noumenon*, therefore, must be admitted as the correlative of phenomena; and, though
such a conception is problematical, it is not only
admissible, but must of necessity be admitted (p. 187).
Phenomena *must* have a transcendental object as a
foundation which determines them as representations (p. 333); and "to this transcendental object
we may attribute the whole connexion and extent
of our possible perceptions, and say that it is
given and exists in itself prior to all experience"
(p. 309).

As Kant assumes the existence of a Transcendental Object as the mental correlate of sense, so
he assumes the existence of a *Transcendental Subject*
as the mental correlate of thought (p. 239). But as
he regards the one as a mere nescio quid, of which,
beyond the fact of its existence, nothing can be
known, so he regards the other as a mere unknown
quantity, the equivalent of an algebraic x. The
Transcendental Object and the Transcendental
Subject are thus the two foci around which the
Transcendental Philosophy revolves. But these

foci are invisible to the eye of sense, and the introduction of these metaphysical elements into the Kantian system does not exercise any influence on the purely psychological development of its world of intuitions, conceptions and ideas. Kant, indeed, gives us a *critical admonition* on the subject. " The transcendental conception of phenomena in space," he says, " is a critical admonition, that, in general, nothing which is intuited in space is a thing in itself, and that space is not a form which belongs, as a property, to things ; but that objects are quite unknown to us in themselves, and what *we* call outward objects are nothing else but mere representations of our sensibility, whose form is space, but whose real correlate, the thing in itself, is not known by means of those representations, nor ever can be, but respecting which, in experience, no inquiry is ever made " (p. 28).

In thus asserting that space, as known to us, is a mere form of our sensibility, and not an independently existing thing, Kant separates himself from all previous philosophers, idealist and realist alike ; and it is by the establishment of this proposition that the *Transcendental Æsthetic* professes to have proved " that all things intuited in space and time, and therefore all objects of possible experience, are nothing but *phenomena*, that is, mere representations ; and that these, whether regarded as extended bodies or as series of changes, have no self-subsistent existence apart from human thought" (p. 307).

What, then, according to the transcendentalist, are Space and Time? By means of the external senses we represent objects as without us, and that in space; and, by means of the internal sense, the mind contemplates the phenomena of its internal state, and represents them as in time (p. 23). But our internal experience is only possible under the previous assumption of external experience (p. 167); for Kant holds, with Locke, that ideas of reflection must be preceded by ideas of sensation. Space, therefore, in this sense, is anterior to time. Time, moreover, is in a state of continual flow, while space is permanent, and determines things as such (p. 176). Let us, therefore, restrict our inquiry to space.

The theories as to the nature of *Space* advanced by the philosophers who preceded Kant were numerous and discordant. The Schoolmen had started a notion, which was afterwards adopted by Gravesande, that space is a self-subsisting but unthinking substance. Newton had broached the doctrine, which was afterwards developed by Clarke, that it is an attribute of the eternal and infinite existence. Locke had maintained that, though space is necessary to the existence of body, the two things are distinct; but, in reply to the question whether space is attribute or substance, had frankly answered that he did not know (II. xiii, 11, 17). Leibnitz regarded it as neither substance nor accident, and, defining it to be nothing but the order of things coexistent, reduced it to a mere relation. Berkeley, as we have seen, maintained that extension, figure, and motion were only ideas existing in the mind (*Prin.* ix.), and that space was nothing but the absence of resistance (*Prin.* cxvi). Collier, in this respect, more philosophical than Berkeley, held that 'the quasi-externeity of visible objects is not only the effect of the will of God,' but 'a natural and necessary condition of their visibility' (*Clavis,* 4). Hume, on the contrary, maintained that 'the idea of space or extension is nothing but the idea of visible or tangible points distributed in a certain order' (i. 80). And, finally, some fifty years before the publication of the Kritik, Law, the translator of the *de Origine Mali* of Archbishop King, anticipated the very phraseology of Kant, and, denying that the idea of space required any external *ideatum,* asserted that its *formality* existed nowhere but in mind, and had no foundation but the power which the mind possessed to form it (*Trans.* 7).

But what was a mere passing conjecture in the mind of Law was converted by Kant into a systematic exposition of the *Transcendental Ideality of Space.* To establish his point Kant employs the formula of Hume in a department of our mental phenomena in which Hume never dreamt of employing it. The idea of space, he said, does not represent any property of objects as things in themselves or any relation between them; for things in themselves are not presented to our intuition (p. 25). Neither is it a general conception; for the idea of space is one, and is not abstracted from a multitude of spaces (p. 24). Neither, he said, can it be derived from our external experience; for before we can represent things as existing in space we must have the representation (p. 23). The representation, therefore, must be regarded as an a priori representation which serves as the foundation for all external intuition (p. 24). Accordingly Kant arrives at the conclusion that 'we find existing in the mind a priori the pure *form* of sensuous intuitions in general, in which the manifold content of the phenomenal world is arranged and viewed under certain relations' (p. 22). It is true 'we cannot convert the special conditions of sensibility into conditions of the possibility of things' (p. 26). It is true that empty space 'may exist where our perceptions cannot exist, inasmuch as they cannot reach it' (p. 158). But space in this sense is not an object of possible experience (*ibid.*); and 'in the human point of view,' space is nothing but a permanent form of sensibility in which the sensations with which we are transcendentally supplied are moulded (p. 26).

The *Empiric Reality of Space* is the necessary consequence of its Transcendental Ideality (p. 27). The objects of external intuition, whenever they may be presented to us, 'must correspond to the formal conditions of sensibility existing a priori in the mind,' because 'without them they could not be objects to us' (p. 76). Phenomena in the future as in the past must necessarily correspond with the formal condition of sensibility, because it is only through such formal condition that phenomena exist

(p. 77). True the phenomenon has its twofold aspect; true it has relation to the transcendental object. But as long as the relation of the object to the subject is maintained (p. 42), as long as the unknown cause of our sensations continues to affect the senses, so long will sensibility, like the cloud in Comus, continue to 'turn forth her silver lining on the night,' and so long will the objective reality of our external intuitions as phenomena in space continue.

If empirical intuition is possible only through the pure intuition of space and time, it follows that what geometry affirms of the latter is indisputably valid of the former (p. 125). But the principle which accounts for the validity of our mathematical preconceptions accounts for their existence also. No synthetic a priori judgment would be possible except by means of some a priori determination of the mind, and the a priori determination of the mind is discovered in the forms of sense. In showing the transcendental ideality of space, therefore, Kant professes to have solved one portion of the grand general problem of the transcendental philosophy. He professes to have shown *how* synthetic a priori propositions are possible in mathematics by showing ' that we are in possession of pure a priori intuitions, namely, space and time, in which we find, when in a judgment a priori we pass out beyond the given conception, something which is not discoverable in that conception, but is certainly found a priori in the intuition which corresponds to the conception, and can be united synthetically with it ' (p. 44).

But this solution, though true as far as it goes, is only a partial solution of the problem, even as far as mathematics are concerned. As 'understanding and sensibility, with¦ us, can determine objects only in conjunction' (p. 189), so 'in no other way than from the united operation of both can knowledge rise' (p. 46). The conclusions of the Transcendental Aesthetic, therefore, require to be supplemented by the *Transcendental Logic*. The Transcendental Logic finds lying before it the manifold content which the Transcendental Aesthetic presents in order to furnish material for the pure conceptions of the understanding; and the spontaneity of thought requires that the diversity presented by the senses should be examined in a certain manner, and connected together, so as to convert it into knowledge (p. 62).

The *Understanding* is variously defined by Kant as the faculty of thinking, the faculty of conceiving, the faculty of judging, and the faculty of rules. But in its most general character it is " nothing but the faculty of *conjoining* a priori, and of bringing the variety of given representations under the unity of apperception," or self-conscious thought (p. 83). It is only by a synthesis of *apprehension* that the manifold in any empirical intuition is combined into the object which we call a phenomenon (p. 98). It is only by a synthesis of *imagination* that the objects which we have once combined in apprehension are permanently associated as objects of experience (p. 63). It is only by a synthesis of *conception* that the scattered data of experience are combined into a system of scientific knowledge, This threefold synthesis is the work of the under-standing, and is presupposed in all a priori empi-rical cognition (p. 63). But even this synthesis necessitates a transcendental pre-conception. It is true we have no intuition of the mind as object; it is true the transcendental subject is an unknown quantity—an algebraic *x*. But in every act of syn-thesis, whether of apprehension, or imagination, or conception, the act is regarded as *mine*, and as per-formed by *me*. The unity of conception, therefore, involves the conception of a unity which Kant styles the *Originally Synthetic Unity of Apperception* (p. 81)—the *Transcendental Unity of Self-consciousness*, to indicate the possibility of any a priori know-ledge (p. 82). This, in fact, is 'the first pure cog-nition of the understanding' (p. 85)—' the supreme principle of all our synthetic judgments' (p. 117). The original synthetic unity of apperception is 'the form of the understanding' in relation to 'the forms of sense' (p. 103); and accordingly the first lesson which the Transcendental Logic teaches is, that it is the supreme principle of the possibility of all *intuition* in relation to the understanding; just as the Transcendental Aesthetic teaches that the formal conditions of space and time are the supreme principle of the possibility of all intuition in relation to our capacities of sense (p. 84).

The synthetic power, which Kant thus attri-butes to the understanding, is merely the scientific expression of what Locke and Hume had intimated in more popular language, when they said that the understanding has the power of perceiving, compounding, and comparing the simple ideas with which it is furnished by the senses, and that the ideas of substances are mere collections of the simple ideas which the understanding joins together. But Kant, in the *Transcendental Analytic*, advanced far beyond this point, and penetrated to the very centre of the subject. He gave an exact analysis of the various a priori conceptions which the understanding employs in dealing with its sensible intuitions, and also an analysis of the various synthetic a priori principles into which those various conceptions enter (p. 53). The Analytic of Conceptions professes to trace the pure conceptions of the understanding to their very germs and beginnings in the mind, until they are developed on the occasions which experience presents (p. 55). And the Analytic of Principles professes to show that 'a priori synthetical judgments are possible, when we apply the formal conditions of a priori intuition, the synthesis of imagination, and the necessary unity of that synthesis in a transcendental apperception, to a possible cognition of experience, and say: the conditions of the possibility of experience in general are at the same time conditions of the possibility of the objects of experience, and have for that reason objective validity in an a priori synthetic judgment' (p. 119).

The first thing to be studied, then, is the *Analytic*

of Conceptions. As the Transcendental Æsthetic professes to have proved that all objects of possible experience are nothing but *phenomena*, which have no self-subsistent existence apart from human thought (p. 307), so the Transcendental Analytic professes to have established that ' the understanding is competent to effect nothing a priori except the *anticipation* of the form of a possible experience in general ' (p. 183). What, then, are the conceptions of the understanding by means of which it anticipates experience ? Here, again, the subject diverges into two branches. The object of the Transcendental Discovery is to determine the precise number of these conceptions, and the object of the Transcendental Deduction is to show that without their aid all anticipation of experience would be impossible for us.

It is in the *Transcendental Discovery* that Kant's claims as a discoverer in mental science are most conspicuous and least disputed. Bacon, it is true, had recognized the necessity of a philosophia prima, which was to be the repository of the conceptions and axioms common to all the sciences, and among his transcendents, had enumerated such conceptions as majus minus; multum paucum; prius, posterius; idem, diversum ; potentia, actus ; habitus, privatio ; totum, partes; agens, patiens ; motus, quies; ens, non-ens; and the like. Hobbes had followed the example of his master, and had acknowledged the importance of a philosophia prima, which should treat of such fundamental notions as body, time, place, matter, form, essence, subject, substance, accident, power, act, finite, infinite, quantity, quality, motion, action, passion, and divers others, necessary to the explaining of man's conceptions concerning the nature and generation of bodies (iii. 671 ; vii. 226). Locke had divided our complex ideas into modes, substances, and relations; and had treated in successive chapters of space, of duration, of infinity, of power, of substances, of cause and effect, of identity and diversity, and of other relations. Berkeley had intimated the necessity of ' an inquiry concerning those transcendental maxims which influence all the particular sciences' (*Prin.* cxviii), and had talked in a vague way of the mind containing all, and acting all, and being to all created things the source of unity and identity, harmony and order, existence and stability (*Siris*, 295). Hume had accepted Locke's division of our complex ideas into modes, substances, and relations; and had classified relations under the heads of resemblance, identity, space and time, quantity and number, quality and degree, contrariety and causation (*Works*, i. 30, 98). But none of them, except Hume, had set any definite aim before them. They followed no guiding principle in their investigations. They fastened on one conception after another as they occurred, and their whole procedure was hap-hazard.

The understanding being the faculty of judgment, Kant conceived that by examining the forms of judgment he would be able to determine the number of the a priori conceptions of the understanding. It was this which supplied him with the *Transcendental Clue* (p. 56). Judgments, according to the logicians, can be contemplated under four aspects only,—those of quantity, quality, relation, and modality; and if a physical content be introduced into these forms of logic, a transcendental element, according to Kant, will be detected (p. 58). The sun is the centre of the planetary system; some of the planets are mere asteroids; all the planets revolve around the sun. What is involved in the words ' the,' and ' some,' and ' all'? Evidently the conceptions of unity, plurality, and totality. The earth revolves around its axis; the sun does not revolve around the earth; glass is a non-conductor. These judgments involve the conceptions of reality, negation, and limitation,—the limitation of a class of things, not by the presence, but by the absence, of a certain characteristic. If we assert categorically that gold has such and such properties, there is implied a conception of inherence and subsistence; when we assert hypothetically that if the sun shines the wax will melt, there is implied the conception of causality and dependence; and if we assert disjunctively that a thing is either this or that or the other, the coordination of the whole, and the reciprocal exclusion of each, involve a conception of community or reciprocity between agent and patient (p. 64). Finally, what is assumed in propositions such as these :—as a matter of fact, man *does* exist upon the earth; as a matter of possibility, life *may* be existent in the moon; as a matter of necessary inference from what we have perceived, man *must* have existed in the glacial period? Clearly the conceptions of actuality, possibility, and necessity. This completes the tale. We have discovered the twelve *Categories of the Understanding.* These are the conceptions which guide the understanding in its anticipations of experience. These suggest the ruling principles which regulate and pre-determine the domain of knowledge. These are the *Di Majores* of the Kantian system.

Or consider the matter in another aspect. We may conceive an object as one, as many, or as at once both one and many; we may conceive it as an object of which something may be affirmed, or of which something may be denied, or of which something may be affirmed with an element of denial; we may conceive it as inherent in some substance, or as produced by some cause, or as reacting on other objects in the form of cause and substance; we may conceive it as possible, or we may conceive it as existent, or we may conceive it as necessary, that is, as existent from the mere fact of the possibility of its existence. We have thus the Categories of Unity, Plurality, and Totality; of Reality, Negation, and Limitation; of Substance, Causality, and Community of Action; of Possibility, Existence, and Necessity. These are the transcendental conceptions elicited from the Quantity, Quality, Relation, and Modality of the logicians. In each of the four classes the number of the categories is three, and in each triad the third is the synthesis of the other two (p. 67). The four forms of judgment are thus like the four rivers of Paradise in the picture in the old Bibles. They are placed at right angles to one another, each with a convenient bridge erected in the middle, and the tree of knowledge, with the serpent round it, is planted in the centre of the four.

Why the Categories should be twelve and twelve only we can no more explain than we can explain why the functions of judgment should be four, or why the kinds of syllogism should be three, or why the forms of sensible intuition should be only two (p. 89). We can only answer that the fact is so. The Transcendental Discovery being completed, Kant proceeds to the *Transcendental Deduction*, the object of which is 'to show that these conceptions are a priori conditions of the possibility of all experience' (p. 78), considered as a system of empirical cognition (p. 160). But the categories are not in themselves cognitions, but are mere forms of thought for the construction of cognitions from given intuitions; so that from them alone no synthetical propositions can be made (p. 174). And this again raises the question, What are the synthetic a priori propositions which the physical sciences assume? And how are such judgments possible?

The *Analytic of Principles* is the complement of the Analytic of Conceptions. Fastening on the four forms of judgment, Kant discovers that 'all intuitions are extensive quantities' (p. 122)—that 'in all phenomena the real, or that which is an object of

sensation, has degree' (p. 125)—that 'in all changes
of phenomena substance is permanent' (p. 136);
and 'all changes take place according to the law of
connexion of cause and effect' (p. 141); and 'all
substances, in so far as they can be perceived in
space at the same time exist in a state of complete
reciprocity of action' (p. 156)—and, finally, that
as a thing agrees with the formal, or coheres with
the material and universal, conditions of experience,
it is possible, real, or necessary (p. 161). These are
the *Axioms of Intuition—the Anticipations of Perception—the Analogies of Experience—and the Postulates of
Empiric Thought* (p. 121). Not only are these principles assumed in all our physical inquiries, but it
would be impossible to form any system of physical
science without assuming them. Unless we assumed
that all phenomena are subject to the laws of mathematics (p. 125), unless we assumed that substance in
the world of phenomena is constant (p. 137), unless
we assumed that the sequence of phenomena is subject to the law of causation (p. 142), we could pre-
determine nothing whatsoever as to the phenomena
with which we are to be presented (p. 141). This
shows the true nature of cognition a priori.
'All cognition by means of which we are able
to cognise and determine a priori what belongs to
empirical cognition may be called an *anticipation*'
(p. 126); and the principles which we are discussing
are only 'rules of synthetic unity a priori by means
of which we can *anticipate* experience' (pp. 160–1).
By means of the Axioms of Intuition we know a

priori that phenomena, when presented to us, will conform to the laws of time and space (p. 125). The Anticipations of Perception enable us to '*forestall* experience' in its very matter, the sensation (p. 127). The Analogies of Experience are merely rules by means of which 'we *anticipate* our own apprehensions' (p. 155), and 'intuite the future by *anticipation*' (p. 164). Even in connexion with the Postulates of Empiric Thought the great objection to the existing systems of idealism was, that by not admitting time and space to be the forms of sense, they gave no objective validity to sensible phenomena, and left the mind without any rational ground for anticipating their recurrence (p. 166). In point of fact, it is only by the existence of the principles of the understanding which *anticipate* experience that our possession of synthetic a priori judgments is proved (p. 463); and, accordingly, the Transcendental Analytic, to repeat the words of Kant, "has this important result, to wit, that the understanding is competent to effect nothing a priori, except the *anticipation* of the form of a possible experience in general' (p. 183); or, as he elsewhere expresses himself, it shows 'how the mere logical form of our cognition can contain the origin of pure conceptions a priori—conceptions which represent objects antecedently to all experience, or rather, indicate the synthetical unity which alone renders possible an empirical cognition of objects" (p. 225).

Kuno Fischer, in his Commentary, tells us that

'the whole summary of the Transcendental Analytic' is contained in the proposition that 'the pure
concepts of the understanding are not produced
by experience, but themselves *produce* experience,
though they cannot produce any other cognition
than experience' (p. 129)—they produce its very
objects like the forms of sense (p. 78). But Kant
asserts the very opposite of this. He asserts that
the conception of the understanding 'does *not* produce the object as to its existence,' but is only 'a
priori *determinative* in regard to that object' (p. 77).
It is true that the word *experience* is used in two
senses by Kant, and sometimes in a single sentence.
Thus in the opening sentence of the Kritik he says
that 'all our knowledge begins with *experience*,' and
then goes on to say that unless our senses were
affected the powers of the understanding would not
be roused 'to compare, to connect, or to separate
our representations, so as to convert the raw material of our sensuous impressions into a knowledge
of objects, which is called *experience*' (p. 1). Here
it is evident that the word experience is used first
as meaning sensuous impression, and afterwards as
meaning scientific knowledge. It is in the latter
sense that the word is used by Kant when he says
that 'the rules of the understanding' form 'the
basis of the possibility of experience.' " These
rules of the understanding," he says, " are not only
a priori true, but the very source of all truth, that
is, of the accordance of our cognition with objects,
and on this ground, that they contain the basis of

the possibility of experience, as the complex—the *inbegriff*—of all cognition" (p. 179).

But this suggests another aspect in which the question must be viewed. If truth be the accordance of our cognition with its objects (pp. 50, 179), how can we guarantee the accordance of objects with our cognition? Our cognition can possess no 'objective reality' unless we are supplied with 'intuitions to correspond with our conceptions' (p. 201)—how, then, can we guarantee that our conceptions will be supplied with the corresponding intuitions? If experience in its higher sense is dependent on the categories for its possibility, it is plain that the categories are dependent on experience in its lower sense for their objective validity and confirmation (p. xxix). How is it, then, that the categories can be 'the keys to possible *experiences*'? (p. 221). In fact, Kant himself suggests the problem. He raises the question, 'how the categories can determine a priori the synthesis of the manifold in nature, and yet not derive their origin from her'—'how it is conceivable that nature must regulate herself according to *them*' when they have their origin not in *her* but in the mind (p. 100). He finds himself 'involved in a difficulty' when he is asked 'how the subjective conditions of thought can have objective validity; in other words, can become the conditions of the possibility of all cognition of objects' (p. 75). He puts it thus :—"That objects of sensuous intuition must correspond to the formal conditions of sensibility existing a priori in the mind, is quite evident from the fact that without these they could not be objects for us; but that they must also correspond to the conditions which the understanding requires for the synthetical unity of thought, is an assertion the grounds of which are not so easily discovered; for phenomena might be so constituted as not to correspond to the unity of thought, and all things might be in such confusion that, for example, nothing could be met with in the sphere of phenomena to suggest a law of synthesis, and so correspond with the conception of cause and effect; so that this conception would be quite void, null, and without significance" (p. 76).

The solution of this enigma as Kant regards it (p. 100) is supplied by the Transcendental Object. Nature in its subjective aspect—*formaliter spectata*—may be regulated by the categories; but nature in its objective aspect—*materialiter spectata*—must be regulated by the object which is the non-sensuous cause of the phenomena presented to the mind (p. 309). ' To this Transcendental Object,' as we have been already told, ' we may attribute the whole connexion and extent of our possible perceptions' (p. 309). The action of this Transcendental Cause when ' phenomenized' is ' in perfect accordance with the laws of empirical causation' (p. 337). It is thus that objects are found to conform to our cognition (p. xxviii). It is thus that the anticipations of the understanding are confirmed by subsequent experience (p. xxix). Hence it is that when

the understanding supplies the conception, experience supplies the case (p. 120). Hence it is that
phenomena are presented to us ' in harmony with
the category' (p. 113). 'The categories never
mislead us,' in short, because ' outward objects are
always in perfect harmony therewith' (p. 394)—
in the words of Hume, because there is ' a kind
of pre-established harmony between the course of
nature and the succession of our ideas' (iv. 65).

The consideration of the Transcendental Object
leads us from the Transcendental Logic to the
Transcendental Dialectic—from the domain of Physical Science to the domain of Metaphysics—from
the region of anticipation which experience can
confirm to the region of anticipation which admits
of no confirmation from experience in our present
state (p. xxix). Here the Understanding expands
its Conceptions into *Ideas*, and assumes the name of
Reason. The ideas of Kant are not, like those of
Plato, the archetypes of things themselves (p. 221).
They are nothing but the categories elevated to the
unconditioned (p. 257), or rather, aspiring to an
unconditioned which they cannot possibly attain
(p. 311). They are necessary conceptions of reason to which no corresponding object can be discovered in the world of sense (p. 228), conceptions
which carry their synthesis far above all possible
experience (p. 263), and of the object corresponding
to which we can have no knowledge (p. 235). And
as the clue to the discovery of the categories was
supplied by the forms of judgment, so the clue to

the discovery of the ideas is supplied by the forms
of syllogism, to which all reasoning is restricted
(p. 225). The three forms of syllogism correspond
to the three categories of subsistence, causality, and
community of action (p. 226); and, following the
thread of these categories, metaphysicians have
attempted to *demonstrate* the nature of the Soul, the
World, and God.

The futility of all these attempted demonstrations, according to Kant, is evinced by demon-
strating the impossibility of making any dogmatical
assertion concerning any object which lies beyond
the boundaries of experience (p. 250). All a priori
knowledge, he says, is obtained either from the
anticipation of possible experience or from the
analysis of conceptions (p. 477). But ' in whatever
way the understanding may have attained to a conception, the existence of the object of the conception
cannot be discovered in it by analysis, because the
cognition of the existence of the object depends
upon the object's being posited and given in itself,
apart from the conception' (p. 392). The objects
which correspond to our ideas are not so given; for
we have no power of intellectual intuition, and the
intuition of the senses can never give the existence
of an object in itself (p. 43). It is in vain, therefore, that the reason poised on the wings of its
ideas attempts to transcend experience. As well
might the dove attempt to pass beyond the atmosphere by which it is supported, and to extend its
flight into the void.

The Transcendental Dialectic is only a development of the principles which are thus laid down. The *Rational Psychology* attempts to demonstrate from the very nature of thought that the Transcendental Subject is a substance—simple in its essence—identical through the whole period of its existence—and distinct from body (p. 239). But the conception of a thing which can exist per se only as a subject possesses no objective reality, because we can never know whether there exists any object to correspond with that conception (p. 244). The argument, therefore, is a mere *Paralogism of the Reason* (ibid.); and the transcendental illusion which gives it plausibility is found in the fact, that the unity of consciousness which lies at the basis of the categories is considered to be an intuition of the subject as an object, and the category of substance is applied to the fancied intuition (p. 249).

The *Rational Cosmology* which attempts to demonstrate the existence of a world resembling our ideas fares worse with Kant than the Rational Psychology. It not only begs the question, but in begging the question it finds itself involved in a variety of contradictions which are styled the *Antinomies of the Reason*. Whether Reason contemplates the composition, the division, the origination, or the dependence of phenomena (p. 260), so long as it supposes that it is dealing with things in themselves, it finds itself involved in a natural antithetic (p. 255). In the discussion of any one of these questions thesis

and antithesis spring from the Reason at the mere
suggestion, just as the two serpents which tormented
Zohab sprang living from his shoulder at the devil's
kiss.   Had the world a beginning or had it not?
Does or does not every composite substance consist
of simple parts?   Is a free causality necessary to
account for the phenomena of nature, or is no
such free causality required?   Does any absolutely
necessary being exist or no? (pp. 266–284).   As
long as we suppose we are dealing with things in
themselves, thesis and thesis may be with equal
plausibility maintained.   But the combatants are
the victims of a transcendental illusion (p. 315).
They fancy that the mere modifications of their
sensibility are things subsisting by themselves
(p. 307).   Once informed that all they are conscious of is phenomenal, they will see that the first
two antinomies are a contest about nothing (p. 313),
and that in the second two the antinomy is only
apparent, as it is not impossible that both the contradictory statements may be true—one, in the world
of sense, the other, in the world beyond it (p. 346).

The Rational Cosmology recognizes the necessity of admitting the existence of a Transcendental
Object as the unknown cause of our known sensations; and the recognition of this necessity is
an inducement to the *Transcendental Theology* to
identify the Transcendental Object, as Berkeley
identified it, with God.   But the fallacy of all
attempts to prove the existence of God by way of
demonstration is shown by the mere definition of

the conception of existence (p. 367)—by the fact that the existence of an object corresponding to a conception cannot be known by a mere analysis of the conception, and can only be shown by actual experience (p. 392). Hence it is that Kant describes the ontological demonstration which Descartes based on the innate idea of a God, as an illusive augmentation of our intellectual wealth by the addition of noughts to our account (p. 370). Hence it is that he describes the cosmological proof, which Leibnitz based on the idea of the contingency of the world, as the ontological demonstration in masquerade, an argument which had changed its dress and disguised its voice, for the purpose of passing itself off as an additional witness before the judgment-seat of reason (p. 372). The claims of the physico-theological argument, based upon the principle of final causes, are treated, it is true, by the critic of the reason with deference and respect (p. 382). But, according to Kant, this argument is merely an introduction to the ontological argument, which contains the only possible ground of proof possessed by the speculative reason for the existence of the Supreme Being (p. 383). Theoretically it is open to the various objections brought against its sufficiency by Hume. It reasons from the analogy of human art, and assimilates the creation of the world to the manufacture of a watch. At most it demonstrates the existence of an architect, but not the existence of a creator, of the world. At most, it proves the existence of a cause proportionate to the order and harmony which we observe, but not the existence of a cause, omnipotent, omniscient, and omnipresent, such as that which reason sees in its supreme ideal. But beyond this, it is open to the one insuperable difficulty in the mind of Kant. The physico-theological argument is unable to bridge the abyss which yawns between reality and thought; and the physico-theologians, after following the path of nature and experience, suddenly turn aside and pass into the region of pure possibility, where they hope to reach, upon the wings of ideas, what had eluded their empirical investigations, and, extending their conceptions over the whole sphere of creation, imagine they have attained to the transcendent reality of which they are in quest (pp. 386, 7).

We have now traversed the whole domain of the Transcendental Philosophy, and pursued our way as best we could in the uncertain glimpses of the moon which illuminates that shadowy realm—

> Quale per incertam lunam sub luce maligna
> Est iter in silvis.

In the *Transcendental Aesthetic* Kant professes to have established that all things intuited in space and time—all objects of possible experience—are nothing but phenomena, which, whether considered as extended bodies or as series of changes, have no existence apart from human thought (p. 307). In the *Transcendental Analytic* he professes to have shown that the understanding is competent to effect nothing a priori except the anticipation of the form of a possible experience in general, and that, as that which is not phenomenon cannot be an object of experience, it can never overstep the limits of sensibility within which alone objects are pre-sented (pp. 183, 225, 429). The *Transcendental Dialectic* professes to have demonstrated that "hu-man reason, in one sphere of its speculation, is called upon to consider questions which it cannot decline, as they are presented by its own nature, but which it cannot answer, as they transcend every faculty which it possesses" (p. xvii); and teaches the lesson that it ought never to attempt to soar above the sphere of possible experience, beyond which there lies nothing for us but the incomprehensible inane (p. 429).

But it is with the Kantian philosophy as with the nether world of Virgil—there is a double exit; and as the Speculative Reason is the porter of the gate of horn which gives egress to mere shadowy shapes, so the *Practical Reason* is seated by the ivory gate from which living realities emerge. Though we surrender the power of 'knowing,' we reserve the power of 'thinking,' supersensible ex-istence (p. xxxiii). There is nothing to prevent us from admitting that the objects which correspond to our ideas of the soul and God have an actual ex-istence (p. 412). We are not only authorised, but we are in fact compelled to realise them, and to posit real objects corresponding to our conceptions, though we cannot be said to know them (p. 415).

Even in a purely theoretical connexion we may assert that we firmly believe in the existence of God, and in a future state, while, in the moral aspect of the question, we are irresistibly constrained to believe in those momentous facts (p. 501). The proofs which have been current among men in justification of these high beliefs not only ' preserve their value undiminished,' but ' gain in clearness and unsophisticated power by the rejection of the dogmatic assumptions of the speculative reason' (p. 251). The practical proofs derived from ' the analogy of nature ' and ' the moral law' remain after the pretended demonstrations have been finally confuted. " This mighty, irresistible proof," says Kant—" accompanied, as it is, by an ever-increasing knowledge of the conformability to a purpose in everything we see around us, by the conviction of the boundless immensity of creation, by the consciousness of a certain illimitableness in the possible extension of our knowledge, and by a desire commensurate therewith—remains to humanity, even after the theoretical cognition of ourselves has failed to establish the necessity of an existence after death " (p. 251).

What then has Kant the Destroyer—the *Alleszermalmender* as he is called by his countrymen—destroyed? He himself informs us. He has effected nothing but a ' destruction of cobwebs' (p. xxxviii). He has confuted all ' metaphysical demonstrations ; ' but he has left us ' practical proofs' to take their place' (p. 251). He denies that we can have any ' logical conviction ' in sup-

port of our belief in God and in a future state, but he
admits that we may have a ' moral certainty' upon
the subject (p. 502). He recognizes the fact as
established on the subjective ground of sentiment
which he refuses to regard as established on the
objective ground of reason (*ibid.*). ' It is not
the *matter* which may give occasion to dispute,' he
says, ' but the *manner*'; and ' even after we have
been obliged to renounce all pretensions to *knowledge*,' it is ' perfectly permissible to employ, in the
presence of reason, the language of a firmly rooted
faith ' (p. 453). Faith fills the space left vacant by
the reason (p. xxxi); and if Kant abolishes knowledge, it is only to make way for belief (p. xxxv).

When knowledge and belief are thus sharply
contrasted, it may be well to examine a little
more closely into the true character of knowledge,
under the conditions of the Kantian system. For
what is Kant's *Cognition*? Kant holds that we
have no intuition but the intuition of the senses,
and that besides the intuition of the senses we
have no mode of cognition, except cognition by
conceptions (p. 57). What, then, is *Cognition by
Conceptions*? According to Kant, ' the conceptions
of the understanding are cogitated a priori antecedently to experience' (p. 219); and, consequently, ' all cognition, by means of which we
are enabled to cognize and determine a priori what
belongs to empirical cognition, may be called an
anticipation' (p. 126). Accordingly, as we have
seen, the Analytic arrives at the result that

" the understanding is competent to effect nothing a priori, except the anticipation of the form of a possible experience in general " (p. 183). But what is the nature of *Anticipation* ? It is not a mere conception of the intuition which will be presented, it is in reality, to use the words of Reid, a conception of the object accompanied by a *belief.* For what, in fact, is the category of substance but a belief that the phenomenal substance of the universe is constant ? What is the category of causation but a belief that the succession of phenomena is subject to a constant law ? What then is the difference in this respect between the conceptions of the understanding and the ideas of the reason ? It is merely this. The conceptions of the understanding, being restricted to the domain of experience, admit of *confirmation,* while the ideas of the reason, attempting to transcend experience, admits of no confirmation in our present state (p. xxix).

Yet it is not exactly true that the ideas of the reason receive no confirmation from experience even here. There are certain principles of the reason which are assumed in physical investigations. With Occam and Leibnitz, Kant has propounded certain laws as to the multiplication of entities, the variety of species, and the continuity of forms, which he denominates the law of parcimony, the law of specification, the law of continuity, and the like (pp. 399–410). These laws, though merely ideas of the reason, have a physical significance and use. They are *presuppositions* that, amid the seemingly infinite

diversity of the phenomena of nature, there will
be found a latent unity of fundamental properties
(p. 400); presuppositions which impose upon the
understanding the duty of searching for sub-species
in every species, and minor differences in every
difference (p. 402); presuppositions which have
their source in reason, and to which no adequate
object can be discovered in experience (pp. 404, 5).
The laws in question are not laws of nature; they
are *Maxims of Reason*—maxims which are not derived from observation of the constitution of the
object, but are subjective principles arising from
the interest which reason has in producing a certain
completeness in its ideas (p. 408). And yet under the
guidance of these principles experimentalists have
determined the nature of the elements (p. 396),
have reduced all salts to alkalis and acids (p. 400),
have ascertained the various species of absorbent
earths (p. 403), and have detected in the orbit of
the planet and the trajectory of the comet the existence and the laws of the all-pervading and continuous force of gravitatiou (p. 406). It might
have happened that reason, in thus following the
path of its ideas, was pursuing a path contrary to
that prescribed by nature (pp. 399, 405), just as
it might have happened that phenomena might
have been so constituted as not to correspond with
our conceptions (p. 76). But in our actual experience it is not so. The preconceptions of these
'anticipatory laws of reason,' as Kant denominates
them, are confirmed (p. 403). They are shown to

possess an 'objective, though undetermined validity' within the sphere of our actual experience (p. 407); and this proof of their validity inspires us with confidence in the other conclusions of reason, and leads us to believe that they too, in some future experience, may be eventually confirmed.*

It is at this point that Kant's approximation to the philosophy of the Scottish school becomes apparent. Reid, as we have seen, had resolved sensible perception into conception and belief, and on the authority of mere belief had assumed the existence of an external world of matter. According to Kant, as we have also seen, it must remain a scandal to philosophy to be obliged to assume the existence of things external to ourselves as an article of mere belief, and not be able to oppose a satisfactory proof to anyone who may call the fact in question (p. xl). We are now in a position to examine how he proposes to remove this scandal to philosophy, and how he proposes to supply a satis-

---

* How nature can regulate herself in accordance with the maxims of reason is presented by the most recent of the Kantian expositors as one of the most difficult problems in the Kritik. How nature must regulate herself in accordance with the principles of the understanding is a question proposed by Kant himself as a transcendental enigma. The two difficulties in reality are but one. Mr. Monck, in his *Introduction to the Critical Philosophy*, follows the German commentators, and answers the question they suggest by saying that without these principles "nature herself (*i.e.* objects of experience) could not exist" (p. 152). I have already given my reasons for rejecting this solution of the difficulty, and shown that the word nature is ambiguous. But while differing from Mr. Monck in this respect, I take this opportunity of expressing my obligations to that acute metaphysician for the numerous hints and suggestions with which he has favoured me during the composition of the present essay.

factory proof of the existence of things external to ourselves.

Kant's 'strict demonstration of the objective reality of external intuition' has been strangely misunderstood. One class of commentators of whom Hamilton is the representative has fancied, that in opposition to the whole scope of his philosophy he attempted to demonstrate the existence of external things as existing in external space. Another class has supposed with Mr. Mahaffy that his object was merely to prove, in opposition to Descartes and Berkeley, that external perception was not mere imagination, and that phenomena were something more than mere appearance (*Fisch.* li). It is difficult to demonstrate the true nature of a demonstration which is left involved in such a mist of words; but the momenta of Kant's argument would seem to be as follows :—I am conscious of my own existence as determined in time ; and all determination with regard to time presupposes the existence of something permanent in perception (p. 167). My existence in time is determined by my intuitions in space (p. 167); and space as the permanent form of my sensibility is permanent, and determines things as such (p. 176). But the permanent something which determines my existence in me cannot be the mere permanent intuition of space, because the permanent intuition of space itself requires to be determined. The external sense of which it is the form implies a relation to something real, which must affect the senses before the form of external sensibility can be evolved (p. xl). There must, therefore, be something permanent in existence, as well as something permanent in representation (p. xli.)—something permanent in existence which is the cause of our representations (p. 167), and which can be no other than the transcendental object (p. 309). But if the transcendental object and the transcendental ideality of space be granted, the objective reality of external intuition, that is, its empirical reality, follows, as a matter of course; and the proof of ‘the objective reality of external intuition’ is all that Kant contemplates by his proof of ‘the existence of things external to ourselves’ (p. xl).

But Kant’s demonstration of the existence of things external to ourselves is in reality a demonstration that things external to ourselves, in the ordinary sense of the term, have no existence. It establishes that when the transcendental object acts it produces certain modifications of our sensibility, and that when these modifications are produced, they are moulded in the forms of sense, of which the transcendental ideality of space is the result. Thus moulded, they are mere *phenomena*, which have no existence apart from human thought; and it is the fundamental position of the Transcendental Æsthetic that these phenomena constitute the only objects of which we have experience (p. 307). It is true, as Hume observes, that by a universal and necessary belief men regard phenomena as things subsisting by themselves (iv. 178). But

Kant, like Hume, though in more learned language, stigmatizes this as a mere transcendental illusion. And this shows the true effect of the Kantian demonstration. It establishes the existence of things external to ourselves, by showing that, properly speaking, they are not external. It demonstrates the objective validity of external intuition by showing that, properly speaking, it is not objective. Kant professes to have removed the scandal to philosophy which, in his opinion, is involved in accepting the existence of things external to ourselves, as an article of mere belief; but he removes the scandal to philosophy of appealing to belief, by the greater scandal of denying the validity of the belief to which philosophy appeals.

It is true that by insisting that all our ideas of sensation are moulded in the forms of sense, and that the forms of sense are constituent and essential elements of human nature, Kant attempted to impart to the sensible world the reality of the human nature in which it is moulded, and by which it is projected into fancied space. But this does not free philosophy from the scandal of accepting the existence of things external as an article of mere belief. It is mere matter of belief that the constitution of human nature, in respect to its capacities of sense, will continue as it is. It is mere matter of belief that the transcendental object will continue to act in its accustomed manner. It is mere matter of belief that the quantity of phenomenal

substance will continue constant. It is mere matter of belief that the succession of phenomena will
continue to be regulated by a constant law. The
law of continuance itself—the law which, in the
words of Bishop Butler, leads us to believe that all
things will continue as they are, except in those
respects in which we have reason to believe that
they will be altered—even this fundamental law,
by its very terms, is nothing but an expression of
belief.

We are now in a position to form an estimate of
Kant's theory of perception by comparing it with
the various theories which he rejects. In the first
place, he rejected, by anticipation, the *Presentative
Realism* which Hamilton proclaimed. He held that
the only manner in which our knowledge relates to
external objects is by means of intuition (p. 21);
and he held that our mode of intuition was sensuous
merely, and could never give the existence of the
object (p. 43). A fortiori he rejected the *Transcendental Realism*, which regards the mere modifications
of our sensibility as things subsisting by themselves
(p. 307). This was a mere transcendental illusion
(p. 315)—a universal and primary opinion of all
men, it is true, but one which, in the words of
Hume, the slightest philosophy was sufficient to
destroy (iv. 177). In the same way the principles
of Kant's philosophy compelled him to reject the
Hypothetical Realism, which supposes the existence
of an external world corresponding to our ideas of
extension. In the first edition of the Kritik, although

he maintains that we must admit the existence of something which, by affecting our senses in a certain manner, produces in us the idea of extension; yet he maintains that this something is not extended, impenetrable, or composite, because all these predicates only concern sensibility and intuition, in so far as we are affected by the transcendental object (*Fischer*, 341). In the Prolegomena he sarcastically exclaims, " I suppose I must say, not only that the representation of space is perfectly *conformable* to the relation which our sensibility has to objects, for that I have said, but also that it is quite *similar* to them—an assertion in which I can find as little meaning as if I had said that the sensation of red has a similarity to the property of vermilion which excites this sensation in me " (p. 56). In the second edition of the Kritik he states his opinion with respect to the fundamental nature of our sensuous cognition to be, " that the things which we intuite are not in themselves the same as our representations of them in intuition, nor are their relations in themselves so constituted as they appear to us " (p. 35). Whether Kant was consistent in making these dogmatic assertions may well be doubted. But his dogmatism goes still further. While he admits that objects corresponding to the psychological and theological ideas may possess ' an objective and 'hyperbolic existence,' he contends that there can be no objects corresponding to the cosmological ideas, because they are antinomial, and involve a contradiction (pp. 300, 412); and he holds that this affords an indirect proof of the transcendental ideality of the phenomena of sense (p. 316).*

And as Kant rejected these various forms of realism, so in recognizing the existence of a transcendental object, he repudiates that form of *Psychological Idealism*, which, ignoring the necessity of conceiving essential substance and efficient cause, regards the sensible world as a mere series of sensations, unsubstantial and uncaused. But he equally repudiated that form of Psychological Idealism which he variously described as *Material Idealism*, to distinguish it from Formal, and as *Empirical Idealism*, to distinguish it from Transcendental. Although Material Idealism recognized a cause by which our sensible ideas are produced, and a substance in which they inhere, it did not recognize the intuitions of space and time in which they are moulded, and thus left them, in his opinion, without form and void. It was upon this ground that he rejected the *Problematical Idealism* of Descartes, which, commencing with the famous *Cogito*, declared the existence of objects in space without us to be doubtful. According to Kant, it ignored the fact

* The most intelligible and compendious comment on the Kantian philosophy which has hitherto been published is to be found in Kant's *Prolegomena to any Future Metaphysic which can claim to be a Science*, and Mr. Mahaffy has laid the philosophical world under great obligation by his translation of that work. To this translation Mr. Mahaffy has appended the principal passages in the original Kritik of the Reason, which were altered in the second and following editions, and by so doing has demonstrated, against the German critics, that there is no substantial difference between the earlier and the later forms of the philosophy of Kant. The same passages are also given in his Translation of Fischer.

that our internal experience is determined by our external experience; and it ignored the fact that our external experience is determined by the Transcendental Ideality of Space.

In the same way he rejected the *Theological Idealism*, or, as he calls it, the *Dogmatic Idealism*, of Berkeley. Berkeley, it is true, admitted that all human experience must commence with sense, and recognized the existence of a non-sensuous cause of our sensations. But he held that space was the mere absence of resistance, and that absolute space was the mere phantom of the geometric mechanical philosophers. Hence he left our sensations without any natural bond or basis. Hence he represented the mind as entirely passive in the reception of its sensible ideas. Hence he reduced phenomena to mere appearance, and regarded the sensible world as a mere vanity of the Divine Art—a mere insubstantial pageant, such as that which the magician exhibited to Miranda in the enchanted isle. But this was not the only ground on which Kant objected to the Theological Idealism of Berkeley. Not only did Berkeley ignore the transcendental ideality of space; but he professed to determine the nature of the transcendental object. Kant, it is true, reproduces the main argument of Berkeley. "The world around us," he says, "opens before our view so magnificent a spectacle of order, variety, beauty, and conformity to ends, that, whether we pursue our observations into the infinity of space in one direction, or into its illimitable divisions on the other, whether we regard the world in its greatest or in its least manifestations, even after we have attained the highest summit of knowledge which our weak minds can reach, we find that in the presence of wonders so inconceivable language has lost its force, and number can no longer reckon, nay, even thought fails adequately to conceive; and our conception of the whole dissolves into an astonishment without the power of expression—all the more eloquent that it is dumb" (p. 382). But while Kant is compelled to recognize the existence of ' something which is primal and self-subsistent— something which, as the cause of this phenomenal world, secures its continuance and preservation' (*ibid.*), he refuses to recognize this primal and self-subsistent cause as God. He is prevented from so doing by the exigencies of his Dialectic. The principle of efficient causation, he says, is a principle without significance in the sensuous world (p. 374). It is impossible to discover any mode of transition from that which exists to something entirely different termed a cause (p. 390). The knowledge of the existence of an object depends upon the object's being posited and given in itself, apart from the conception (p. 392). The fact is not susceptible of demonstration. It is strange that Kant should have forgotten that, on his own showing, what cannot be mathematically demonstrated may be practically proved, It is stranger still that he should have recognized the principle of efficient causation when he assumed the existence of a Transcendental Object, but should have repudiated its authority when he came to prove the existence of a God.

Kant was more self-consistent when he declined to adopt the *Egoistical Idealism* of Fichte, and to hold that there is only one single substance in the universe—the Ego. We are told by Schwegler that Kant, in his first edition, stated it to be possible that the ego and the thing in itself, which lies behind the appearances of sense, might be one and the same thinking substance, and that in his second edition he expunged the conjecture (*Schw.* 220). But this is a mere misapprehension. In the second edition Kant repeats the language of the first. He gives a premonition that the two fountains of human knowledge may possibly spring from a common but an unknown source (p. 18). He states "that it is quite possible that the cause of our representations may lie in ourselves, and that we ascribe it falsely to external things" (p. 167). He considers that "that which lies at the basis of phenomena, as a thing in itself, may not be heterogeneous" from the object of the inner sense, the soul (p. 252). But he declined to accept an admitted possibility for an established fact. All the manifestations of our consciousness are determined by our external intuitions (p. 167); but though our external intuitions are determined by some transcendental object, we possess no intuition which gives the determining in ourselves prior to the act

of determination (p. 96). On the contrary, we have
the consciousness, not of a determining, but only of
a determinable, self (p. 241). In one passage Kant
seems to agree with Berkeley, that the permanent
something to which we are related cannot be ' something in us' (p. 167); but he subsequently modifies the statement, and contents himself with saying
that this permanent cannot be an ' intuition in us'
(p. xl). Nor could Kant consistently have made
any dogmatic assertion on the subject. His official
doctrine, constantly repeated, is expressed in language which admits of no dispute. He does not
hold, as Fichte seems to have imagined him to hold,
' that sensation is to be explained by reference to a
transcendental object independently existent without us' (*Schw.* 260). What he holds is, that the
transcendental object which is the basis of phenomena is a mere nescio quid (p. 206). He insists
that the transcendental ground of the unity of
subjective and objective lies too deeply concealed
for us, who know ourselves only through the internal sense, and consequently as phenomena, to
be able to discover in our existence anything but
phenomena, the non-sensuous cause of which constitutes the mystery of the origin and source of sense
(p. 200). In fine, he persistently maintains, against
Fichte as against Berkeley, that the transcendental
object which is the cause of phenomena is ' an
object of which we are quite unable to say whether
it can be met with in ourselves, or out of ourselves—
whether it would be annihilated together with

sensibility, or, if this were taken away, would continue to exist' (p. 206).

But while Kant thus protested his ignorance of the nature of the transcendental object, he entertained no misgivings as to the transcendental ideality of space. It is in this transcendental ideality that the peculiarity of his *Transcendental Idealism* is to be sought and found. It is true he admitted that the faculty of cognition could not be awakened into exercise unless our senses were affected (pp. i. 21, 45). It is true he held that our senses could not be affected except by the operation of some efficient cause (pp. 206, 333, 337). It is true he recognized as 'the non-sensuous cause of phenomena' (p. 309) 'a non-empirical and intelligible causality' which 'phenomenises' itself though it is not 'phenomenal' (p. 337), and which as transcending the sensations of which it is the cause may be styled the transcendental object (pp. 200, 309, 333, 337). But the transcendental object merely supplies the *material* of knowledge, and it is the transcendental ideality which supplies the *form* (p. 36). Our sensations are nothing till they are moulded in the forms of sense. Accordingly Kant contended, not only that the rainbow with its various colours has no existence, except in the mind, but that even the raindrops themselves, with their globular form and the space through which they fall, are merely fundamental dispositions of our sensuous intuition (p. 38). It was by the establishment of this that the Transcendental Æsthetic established the fundamental position

of Transcendental Idealism, which proclaims that all
things perceived by us in space and time, and therefore all objects of any experience which is possible
to us—whether they be regarded as extended bodies,
or whether they be regarded as series of changes—
are nothing but phenomena which have no existence
apart from human thought (p. 307).

Kant tells us that we are not justified in con-
verting the forms of our sensibility into conditions of the possibility of things (p. 27). He tells
us that he does not deny that empty space may
possibly exist, though he holds that we cannot
possibly perceive it (p. 158). But he maintains
that, from 'the human point of view,' space is
nothing but a form of human sensibility (p. 27);
and that, though things may be related *in* space as
a form of sense, they have no relation *to* space
considered as a reality independent of the senses
(p. 267).* To test the doctrine which thus reduces
space, from the human point of view, to a mere
transcendental ideality, let us take the famous pas-

---

* Mr. Mahaffy considers that I am wrong in my view of Kant's theory of space. In his Translation of Fischer's Commentary he says—"How, in the face of these reiterated assertions, Professor Webb could write (*Intellectualism*, p. 173), 'whether Kant held that space was nothing but a form of sensibility may be doubted,' seems to me marvellous. And the ground of the assertion is still more so: 'it is inconceivable that so systematic a thinker should have denied the possibility of a knowledge of the objective, and yet dogmatically have affirmed the objective non-existence of what possesses empiric reality'" *Mahaffy's Fischer*, p. 55. But Kant expressly says that it is only from the human point of view that *we* can speak of space (p. 26); and he expressly says that he does not intend to combat the notion of empty space; for, he says, "it may exist where our perceptions cannot exist, inasmuch as they cannot reach thereto" (p. 158).

sage in the *Theory of Ethics* which is familiar to every student of philosophy. "Two things there are," says Kant, "which, the oftener and the more steadfastly we consider them, fill the mind with an ever new and ever rising admiration and reverence —the Starry Heavens above and the Moral Law within. Of neither am I compelled to seek out the reality, as veiled in darkness, or only to conjecture the possibility, as beyond the hemisphere of knowledge. Both I contemplate lying clear before me, and I connect both immediately with my consciousness of existence. The one departs from the place I occupy in the outer world of sense—expands, beyond the bounds of imagination, the connexion of my body with worlds rising beyond worlds, and systems blending into systems—and protends it into the illimitable times of their periodic movement, its commencement and perpetuity. The other departs from my invisible self, from my personality, and represents me in a world truly infinite, indeed, but whose infinity can be tracked out only by the intellect, and my connexion with which, unlike the fortuitous relation in which I stand to the world of sense, I am compelled to recognize as universal and necessary. In the one, the first view of a countless multitude of worlds annihilates, as it were, my importance as an animal product, which, after a brief and incomprehensible endowment with the powers of life, is compelled to refund its constituent matter to the planet—itself an atom in the universe—on which it grew. The other, on the contrary, elevates my worth as an intelligence, even without a limit, and that through my personality, in which the moral law reveals the faculty of life independent of my animal nature, nay, of the whole material world —at least, if it be permitted to infer as much from the regulation of my being, which a conformity with that law enacts, proposing, as it does, my moral worth for the absolute end of my activity, conceding no surrender of its imperative to a ne- cessitation of nature, and spurning in its infinity the conditions and boundaries of my present transitory life."*

This passage shows how difficult it is for any idealist to realise his own idealism, or to reconcile it with the unsophisticated view of common sense. For why contrast the moral law within with the starry heavens above, if the starry heavens above in reality exist within?   Why talk of my con- nexion with worlds upon worlds, and systems upon systems, if worlds upon worlds, and systems upon systems, have no external existence, and are but modifications of myself?   Why should the countless multitude of worlds annihilate my importance as an animal nature, when it is in my nature alone that all the countless multitude of worlds exists?   How is the constituent matter of the animal product to be given back to the planet it inhabits, if the matter of

---

* I have slightly modified the trans- lation of this magnificent passage as given in Hamilton's Discussions (p. 310). A more literal translation is to be found in Kant's *Theory of Ethics* or *Practical Philosophy*, by the Rev. T. K. Abbott, Fellow of Trinity Col- lege—another valuable contribution to the study of the Kantian Philosophy supplied by the University of Dublin.

which it is formed, and the planet which it inhabits, and the universe of which that planet is a speck, are all mere transcendental idealities, which have no existence whatever apart from human thought? And where is the majesty of the moral law in a world which exists only in idea? The moral law supposes me to be a member of a moral system—a system in which I am related to other beings, and in which each member has his rights and duties, and is under obligation to the others. But if there is no external world, there are no external bodies; and if there are no external bodies, what proof have I of the existence of other moral beings? How can I prove, or believe in, the existence of my fellow-creatures, if I cannot prove, and am not to believe in, the existence of the corporeal frames in which they are embodied, and by which they are revealed? On the principles of idealism not only is the sublimity of the contrast lost, but its very significance is gone. The starry heavens fade away into a sensuous image, and the empire of the moral law dissolves into a domain of dreams.

The imagination encounters still greater difficulties when it attempts to realise the purely idealist conception of *time*. Hegel ridicules the passage in which Haller describes eternity as awful, with its mountains of millions, its ages piled on ages. The only really awful thing about it, he says, is the awful wearisomeness of ever fixing, and anon unfixing, a limit, without advancing a single step (*Log.* s. 104). But the wearisomeness of the effort

Q

to contemplate the everlasting Now, which is the
only idea of objective time which the idealist
admits, is quite as awful. The effort, moreover,
from the very nature of the case, must prove
abortive. We cannot divest ourselves of the idea
of an objective time in which all objective change
occurs. Changes are real. Time may be a mere
form, in so far as it is the form of the continual
change in our representations (p. 32). But there
are objective changes. We ourselves, whatever we
may be, begin to exist, and have therefore an objective beginning of existence. Of such an objective fact no subjective form can be the explanation.
As far as we can judge objective changes can only
occur in an objective time. Nor does Kant, when
properly understood, deny the existence of such an
object. It is true, he says that time is not something which subsists of itself (p. 30)—that if we
take objects as they are in themselves then time is
nothing (p. 31)—that time cannot be reckoned as
subsisting or inhering in objects as things in themselves, independently of its relation to our intuition
(p. 32). But, in this connexion, what are we to
understand by *time?* According to the doctrine of
the Kritik, time regarded as a real object is not
presented to any of our perceptive powers (p. 30).
As in the case of every other real object, the only
mode in which our knowledge can relate to it is by
means of our intuition (p. 21); and here, as elsewhere, our intuition, being merely sensuous, can
never give us the object of intuition in itself (p. 43).

But if the object be not given by intuition, its existence, according to the teaching of the Kritik, can never be discovered by any analysis of our conceptions (p. 392). Time, therefore, as an absolute reality, is something which, for us, remains unpresented and unknown. It is only presented to us as a form of sense. Consequently it is only as a necessary representation lying at the foundation of all our intuitions of sense (p. 28), and all our conceptions of change (p. 29) that *we* have any cognisance of time. As the real form of our internal intuition, it is something real (p. 32), but this reality is not the absolute reality of a thing subsisting by itself (p. 34). To regard any mere modification of our sensibility as a thing subsisting by itself would be to maintain that obnoxious transcendental realism against which the whole Kritik is one continued protest (p. 307). As a form of intuition, therefore, time is nothing when abstracted from the phenomenon of sense (p. 31); as a form of intuition, it cannot be reckoned as an attribute of things (p. 32). But the existence of things in themselves is recognised by Kant, and in addition to the time which is a form of sense there *may be* a time which is an existing thing. If time, as an absolute reality, is not given, it does not follow that it does not exist. If time, as an objective existence, is not known, it does not follow that its existence may not be an object of belief. Kant has met all such inconsequential reasoning in advance. He answers both those who deny his doctrine and those who would extend it. They do not reflect, he says, that both space and time, without question of their reality as representations, belong only to the genus phenomenon, which has always *two aspects*—the one, the object considered as a thing in itself, the other, the form of our intuition of the object (p. 33).

To conclude that space and time have no existence because we do not know them as existing would be to disregard the wisest lesson and the most earnest warning of the Kritik. True, the great metaphysician professed to have abolished metaphysics. True, he ridiculed the so-called science with all the richness of metaphor which his imagination could supply. It was a stormy ocean in which nothing could be discerned but the fog-bank and the mist. It was a Serbonian morass in which man could neither stand nor swim. It was a shadowy Walhalla which was the everlasting battle-field of shades. It was a Babel of confusion in which men, like the builders on the plain of Shinar, strove in vain to build them a city and a tower which might reach to heaven. But, in the opinion of Kant, the very severity of his criticism had rendered an important service to the interest of thought. By showing the impossibility of making any dogmatical affirmation concerning objects beyond the boundaries of experience it had fortified the mind against all counter affirmations (p. 250). If it had shown the inability of human reason to supply any demonstration of the existence of a Supreme Being, it had also shown the utter fatuity of denying his existence (p. 393). If it had shown that mere reason is incompetent to demonstrate the freedom of the will and the immortality of the soul, it had shown that reason was equally incompetent to demonstrate that we are not immortal and that we are not free (p. 458). In fact, according to Kant, the greatest if not the only use of a philosophy of pure reason was to be found in its purely negative character (p. 482)—in the protection which its very negation of knowledge supplies to our practical beliefs in freedom, immortality, and God (p. xxxv).

But our practical beliefs in freedom, immortality, and God can scarcely be considered stronger than our practical belief in the absolute reality of space and time. The principles of space and time stand on the same level of authority as the principles of causation, which Kant recognises without reluctance or reserve. Kant admits that there is an objective course of physical causation which confirms all the anticipations of experience suggested by the categories of the understanding. He admits the objective existence of an efficient cause which operates beyond the region of mere physical causation, and which he styles the transcendental object. He even admits the validity of the principle of final causes, and again transcending the domain of nature, insists on the existence of a great first cause which sustains and regulates the world of sense (pp. 251, 382). In all these cases belief surpasses knowledge. In all these cases belief supplies a ground of expec-

tation and a principle of action. But what principle
of action can be justified, if one of the most powerful of our practical beliefs is to be belied? The
belief in the existence of space and time is as strong
as any belief which the human mind can entertain
and to give that belief the lie is to destroy all confidence in our faculties and to cut the very nerves
of action.

The tendency of the mind of Kant was essentially idealistic. It was his boast that the Kritik
had struck at the root of materialism and destroyed
the fatalism and atheism which are its malignant
growth (p. xxxvii.). Nor was the boast unfounded.
In spite of its loud appeals to experience, materialism is nothing but a form of metaphysic. The metaphysic of matter is as incapable of verification as
that of mind. To convert the principles of experience
into conditions of the possibility of things, and to
reduce the universe to matter, is just as transcendent
a procedure as that which appeals to the principles
of thought, and affects to demonstrate the existence
of the objects of our ideals and ideas (p. 474).
Materialism may be one of the possibilities of
things; but even if materialism be possible it does
not exhaust the sphere of possibility (p. 474). There
are other possibilities which are equally worthy of
regard. It is possible, for instance, that our actual
life is nothing but a sensuous representation of a
pure spiritual existence—that the sensible world is
but an image hovering before our faculty of sense—
that, if we could see ourselves as we actually are,

we should see ourselves in a world of spiritual natures, our connexion with which did not begin at our birth, and will not cease with the destruction of our bodies (p. 473). But Kant struck at the root of idealism as vigorously as he struck at the root of materialism (p. xxxvii.). Idealism, he said, is not to be obtruded as a dogma—it is not even to be regarded as a fixed opinion (p. 474). It is a mere *transcendental hypothesis* (p. 473)—a hypothesis which is not to be valued as an instrument of discovery, but as a weapon of defence (p. 472). As a weapon of defence it is available against the attacks of materialism, but that is all. It is a weapon which has not been steeled in the armoury of experience— its metal is not steel, but lead (p. 473).

But this wise reserve was contemptuously disregarded by the philosophers of Germany who succeeded Kant. They professed to be in earnest about idealism. They proclaimed the transcendental ideality to be the only valuable portion of the philosophy of their master. They denied that space and time had any ontological existence. They treated the principles of substance and causation as they treated the principles of space and time. They repudiated the transcendental object. Resolving the World into a sensuous phantom, and God into the moral order, Fichte declared the Ego to be the only substance (*Schw.* 267), while Hegel resolved the Ego itself into its ideas—left ideas without any origin in causation or any support in substance —made the Absolute Idea the sum total of existence

—and declared Absolute Idealism to be the last word of philosophy, the culminating point of human thought (*Schw.* 435).

But every revolutionary excess is followed by reaction. In opposition to these extravagances the Neo-Scottish school reverted to the principles of Reid. They recognised the practical authority of belief, and reasserted the objective validity of the principles of space and time, and substance and causation. But they also, with a certain reserve, adopted the principles of Kant. They admitted that unless the object were actually given, its existence could never be positively known; and they admitted that in whatever way our knowledge relates to material objects, it can only immediately relate to them by means of an intuition. But is our intuition merely sensuous? Is all our knowledge essentially subjective? Is it true that the object is never given to us in intuition? Is it true that the object is never actually known? These were the questions which engaged the attention of the Neo-Scottish school, and they cannot be more satisfactorily discussed than in connexion with the philosophy of Hamilton, its founder.

CATALEPTIC IDEALISM:

OR

HAMILTON.

CATALEPTIC IDEALISM:

OR

HAMILTON.*

◆

Tactus enim, Tactus, proh Divóm numina sancta !
Corporis est sensus.

LUCRETIUS.

THE history of philosophy is little more than a history of refutations. For upwards of two hundred years the church militant was thundering on the morion of Hobbes. A whole library might be formed of the answerers of Locke. The name of the antagonists of Hume is legion. But nowhere has this rage of refutation been more conspicuous than in the Scottish School. In the succession of

* The substance of this Essay was originally published under the title of *The Metaphysician* in *Frazer's Magazine* for April, 1860, four or five years before the publication of Mr. Mill's Examination. Any coincidences, therefore, which may be detected between the Examination and the present Essay are coincidences only. Those who travel the same road will see the same objects, and those who see the same objects will describe them in similar terms and make the same observations on them.

writers, by whom it is represented, we have not
only a series of refutations, but a series of refutations in which the great man, who for the moment
was lord of the ascendant, refuted the refutation of
his predecessor. The philosophy of Reid was nothing
but an attack on the speculative edifice which was
reared by Hume. But as Reid refuted Hume, so
Brown refuted Reid; and as Brown refuted Reid, so
Hamilton refuted Brown; and as Hamilton refuted
Brown, so the whirligig of time brought in its
revenges, and Mill, in his turn, refuted Hamilton.
The whole intellectual movement, in fact—if it
is not beneath the dignity of the subject to employ
such an illustration—is the exact counterpart of the
performances of the cow, the dog, the cat, and the
rat, which are celebrated in the jingling history of
the House that Jack built.

Hamilton, after Hume, is the greatest of the
metaphysicians whom Scotland has produced. He
occupied a large space in the view of his contemporaries; and of all his contemporaries none, perhaps, exerted a greater influence upon thought. Of
the state of philosophy in the year 1833, when he
first appeared as a writer, we cannot require better
evidence than that of a celebrated work which
was published in that year—the *England and the
English* of the first Lord Lytton. According to that
brilliant writer, it was the age of political econo-
mists. The stream of thought had been diverted
into political science, and had left the fountains of
metaphysics and of ethics dry. All the recent

moralists were of the school of Helvetius, and all
the recent metaphysicians were of the school of
Hartley. There was no idealizing school to coun-
terbalance the attraction towards speculations which
dealt with the unelevating practices of the world.
The lamp of a purer naphtha, to use Lord Lytton's
expression, was extinct. Compare this description
with the present state of thought, and it will be
seen how wide a distance separates the epochs.
The lamp which was extinguished is re-lit. The
fountain which had run dry is all aflow. Instead of
metaphysics being material, physical science has
become metaphysical. In this revolution by far
the most conspicuous figure is that of Hamilton;
and the power of his personality is evidenced by
the influence which he exercised upon such minds as
Mansel, and Fraser, and M'Cosh, and Veitch.

The first thing which strikes the student of the
works of Hamilton is the appearance of stupendous
learning. The philosophy of Aristotle and Plato,
the mystical speculations of the Alexandrine and
Arabian schools, the infinite subtilties of the Schoolmen, and all the developments of modern thought—
whether British, French, or German—appear to be
reflected in his mind. Nay, the physiologists and
anatomists of all ages seemed to have been as
familiar to him as the philosophers; and even on
the question of the worms in the frontal sinus,
when attacking the phrenologists, he could in his
medical ignorance, as with the pride which apes
humility he styles it, refer to authorities which he

could scarcely summon patience to recount (*Lect.* i.
427). But if we test his knowledge by a reference
to the writers with whom we are familiar—if we
test it by a reference to Locke, to Berkeley, or to
Hume—it will be apparent that his learning was
too multifarious to be precise. Take, for example,
the case of Hume. Hamilton conceived that Hume
had no philosophical principles of his own, but
merely accepted the principles adopted by the
previous schools. He did not see that while Hume
rejected Locke's theory of the origin of ideas, he
accepted his theory of the origin of knowledge.
He did not perceive that on the question of the
existence of an external world Hume recognised
the practical authority of the common sense of
Reid. He did not see that in his discussion of
the question of causation Hume enunciated and
employed the method which is deemed the discovery of Kant. He identified Hume with the sensualistic school, though Hume insisted on the a priori
character of mathematics. He saw in Hume nothing but the sceptic, and even the nature of his
scepticism itself he misconceived, identifying him
with Pyrrho and with Sextus, instead of identifying him with Pascal and with Kant.

And yet the view of his enormous intellectual
acquisitions occasions a feeling of regret that he did
not employ them in satisfying the one great desi-
deratum of the philosophic world. Studious, subtle,
and systematic, the intellect of Hamilton was pecu-
liarly fitted for the task of contabulating all the

various speculations of philosophers, exhibiting them in their mutual relations, and presenting a synopsis of the various systems. His analysis of all the possible theories of causation, and his analysis of all the possible theories of perception, show what he could have effected on a larger scale. But Hamilton mistook his mission. He aspired to be a great original thinker, and despised the humbler function of expounding the various possibilities of thought. He did not see that the resources of conjecture were practically exhausted, and instead of supplementing the work of Kant by giving the world a Kritik of Systems, he added to the confusion and the conflict which distract philosophy by elaborating a system of his own.

Regarded as a system, the philosophy of Hamilton presents an appearance which is strangely unsystematic. He seems to have been overwhelmed with the mass of his materials. His sentiments are to be collected with infinite labour by a collation of passages extracted from a variety of dissertations—historical, critical, and dogmatic. His works are full of repetitions, and inconsistent statements of opinion. Not one of them, in a literary point of view, is artistically complete. He had collected materials for a noble superstructure, but his philosophy presents the appearance of a builder's yard rather than the appearance of a building.

Unfortunately for his permanent influence, Hamilton was misled by his patriotic bias as a Scotchman, and mainly applied his genius to the service of

the Scottish School. With the self-abnegation of a
Dumont, he devoted himself to the exposition and
development of the philosophy of Reid—with this
difference, however, that Reid was as inferior to
Hamilton as Mirabeau and Bentham were superior
to Dumont. But it was clearly impossible for a
mind so enterprising and so energetic to confine
itself within the narrow limits of the philosophy of
common sense. It would have been strange, indeed, if the genius of Kant had not fascinated the
imagination, and cast a spell over the intellect, of
Hamilton. Hamilton, in fact, was a composite of
Reid and Kant. His philosophy was a confluence
of the two streams of speculation which had their
fountain-head in Hume. But, like the rivers in the
Iliad, the two incongruous tides would never mingle;
and hence, while the professions of common sense,
like the stream of oil, lay glistening on the surface
of his philosophy, the Kantian stream, like the off-
shoot of the waters of the Styx, rolled deep and
dark beneath.

The influence, however, which Reid exerted
over the mind of Hamilon was so great that, in his
view, it invested with paramount importance the
primary question of Reid's philosophy—the theory
of perception, and the proof of the existence of the
world of matter. This question had been brought
into prominence by Berkeley, and had been pronounced to be incapable of solution in the way of
philosophy by Hume. Reid undertook to solve it.
Hume's position was that the opinion of external

existence, if rested on natural instinct, is contrary
to reason, and if referred to reason is contrary to
reason, and at the same time carries no rational
evidence with it, to convince an impartial inquirer
of its truth (iv. 181). This position Reid undertook
to turn; but his mode of procedure was peculiar.
He conceded the premises of Hume. He conceded
that in perception there is nothing present to the
mind but the perception. He conceded that there
is no immediate intercourse between mind and
matter, and that we have no experience of the
connexion between our perceptions and material
things. He conceded that the existence of the world
of matter cannot possibly be proved by reason. It
is true he insisted on what Hume admitted—that
we are irresistibly led by a natural instinct to
believe in the existence of an external world which
is independent of our perceptions; but it is equally
true he admitted what Hume insisted on—that when
we yield to this natural instinct we are irresistibly
led to believe that our perceptions are themselves
external. Reid, therefore, could not deny the existence of the conflict signalised in Hume's dilemma.
All he could say was what had been previously said
by Hume—that, conflict or no conflict, we must
follow the instincts of our nature. It was the
governing principle of his doctrine, according to
Hamilton, to reconcile philosophy with the necessary convictions of mankind (*Reid*, 820); but his
only resource was to disguise the conflict between

R

them by conferring on each of the conflicting principles the equivocal name of common sense.

The impossibility of basing a system of philosophy on common sense in any consistent meaning of the term is apparent from Hamilton's treatment of the subject. "Common Sense," he says, " is like Common Law—each may be laid down as the general rule of decision; but in the one case it must be left to the jurist, in the other to the philosopher, to ascertain what are the contents of the rule; and, though in both instances the common man may be cited as a witness, for the custom or the fact, in neither can he be allowed to officiate as advocate or judge " (p. 752). But Hamilton does not seem to have perceived the inevitable consequences of this distinction. For observe the results of the examination of the common man if he be cited as a witness for the custom or the fact on this question of perception. Undoubtedly the common man would depose, if he could express himself in the language of philosophers, that he believes the world to exist, because he is immediately cognisant of its existence (*Reid*, 750). But submit the witness to cross-examination, and what will be the result? He will inevitably admit to Hume that he believes the images presented by the senses to be the external objects (iv. 177). He will inevitably admit to Hume that the sensible qualities, such as colour, heat, and cold, which are mere sensations of the mind, are, in his opinion, inherent in the object

(iv. 180). He will admit, in fine, that he thinks he sees the sky above him, and the fields around him, and the fruit tree in his garden, and that to the best of his belief the sky is blue, and the fields are green, and the cherries on the cherry-tree are red. But these beliefs Hamilton admits to be at once inevitable and erroneous. He holds that it is incorrect to say that the sun, or moon, or stars are, or can be, perceived by us as existent, and in their real distance in the heavens (*Reid*, 299); and he repudiates the natural realism of the vulgar, which transfers our sensations of colour to the object (*Reid*, 816). But in admitting this, Hamilton admits everything for which Hume contends. He admits that reason and natural instinct are in conflict. He admits that what is common is not sense, and that what is sense is not common— that what is natural is not real, and that what is real is not natural, In short, he virtually admits that Common Sense and Natural Realism, as far as perception is concerned, are contradictions.

Nor is Hamilton more fortunate in his appeal to the philosophers on the question of law than he is in his appeal to the common man on the question of the facts. " For reasons to which we cannot at present advert," he says, "it has been almost universally denied by philosophers, that in sensitive perception we are conscious of any external reality —on the contrary, they have maintained, with singular unanimity, that what we are immediately cognitive of, in that act, is only an *ideal object* in the

mind itself" (*Disc.* 193). He repeats this in his
edition of Reid (pp. 749, 817); he repeats it in his
Lectures (i. 295). What then, according to Hamilton, is common sense? Not the common sense of
the vulgar, for they are incompetent to form a
judgment; not the common sense of the philosophers, for the judgment *they* pronounce is wrong.
Hamilton's common sense, therefore, would appear to
be merely the common sense of one uncommon man;
and, as far as his immediate purpose is concerned,
he is merely in a position to verify the saying which
Voltaire borrowed from Buffier—that common sense
is anything but common. The fact is, that common
sense is incompetent to give any satisfactory answer
either as to law or as to fact; and the appeal to
such an authority can have no result but that of
arraying the prejudices of the vulgar against the
speculations of an opponent. It is not an argument
addressed to a judge, neither is it the examination
of a witness. To carry out the analogy, it is a
mere speaking to the gallery—an appeal to the
prejudices of the mob.

Abandoning the shifting ground of common
sense, and taking his stand upon the ground of
reason, Hamilton deviated from the procedure
of Reid in dealing with the idealistic question.
In reducing perception to mere conception and
belief, Reid had unconsciously admitted that in
perception there is nothing present to the mind but
its ideas, and had gone off on a false track, misled
by the idle fancy that the idea of the philosophers

was a tertium quid. Hamilton was too subtle to be
betrayed into any such fiasco. He attacked Hume
in his central position. Hume had laid it down as a
principle, conceded by all philosophers, that, in perception 'the mind has never anything present to it
but the perceptions and cannot possibly reach any
experience of their connexion with objects' (iv. 177,
179). This Hamilton denied. 'In the act of perception,' he said, 'I am conscious of two things—
of myself, as the perceiving subject, and of an external reality, in relation with my sense, as the
object perceived' (*Reid*, 747). This he said was
'the cardinal point of philosophy' (*ibid.*), and it was
to the establishment of this point that his philosophy of perception was devoted.

As this theory must be regarded as one of the
permanent possibilities of speculative thought, it
may be well to consider it in the various lights in
which it was presented by its author. What Hamilton conceived himself to have conclusively established was a system of *Natural Realism* founded on
'the datum of the natural consciousness, or common sense, of mankind' (*Reid*, 816), which proclaims that 'in perception we are conscious of the
external object immediately and in itself' (p. 866).
He maintained that we have an *Immediate Knowledge*
of the existence of the external world (pp. 750, 805).
He maintained that we have *Intuitive Perception*
of things, and that 'the mind, when a material
existence is brought into relation with its organs
of sense, obtains two concomitant and immediate

cognitions'—one 'the consciousness of certain subjective modifications in us, which we refer, as effects,
to certain unknown powers, as causes in the external reality'; the other 'the consciousness of certain
objective attributes in the external reality itself, as,
or as in relation to, our sensible organism' (*Reid*,
820). He developed a doctrine of *Real Presentation-
ism* which asserts ' the consciousness, or immediate
perception, of certain essential attributes, of matter
objectively existing, while it admits that other
properties of body are unknown in themselves, and
only inferred as causes to account for certain subjective affections of which we are cognisant in ourselves' (p. 825). What he advanced was a theory of
Dualistic Realism the fundamental position of which
is that ' our cognitions of extension and its modes
are not wholly ideal—that although space be a
native, necessary, a priori, form of imagination,
and so far, therefore, a mere subjective state, there
is, at the same time, competent to us in an immediate perception of external things, the consciousness of a really existent, of a really objective,
extended world ' (p. 840).

The theory of Natural Realism was intended to
displace the *Hypothetical Realism* of the Cosmothetical Idealists—a compromise between common sense
and speculation, which was the favourite theory
of the philosophers (p. 749), and which supposed
'that behind the non-existent world perceived
there lurks a correspondent but unknown world
existing' (p. 817). The Cosmothetical Idealist

argues that 'the external world exists, because
we naturally believe it to exist'; but this illation
Hamilton conceived to be incompetent (p. 749).
In a remarkable passage he contrasts his views on
this subject with those of Reid. " Our belief
of a material universe," he says, "is not ultimate,
and that universe is not unknown. This belief
is not a supernatural inspiration, it is not an in-
fused faith. We are not compelled by a blind
impulse to believe in the external world as in an
unknown something; on the contrary, we believe
it to exist only because we are immediately cognisant of it as existing. If asked indeed—how we
know that we know it?—how we know that what
we apprehend in sensible perception is, as consciousness assures us, an object, external, extended, and
numerically different from the conscious subject?—
how we know that this object is not a mere mode
of mind, illusively presented to us as a mode of
matter?—then indeed we must reply, that we do
not in propriety *know* that what we are compelled
to perceive as not self is not a perception of self,
and that we can only on reflection *believe* such to be
the case, in reliance on the original necessity of so
believing imposed on us by our nature " (*Reid*, 750).

This resolves the question at issue between
Hamilton and the philosophers into one of fact.
We know that we necessarily believe in the existence of the material world. Do we necessarily
believe that we know it as existing? To test the
necessity of such a belief, let us take the condi-

tions of the possibility of such a knowledge as laid down by the natural realist himself. They are laid down with italicised precision. "A thing to be known *in itself* must be known as *actually existing;* and it cannot be known as actually existing, unless it be known as existing in its *When* and its *Where.* But the When and Where of an object are *immediately* cognisable by the subject, only if the When be *now* (*i.e.* at the same moment with the cognitive act), and the Where be *here* (*i.e.* within the sphere of the cognitive faculty); therefore a presentative or intuitive knowledge is only competent of an object *present* to the mind, both in *time* and *space*" (*Reid*, 809). Let us mark the consequence of this.

The first consequence is the exclusion of the whole *World of Vision* from the range of intuitive perception and immediate knowledge, and a divergence from the views of Reid and Stewart as to the object of perception (*Reid*, 814). If 'we are percipient of nothing but what is in proximate contact, in immediate relation, with our organs of sense,' it follows that we can never be said to perceive a distant object (*ibid.*). 'Distant realities we reach, not by perception,' says Hamilton, 'but by a subsequent process of inference founded thereon : and so far, as Reid somewhere says (p. 284), from all men who look upon the sun perceiving the same object, in reality every individual perceives a different object, nay, a different object in each several eye' (p. 814). 'Vision,' he says, 'is only a perception, by which we take immediate cognisance of light in relation to our organ'; and 'the total object of visual perception is neither the rays in themselves nor the organ in itself, but the rays and living organ in reciprocity' (p. 160). Whether this be the total object of visual perception may possibly be disputed. It may be said that we see neither the organ nor the ray, whether in their reciprocity or in their isolation. It may be said that the total object of visual perception is the coloured and extended object which is seen. But how is it that we see the coloured and extended object? A ray alights upon the eye—an inverted image is depicted on a small expanse of nerve—and on the instant, as if by the touch of an enchanter's wand, an ideal universe exists. In this ideal universe the material reality is absent—the existence of the inverted image is unknown—the idea, the inference, is all in all. Vision is literally what Swift described it to be—the art of seeing things which are invisible. Malebranche was right in saying that the science of optics is merely an explanation of our optical illusions. The theory of Berkeley is triumphant, and the world of vision turns out to be nothing but the vision of a world.

And yet sight, if we regard the information which it conveys, is the most objective of the senses. "If," says Reid, "we shall suppose an order of beings, endued with every human faculty but that of sight, how incredible would it be to such beings, accustomed only to the slow informations of touch, that, by the addition of an organ, consisting of a ball and

socket of an inch in diameter, they might be enabled in an instant of time, without changing their
place, to perceive the disposition of a whole army,
or the order of a battle, the figure of a magnificent
palace, or all the variety of a landscape" (*Works*,
133). It is no marvel that Reid should have regarded such a perception as a revelation, as an
inspiration, as a species of natural magic. This
language Hamilton denounces. "These expressions," he says, "in which the cosmothetic idealists shadow forth the difficulty they create, and
attempt to solve, are wholly inapplicable to the
real fact" (*Reid*, 749). But in visual perception
the real fact, as stated by Hamilton himself, supplies their justification. Here at all events we
cannot believe that we are immediately cognisant
of the world of matter as existing. The world of
vision, so far as it is perceived, exists merely in idea,
and, natural realism, so far as it recognises the existence of a world beyond perception, is cosmothetical
idealism, open and avowed.

Abandoning the world of vision, the natural
realist takes his stand upon the *World of Touch*.
"There is in reality no medium in any sense,"
says Hamilton, "and, as Democritus long ago
shrewdly observed, all the senses are only modifications of touch" (*Reid*, 104). But here again
let us attend to Reid. "If a man were by feeling
to find out the figure of the Peak of Teneriffe," he
says, "or even of St. Peter's Church at Rome, it
would be the work of a lifetime" (*Works*, 133).

" The thing would be impossible," says Hamilton
—"let anyone try, by touch, to ascertain the
figure of a room, with which he is previously un-
acquainted, and not altogether of the usual shape,
and he will find that touch will afford him but
slender aid." (*ibid.*).   On such slender aid, however,
the natural realist is necessitated to rely.   And
what is the result?   Once more, let us apply his
own condition.   Select the simplest phenomenon of
touch.   You touch an object with the tip of your
finger ; you have a sensation in the organ of sense :
do you know the object?   On Hamilton's own
showing, only if the percipient knows it in its *where.*
But if, as the Cartesians held, the soul be seated on
the pineal gland—if, like a spider in the centre of
its web, it be localised at any point within the body
—it is seated at a distance from the scene of sense.
The informations of sense must be *telegraphed*, as it
were, along the nerves, and the recognition of the
object can never be regarded as immediate.   Before, therefore, we can accept the doctrine of natural
realism, we must reject the Cartesian doctrine, which
centralizes the seat of thought—we must maintain
that the soul is literally at our finger's end—we
must adopt the doctrine of Aristotle, that the soul
contains the body, rather than the body the soul—
we must embrace the dogma of the schools, that the
soul is all in the whole body, and all in every of its
parts (*Reid*, 861).   But even this will not avail us.
In order to cognise the object in its *where*, not only
must we assume that the soul is at the finger's end

—we must assume that the finger's end is in *contact* with the object touched. But if the theory of Boscovich be true—if matter be nothing but a system of acting and reacting forces—it is impossible that there should be any such thing as contact; and, on Hamilton's concessions, if there be no contact there can be no cognition. If the organ and the object be separated by the merest differential which the mind of the mathematician can conceive, it is evident that, for all purposes of intuition, they might as well be separated by what Norris calls the whole diameter of existence. Before we can accept the conclusions of natural realism, therefore, we must reject the theory of Boscovich, which reduces matter to a system of forces, and adopt the theory of Democritus, which not only reduces every sense to a modification of touch, but explains touch by a contiguity of atoms. But suppose the contiguity effected, we are as far from a cognition of the objective as ever. For what is contact? A mere community of surface, which of itself conveys no knowledge of diversity of being. "Suppose a man," says Hume, "to be supported in the air, and to be softly conveyed along by some invisible power, it is evident he is sensible of nothing, and never receives the idea of extension, nor indeed any idea from this invariable motion" (i. 82). Sense, therefore, might be in contact with an object, and yet receive no knowledge of its existence from the contact. If the object should exert pressure and evoke resistance

253

253

The253

a new sensation would be determined, a new inference drawn; but consciousness would be affected,
not by contact, but by pressure. Here, then,
it is evident we must abandon atoms and have
recourse to force; and as the theory of Boscovich
was abandoned for that of Democritus to effect a
contact, so the theory of Democritus must be abandoned for that of Boscovich to secure resistance.

And it is to force that Hamilton avowedly has
recourse in order to secure the knowledge of a
world without. "The existence of the *Extra-
organic World*," he says, "is apprehended, not in a
perception of the primary qualities of matter, but
in a perception of the quasi-primary phasis of the
secundo-primary; that is, in the consciousness that
our locomotive energy is *resisted*, and not resisted by
aught in our organism itself" (*Reid*, 882). This at
first sight would seem to be the theory maintained
by Brown. Brown virtually argues, "I am conscious of the feeling of resistance; in myself I am
conscious of no difference; and I therefore infer
the cause to be something not myself on the ground
that a different consequent necessarily implies a difference of the antecedent" (*Lect.* xxiv.). But Hamilton denies that the conclusion rests on inference.
"I am *conscious*," he says, "that my locomotive
energy is not resisted by aught in my organism
itself." That is the pinch of the whole question. As incubus originates within, though it appears to be an oppression from without, why may
not the external world be what Fichte conceived it

to be, an *anstoss*, a self-limitation, in which the radiating activity of the ego is drawn backward on itself? (*Schw.* 268). " I cannot," says Hamilton, " be conscious of myself as the resisted relative, without at the same time being conscious, being immediately percipient, of a not-self as the resisting correlative" (*Reid*, 866). But why may not this correlative be the transcendental cause of Kant ? Why must it necessarily be the material thing of Reid ? " The experience of external resistance," says Hamilton, " supposes a possession of the notions of *space* and *motion* in space" (*Reid*, p. 882). But here the natural realist is involved in a dilemma. Is the notion of space a mere idea ? Then external space, and all that it embosoms, may, for aught we know, be a mere objectification of a form of sense, a self projection of the mind, a mere metaphysical mirage ; and natural realism is lost in the transcendental idealism of Kant. Is this notion of space an apprehension of space in its objective externality ? In this case we believe in the existence of an external world of matter, because we believe in the existence of motion in an external world of space ; and natural realism is enveloped in a mist of paralogism and again is lost.

In fact, the extra-organic world of touch, like the extra-organic world of vision, is at last avowedly abandoned to the cosmothetical idealist. " The primary qualities of things external to our organism," says Hamilton, " we do not perceive—i. e. *immediately know*—for these we only learn to *infer*, from

the affections which we come to find, that they
determine in our organs; affections which, yielding us a perception of organic extension, we at
length discover, by observation and induction, to
imply a corresponding extension in the extra-
organic agents" (p. 881). But how can we know
that the extension of the extra-organic agent which
ex hypothesi is unknown, corresponds to the organic extension which, for the moment, we may
admit that we perceive? Here it is evident that
Hamilton is betrayed into the very absurdity with
which he constantly taunts his opponents, and
which he regards as decisive of the fate of that
form of philosophy which the cosmothetical idealist
maintains. How can you deny to mind all cognisance of matter, he asks, yet bestow upon it the
inconceivable power of truly representing to itself
the external world which is ex hypothesi unknown? This was the argument which Hamilton
constantly employed (p. 755). It was by this
question that he demolished the Master of Subtilties (p. 815). It was by this question that he
overwhelmed Descartes and Locke (pp. 839, 840).
It was by this question that he annihilated Brown
(*Disc.* 64). It was by this question that he held up
the whole race of cosmothetical idealists and hypothetical realists to scorn (*Reid*, 749). But here his
argument unexpectedly recoils upon his own philosophy; and it recoils with a peculiar force. The
cosmothetical idealist does not profess to *know* that
the idea corresponds to the unknown; he only

professes to *believe* it. The natural realist, on the
contrary, professes to know that an extra-organic
extension, which is confessedly unknown, corresponds with an organic extension which, as we shall
see, itself escapes his knowledge.

Driven from position to position, the natural
realist falls back upon the *Organic World*, the mi-
crocosm of the organs. 'The organism,' says
Hamilton, 'is the field of apprehension, both to
sensation proper and perception proper' (*Reid*, 880).
And here again he calls upon us to concede a paradox. 'The organism,' he says, 'is, at once, within
and without the mind; is, at once, subjective and
objective; is, at once, ego and non-ego' (*ibid.*).
'Such is the fact,' he says; 'but how the immaterial can be united with matter, how the unextended can apprehend extension, how the indivisible
can measure the divided—this is the mystery of
mysteries to man' (*ibid.*). To preclude all confusion
and ambiguity with respect to this cardinal distinction, Hamilton maintains that " our nervous organism, in contrast to all exterior to itself, appertains
to the concrete human ego, and in this respect is
subjective, internal; whereas, in contrast to the abstract immaterial ego, the pure mind, it belongs to
the non-ego, and in this respect is *objective, external*"
(p. 858). But even, in so far as our organism is
objective and external, a discrimination must be
made; for the body may be viewed as a body
simply or as an animated body. Hence, while
some of its phenomena are " to be considered as

subjective, being the modes of our organism as animated by, or in union with, the mind, and therefore states of the ego," there are other phenomena which are "to be considered as *objective*, being modes of our organism, viewed as a mere portion of matter, and in this respect a non-ego" (*ibid.*). 'As an animated body' our nervous organism, we are told, 'actually exists, and is actually known to exist, only as it is susceptible of certain affections, which, and the causes of which, have been ambiguously called the secondary qualities of matter,' while 'as a body simply it can possibly exist, and can possibly be known as existent, only under those necessary conditions of all matter, which have been denominated its primary qualities' (*ibid.*). Of these primary qualities we are conscious. Hamilton concedes that "by a law of our nature we are not conscious of the existence of our organism, consequently not conscious of any of its primary qualities, unless when we are conscious of it as modified by a secondary quality, or some other of its affections, as an animated body" (*ibid.*). But he holds that while the object of the one consciousness is merely 'a contingent passion of the organism, as a constituent of the human self,' which is recognised as 'a *subjective object*,' the object of the other consciousness is 'some essential property of the organism as a portion of the universe of matter'—a property which, 'though apprehended by,' is 'not an affection proper to, the conscious self at all' and which, 'as a common property of

s

matter,' must be 'recognised to be an *objective object*' (*ibid.*).

But even from this position Hamilton finds himself necessitated to retreat. He is compelled to admit that, as far as our knowledge of the primary qualities of objects in immediate contact with our organs is concerned, our ignorance of their real magnitude is as complete as our ignorance of the magnitude of the most distant object. He acknowledges that magnitude appears greater or less in proportion to the different size of the tactile organ in different subjects; as an apple seems larger to the hand of a child than to the hand of an adult (*Reid*, 303). Experiment, he admits, establishes the curious fact that even in the same individual the same object appears greater or less, according as it is touched by one part of the body or by another (pp. 126, 303). In short he is compelled to allow that 'the magnitude perceived through touch is as purely relative as that perceived through vision or any other sense' (p. 885).

Nor, on Hamilton's own admission, have we any more accurate knowledge of the real extension of our organism than we have of that of objects in contact with our organs. Here again physiology is fatal to his claims. 'As perceived,' he says, 'extension is only the recognition of one organic affection in its outness from another' (p. 882). But, 'as a minimum of extension,' he continues, 'is thus to perception the smallest extent of organism in which sensations can be discriminated as plural; and as in one part of the organism this smallest extent is perhaps some million, certainly some myriad, times smaller than in others; it follows that, to perception, the same real extension will appear, in this place of the body, some million or myriad times greater than in that' (*ibid.*). Hamilton, accordingly, admits that 'in no part of the organism have we any apprehension, any immediate knowledge, of extension in its true and absolute magnitude' (p. 881) — an admission which leaves no pretence for saying that we are, or can be, conscious of any essential property of our organism as a portion of the universe of matter.

As far, then, as our knowledge of the primary qualities of the universe of matter is concerned, the natural realist takes his final stand on the position that, 'Perception proper is an apprehension of the *relations of sensations to each other*, primarily in Space, and secondarily in Time and Degree' (*Reid*, 881). But whatever may be our ultimate opinion of the logical coherence or philosophic value of this theory of perception, it is evident that it is not the theory of perception which Hamilton originally led us to expect he would establish. The consciousness of the relations of sensations to each other is not the consciousness which gives us an immediate knowledge of the world of matter in itself (p. 747) as actually existing (p. 805), as existing in its when and where (p. 809). It is not 'the consciousness, or immediate perception, of certain essential attributes of matter objectively existing' (p. 825). It is not 'the immediate perception of external things, the consciousness of a really existent, of a really objective, extended world' (p. 841). It is not 'the immediate knowledge or consciousness of the external object, *as extended*' (p. 842). It is not the 'sensitive perception,' in which 'the extension as known, and the extension as existing, are convertible—known, because existing, and existing, since known' (*ibid.*). Indeed so far is it from being so that it is a perception in which extension as existing, whether in things external to our organism or in the organism itself, is confessedly unperceived, unapprehended, and unknown (p. 881).

Hamilton nevertheless contends that 'an extension is apprehended in the apprehension of the *reciprocal externality of all sensations*' (*Reid*, 885). He holds that "in the consciousness of sensations out of each other, contrasted, limited, and variously arranged, we have a perception proper of the primary qualities, in an externality to the mind, though not to the nervous organism, as an immediate cognition, and not merely as a notion or concept of something extended, figured, &c." (p. 883). Nay he asserts that even when consciousness projects its sensations beyond the bounds of the existing organism into external space, as in the case of an amputated limb, the sensations thus falsely localised 'being now, as heretofore, manifested out of each other, must afford the condition of a perceived extension, not less real than that which they afforded prior to the amputation' (p. 861). But in what sense can the extension thus perceived be said to be real? and in what sense can it be said to be external to the mind? As perceived, extension is defined to be the recognition of one organic affection in its outness—not from the mind, but—from another (p. 882). The term ' outness,' therefore, is used in the sense not of externality but of distance. To speak of the distance between one sensation and another is sheer nonsense; and, accordingly, the distance to be considered is the distance between one sentient point in the organism and another. But this is admittedly unperceived. All that we perceive is admittedly an extension which varies with the sentient mind — which differs with the seat of sense — which may be presented by a falsely localised sensation—which corresponds with nothing that is real in the proper acceptation of the term—and which, appearing in this part of the body some million or myriad times greater than in that, can be nothing but appearance. If this be so, what is presented to us is not extension but an idea of extension; and what Hamilton calls the intuitive perception of extension is only another name for what Kant has termed its empiric intuition.

If we wish to see how thin is the partition which divides the bounds of Hamilton's intuitive perception from those of the transcendental ideality of Kant, we have only to examine the views of the Scottish philosopher with regard to *Space.* In his notes to Reid, he tells us that 'we have a twofold cognition of space—an *a priori* or native imagination of it, in general, as a necessary condition of the possibility of thought; and, under that, an *a posteriori* or adventitious percept of it, in particular, as contingently apprehended in this or that actual complexus of sensations' (p. 882). In his Lectures, he designates this adventitious percept by the word *extension*, and reserves the term *space* for space considered as 'a form or fundamental law of thought' (ii. 114). But what is the source to which this adventitious percept is indebted for its advent? It is not furnished to the mind by the extension of external things ; for Hamilton admits that the extension of external things is only an inference from *it*. Neither is it furnished to the mind by any organic extension ; for Hamilton concedes that our actual organic extension is not apprehended by perception. The adventitious percept, therefore, must be essentially subjective—as subjective as the sensations of the relations between which it is the apprehension. We are led to the same conclusion if we consider Hamilton's theory of *space*. In the first edition of his Discussions he tells us that "it is one merit of the Philosophy of the Conditioned that it proves space to be only a law of thought, and not a law of things" (p. 582). True, in his second edition, published a year after the first, he modifies his statement. The merit of his philosophy, he says, consists in this—" that it proves space to be *by* a law of thought and not *by* a law of things " (p. 607). But in what sense can Hamilton maintain that space exists only by a law of thought ?

As a natural realist he must maintain that, independently of our perceptions and conceptions, there
is an external universe of things existing in an external infinitude of space. His proposition, therefore, must mean that it is only by a law of thought
that space exists *for us*—that the space of consciousness is not a conception which has been
derived from outward experience, or an intuition
which presents any property of objects as things in
themselves, or which presents their objective relations to each other (*Kritik*, 23–26)—in other words,
that space, as known by us, is merely an evolution
of the a priori form of sense, which Hamilton describes as a necessary condition of the possibility
of thought. But if this be so, what is the doctrine
of the natural realist but the doctrine of the cosmothetical idealist whom he derides? To use his
own emphasised expressions, ' the qualities which
we call material—extension, figure, &c.—*exist for
us* only as they are *known by us ;* and, on this hypothesis, they are known by us only as *modes of mind*'
(*Reid*, 751).

The affinity which exists between the natural
realism of Hamilton and the transcendental idealism
of Kant will be brought into evidence if we view
the subject in another light. Hamilton, as we have
seen, resolves perception into an apprehension of
relations. Now this is the very fact on which Kant
relies as affording confirmation to his theory of the
ideality of the external as well as the internal sense
(*Kritik*, 40). He remarks that ' all in our cognition that belongs to intuition contains nothing more

than mere relations' (*ibid.*) ; he observes that 'by means of mere relations, a thing cannot be known in itself' (*ibid.*) ; and he thinks 'it may be fairly concluded that, as through the external sense nothing but mere representations of relations are given us, the external sense in its representation can contain only the relation of the object to the subject, but not the essential nature of the object as a thing in itself' (*ibid.*). From this conclusion Hamilton recoils. He admits that in saying 'a thing is known in itself,' he does 'not mean that this object is known in its absolute existence, that is, out of relation to us '—'this,' he says, 'is impossible, for our knowledge is only of the relative' (*Reid*, p. 866). He admits that 'of things absolutely or in themselves, be they external, be they internal, we know nothing, or know them as incognisable, and become aware of their existence only as this is indirectly and accidentally revealed to us, through certain qualities related to our faculties of knowledge, and which qualities, again, we cannot think as unconditioned, irrelative, existent in and of themselves' (*Disc.* 643). He admits, in fine, employing the very phraseology of the Kritik, that 'all we know is phenomenal—phenomenal of the unknown' (*ibid.*). But instead of acquiescing in Kant's conclusion, that what is thus confessedly unknown is to human consciousness a mere nescio quid, he conceives that its nature is partially revealed to us through certain qualities related to our faculties of knowledge. But what are the qualities of external things which are thus related? Not the primary qualities, for they are confessedly unknown (p. 881); not the secondary qualities, for, as manifested to us, they are merely phenomenal affections determined by causes which are essentially occult (p. 854). This brings the question to the very point to which it was brought by Hume—'bereave matter of all its intelligible qualities, both primary and secondary, and you in a manner annihilate it, and leave only a certain unknown inexplicable something, as the cause of our perceptions' (*Hume*, iv. 181).*

Hamilton holds that, at all events, we have the perception of 'a resisting something *external to our body*' (p. 883). But it is as difficult to show that this something is external, as it is to show that it is extended. It is in reality something transcendental. Yielding to the coercion of the principle of metaphysical causality, Kant postulates its existence as an efficient cause; yielding to the natural instinct of the human race, Hamilton professes to apprehend it as an external object. Regarding it as an efficient cause, Kant accepts the conclusion of Hume (iv. 178), and insists that by no argument can

---

* Since writing the above, I have had the privilege of reading Professor Veitch's valuable monograph entitled *Hamilton*, and it is a source of satisfaction to be able to cite the following passage from the work of the disciple, to show that in the foregoing criticism I have been guilty of no injustice to the master: "This reference [to the thing in itself]—what we may ask the Ontological—is, no doubt, the least explained point in Hamilton's philosophy of Perception. Do we actually perceive and conceive in those primary qualities body as body, *per se*—as that which exists and subsists whether we perceive it or not—in its own actual, absolute reality—the transcendent thing in existence? My view is, that Hamilton says no to this question" (*Hamilton*, 145-6). Mr. Veitch even questions whether Hamilton held that perceived extension subsists after the act of perception (p. 179).

it be proved that our perceptions do not arise either from the energy of the soul itself, or from the suggestion of some invisible spirit, or from some other cause which is equally unknown (*Kritik*, 206). Regarding it as an external object, Hamilton accepts, in a modified form, the conclusions of Reid and Brown, and insists that its existence is given in the *consciousness* that our locomotive energy is resisted, and not resisted by aught in our organism itself (*Reid*, 882). But what is the consciousness to which Hamilton appeals? Undoubtedly, in the world of motion we seem to be resisted from without, and we seem to behold the very objects which resist us. But sight is, confessedly, mere inference, and why should we not regard this seeming of material resistance as mere inference also? The great philosophers who have written on the subject must be presumed to have known what they were conscious of, and to have been conscious of what they knew. And yet what are the philosophical conclusions as to the true nature of this resisting object? To Hamilton, it is true, it was a material thing; but to Berkeley it was a divine agent—to Fichte it was a subjective anstoss—to Kant it was a nescio quid—and to Hegel it was nothing. The philosophical difficulties which Hamilton's theory encounters are not less than those encountered by the theories of Berkeley and Fichte. The fact is, that Hamilton's criticism of Kant's only possible demonstration of the reality of an external world recoils upon himself, and he only reaches his external reality by a double *saltus*, which overleaps the foundations of both the egoistic idealism and the mystic (*Disc.* 93).

In these interesting discussions, however, there is one point on which Hamilton is entitled to peculiar credit. He saw more clearly than any contemporary philosopher where the real pinch of the difficulty lay. He accepted the position of Kant, that " in whatever way the understanding may have attained to a conception, the existence of the object of the conception cannot be discovered in it by analysis, because the cognition of the existence of the object depends upon the object's being posited and given in itself apart from the conception" (*Kritik,* 392). He adopted the words of Fichte when he says : " From cognition to pass out to an object of cognition—this is impossible ; we must, therefore, depart from the reality, otherwise we should remain for ever unable to reach it " (*Reid,* 799). Hence it was that he declared it to be the very cardinal point of philosophy to show that in the act of sensible perception we are conscious not only of ourselves as the perceiving subject, but of an external reality, in relation with our sense, as the object perceived (*Reid,* 747) ; and hence it was that he concentrated all his powers on the attack of Hume's position—that in perception the mind has never anything present to it but its perceptions, and cannot attain any experience of their connexion with resembling objects (*Hume,* iv. 178).

But, notwithstanding the loud promise of the new departure, Hamilton is eventually forced to yield the supremacy to Hume. He is compelled to confess that " the primary qualities of things external to our organism we do not perceive, that is, immediately know " (p. 881). He is compelled to confess that " in no part of the organism have we any apprehension, any immediate knowledge, of extension in its true and absolute magnitude" (p. 881). He is compelled, in fine, to resolve our perception of extension into a mere recognition of one organic affection in its outness from another (p. 882)—a recognition which is infinitely variable and confessedly deceptive—an extension which is not extension in its reality, but only an idea of extension. To avoid the inevitable conclusion that in perception the mind has nothing present to it but its perceptions, Hamilton exhausts the resources of his learning, but in vain. In vain he contends that all our senses are modifications of touch. In vain he revives the scholastic doctrine that the soul is all in the whole body, and all in every of its parts. In vain he calls upon us to admit that the organism is at once within and without the mind. In vain he distinguishes between the abstract immaterial ego and the concrete human ego incorporate in matter; between the animated organism and the material things without it; between the contiguous world of touch and the distant universe of vision. The world of vision, the extraorganic world of touch, and the world of the sentient organism are successively surrendered to the idealist and sceptic. Natural realism is foiled at every point. Thrice has it essayed to grasp reality, but thrice has reality escaped its grasp.

> Ter conatus ibi collo dare brachia circum—
> Ter frustra comprensa manus effugit imago.

Hamilton's theory of Perception is not, in fact, the Natural Realism of common sense, but a *Cataleptic Idealism*, similar to that which Cicero attributes to the Stoics (*Acad.* i. 11). The propositions on which Hume challenged contradiction from the philosophers were three. Nothing, he said, can ever be present to the mind but an image or perception; true, we are carried by a natural instinct to suppose an external universe, which exists independently of our perceptions; but when we follow this natural instinct, we suppose the images presented by the senses to be the external objects (*Hume*, iv. 177). Regarding these propositions as the expression of the facts of consciousness, Hume accepted what he calls the whimsical condition of mankind, who must act, and reason, and believe, though they are not able, by their most diligent inquiry, to satisfy themselves concerning the foundation of these operations, or to remove the objections which may be raised against them (iv. 187). In this admixture of speculative scepticism with practical belief, Philosophy refused to acquiesce, and proceeded to deal with the three propositions of Hume as best it could. Rejecting the natural instinct which leads us to believe in the existence of an external world, Berkeley accepted the natural instinct which leads us to believe that our sensible ideas are external objects, and boldly identified object and idea. Accepting the natural instinct which leads us to believe in the existence of an external world, Reid rejected the natural instinct which identifies the object with the idea, and, in effect, regarded the idea as a representation of the object. Struck with the inconsistency of rejecting one natural instinct and relying on another, Hamilton neither identified the object and the idea with Berkeley, nor made the idea the representative of the object with Reid, but recognizing the co-existence of object and idea, brought the idea into contact with the object, and conceived that the material thing was apprehended—κατάληπτον—manu comprehensum—in the contact.

But Hamilton seems to have closed his eyes to the difficulties and inconsistencies in which his system is involved. His system postulates the absolute veracity of consciousness in every instance (*Reid*, 745). He holds that 'the immediate or mediate repugnance of any two of its data being established, the presumption in favour of the general veracity of consciousness is abolished, or rather reversed' (p. 746). He appeals to the judgments of consciousness, in fact, as Torquatus appealed to the judgments of the senses—quibus si semel aliquid falsi pro vero probatum sit, sublatum esse omne judicium veri et falsi putat (*De Fin.* i. 7). But he admits that to consciousness 'it appears as if the sense actually apprehended the things out of itself, and in their proper space' (*Reid*, 748), and nevertheless holds that we reach distant realities, not by perception, but by a subsequent process of inference founded thereon (p. 814). Ubi igitur illud *semel*? Even if it could be established against Hume, that in certain limited relations of contact we apprehend the object in the image, this would not evince the veracity of consciousness in those wider relations of vision where we admittedly mistake the image for the object. Hamilton, then, at the outset is met with the dilemma with which he confronted Brown—if he adhere to his hypothesis, he must renounce his argument; and if he apply his argument, he must renounce his hypothesis (*Reid*, 750). But, apart from this, what is the value of the inference by which he professes to bring distant realities within his reach? He insists that when Locke is asked, how he became aware that the known idea truly represents the unknown reality, he can make no answer (*Reid*, 839). But what answer can Hamilton make when the same interrogatory is administered to himself? He stands confronted by Hume's dilemma, and has nothing to say when the great Academic maintains that 'the opinion of external existence, if rested on natural instinct, is contrary to reason, and, if referred to reason, is contrary to natural instinct, and at the same time carries no rational evidence with it to convince an impartial inquirer.' Hamilton insists that we know from consciousness that the agent which produces the sense of tension, and

pressure, and resistance, is something beyond the
limit of the mind and its subservient organs (*Reid*,
859, 883). But the testimony of consciousness to
this is not more to be depended on than its testimony to the effect that in vision we apprehend the
external object in external space. Hamilton admits
that " sensations of light and colours are determined,
among other causes, *from within*, by a sanguineous
congestion in the capillary vessels of the optic nerve,
or by various chemical agents which affect it through
the medium of the blood ; *from without*, by the application to the same nerve of a mechanical force, as a
blow, a compression, a wound, or of an imponder-
able influence, as electricity or galvanism" (p. 855).
Natural Realism therefore supplies no proof, in
opposition to Hume, that "the perceptions of the
mind must be caused by external objects entirely
different from them, though resembling them, if that
be possible" (*Hume*, iv. 178). It stands confronted
by Berkeley's dilemma, and has no answer to give
when the idealist contends that " if there were external bodies, it is impossible we should ever come
to know it ; and, if there were not, we might have
the very same reasons to think there were that
we have now" (*Prin.* xx.).

ABSOLUTE IDEALISM:

OR

HEGEL.

ABSOLUTE IDEALISM:

OR

HEGEL.

Quid Democritus, qui tum imagines earumque circuitus in Deorum
numero refert, tum illam naturam quae imagines fundat ac mittat,
tum scientiam intelligentiamque nostram, nonne in maximo errore
versatur?—Cic. *de* NAT. DEOR.

THE nature of the Scottish reaction against the philosophy of Kant has been described. The counter-revolution which occurred in Germany remains to be considered.

Kant, as we have seen, regarded it as a scandal to philosophy that it should assume the existence of things external to ourselves as an article of irrational belief (*Kritik*, xl.) He admitted that the external object is not given by any faculty of intuition; and he showed that, if the external object be not originally given, its existence is incapable of proof. But while Kant made these concessions to philosophy, he made concessions more important still to common sense. The phenomena of sense, he acknowledged, must be produced by some efficient cause, and relying upon what he called the " intellectual conception " of causality, he admitted the existence of a transcendental cause of sensation, which he styled the transcendental object. Our anticipations of the future he saw could never be explained by our recollections of the past, and presuming the existence of the law of physical causation, and others of the same character, in the course of nature, he postulated certain anticipations of these natural laws in thought, and named them the categories of the understanding. All physical science was thus the result of the categories of the understanding applied to the experience of the past ; and all experience whatsoever was due to the conjoint action of the transcendental object and our faculties of sense.

The impossibility of building a system of philosophy on mere irrational belief is obvious; for if natural instinct accredits natural realism by asserting the existence of external things, reflection accredits absolute idealism by asserting that what we assume to be external things are nothing but our own ideas. It is the same with regard to demonstration. That the existence of external things cannot be proved by any process of reasoning is admitted by Reid as readily as by Hume, and by Hamilton as readily as by Kant. But the proposition that the external object is not given by any faculty of intuition has not received as general an acceptance. Hamilton, as we have seen, contended that in certain limited relations the external object is given by the intuition of the senses. But in Germany a still bolder attempt to show that objective reality, even in its highest forms, might be grasped, was made by Schelling, who, soaring high above the region of the senses, revived the doctrine of Plotinus, and maintained that absolute reality might be reached by the vision and the faculty divine, which he denominated intellectual intuition. The possibility of such a philodoxy, as he would have styled it, had been clearly seen by Kant; but here, as everywhere, the common sense of that illustrious man preserved him from illusion. He disclaimed the exercise of the arts of magic. He was a plain man, he said, who knew of no intuition but the vulgar intuition of the senses. He saw nothing in the understanding but a certain faculty of judgment; and the intellectual intuition, with its ecstacies and its absorptions and its unintelligible swoons, he left with the Teutonic Theosopher, the Alexandrine Mystic and the Indian Mouni.

But it was not on the side of intuition that the serious attack was made on the philosophy of Kant; it was on the side of the categories and the transcendental object. If the existence of objects external to ourselves can neither be perceived nor proved, why, it was asked, should we insist on their existence? Philosophy for centuries had plagued

itself with abortive attempts to determine the relations subsisting between the subject and the object.
Kant had shown that the development of the subject was not the mere result of the action of the
object; why not assume that the object is the mere
creation and projection of the subject? Kant himself had approached this point of view, but with his
characteristic caution he had declined to take it as
his standpoint. In assuming the existence of the
transcendental object, he had taken care to guard
himself by saying that it was " an object of which
we are quite unable to say whether it can be met
with in ourselves or out of us; whether it would be
annihilated together with sensibility, or if this were
taken away, would continue to exist" (*Kritik*, 206).
But what Kant was unable to say, his successors
dogmatically said. They professed to be in earnest
about idealism. They gave out a series of ideal-
isms—subjective, objective, and absolute—as bewildering and as transient as the northern lights.
Fichte, a self-confident and overbearing thinker,
commenced the revolution. Schelling—first the follower of Fichte, then the successor of Spinosa, then
posing as a new Plotinus, and finally lost in the
Aurora or Morning Red of Jacob Boëhmen—astonished the world by his versatility and genius, but
was too fitful and erratic to produce any permanent effect upon the world of thought. He was
succeeded by a more imperial spirit. Idealism
was in the ascendant in Germany, and the crown-

ing victory of German idealism was achieved by Hegel.

The influence exerted by this extraordinary man is one of the most remarkable events in the history of modern speculation. At first he was rapturously hailed as the founder of a new religion. He was regarded as a new Messiah. He was styled a God. Even among the more sober of his admirers the language in which he was described, if less blasphemous than that of Marheinecke, was equally extravagant. He was styled the King of Thought. Förster compared him to Alexander, and said that on his death the throne of philosophy became vacant, and the provinces of thought could only be governed by his satraps. Scherer compared him to Napoleon, and Professor Graham, making the same comparison, exclaims, " they were two lions littered in one year, but the elder and more terrible was Hegel." *

Nor, if Hegel had accomplished all that he is said to have accomplished, would he have been unworthy of his fame. Professor Graham tells us that the system of Hegel is the most transcendant attempt ever essayed by the aspiring sons of men to solve at once, and by one principle, all the problems of philosophy, and all the sphinx enigmas of existence,

---

* *Idealism :* An Essay, Metaphysical and Critical, by William Graham, M.A., of Trinity College, Dublin—a work of great eloquence, and full of suggestiveness, even to those who do not accept the doctrine which it preaches, or the estimate of Hegel which it forms.

as well as the riddle of the painful earth (*Ideal.* 69). But even this falls short of the pretensions of the great hierophant himself. His logic, he said, was not the mere scientific exposition of the pure notions of the reason; it was the exhibition of truth without her veil—it was the exposition of God in his eternal essence—it was the display of the diamond net in which the universe is held (*Schw.* 323).

Mr. Graham maintains that for years to come it will be the business of philosophy not to refute Hegel, but to try and understand him (p. 41). Confessedly this is not an easy task. Hegel himself has said that to learn his system is to learn to walk upon one's head; and in speaking of his philosophy, shortly before his death, he was fain to admit that of all his disciples one only understood it—and that even *he* did not. Ferrier tells us that, with peaks more lucent than the sun, his intervals are filled with a sea of darkness, unnavigable by the aid of any compass, and overhung by an atmosphere, or rather by a vacuum, which no human intellect can breathe. Stirling, who has devoted a lifetime to the study of his system, and who has written two large octavos on his *Secret,* is no less eloquent on the obscurity of the modern Heraclitus. His system is a Cyclopean edifice—a palace of Oriental dream—a Chinese puzzle—a thing of infinite meddle and make—a map of infinite joinings, of endless seams and sutures, whose opposing edges no cunning of gum, or glue, or paint, can

ever hide. Mr. Wallace, who has translated his
Logic, has to confess that to the neophyte the
atmosphere of Hegelian thought is a vacuum which
we cannot breathe, and which is merely tenanted
by ghosts.* In point of fact the most practised and
patient of metaphysicians is at fault when he strives
to catch the evanescent meanings and interpret the
uncouth phraseology of this portentous thinker,
while the ordinary man of letters who dips into
his works is compelled to quit them in despair,
reminded only of the Rosicrucian jargon with which
the Adept endeavoured to confound the Antiquary,
or the problematical dialogisms, and the conca-
tenations of self-existence with which the Squire
smoked Moses in the parlour of the Vicar.

Mr. Graham tells us that the Hegelian system
is the final result of philosophy, and that Hegel had
the genius to discover and the courage to proclaim
that a universal thought is the absolute, and the
sole existence (*Ideal.* 19). But if the position that
thought is the sole and absolute existence is the last
result of philosophy, it was also one of its earliest
results. The Greeks, who anticipated everything,
anticipated even this. Centuries before the Christian era Parmenides had proclaimed in sounding
hexameters that thought and its objects are the

* *The Logic of Hegel* translated from the Encyclopaedia of the Philosophical Sciences, with Prolegomena by William Wallace, M.A., Fellow and Tutor of Merton College, Oxford. This is the most intelligent and the most intelligible account of Hegel's system that the English reader can be referred to.

same.   Gorgias had amused the youth of Athens
with the paradox which proclaims the identity of
Nought and Being.   In fact Heraclitus, in metaphors which darkened knowledge, had given forth
adumbrations of the whole Hegelian doctrine.
When he said that all things are in ceaseless flow,
he announced the dogma, according to Hegel himself, that Becoming was the fundamental category
of all that is (*Log.* 144).   When he proclaimed that
strife is the parent of all things, he proclaimed the
Hegelian axiom that plurality and contrast were
the conditions of knowledge and perception.   Nay,
when he said that the world is an ever-living fire
which is alternately extinguished and rekindled by
itself, he merely anticipated the words of Hegel
when he said, " the Becoming is as it were a fire,
which dies out in itself, when it consumes its material " (p. 146).

Nor was the theory of Absolute Idealism unknown in modern Europe.   The marvellous metaphysical genius which had anticipated Kant had
also anticipated Hegel.   In his youthful Treatise
of Human Nature, Hume had unconsciously reproduced the ideas of Parmenides and Heraclitus,
and laid the lines of the Hegelian Logic.   He
said to himself that " as long as we confine our
speculations to the *appearances* of objects to our
senses, without entering into disquisitions concerning their real nature and operations, we are safe
from all difficulties, and can never be embarrassed

by any question" (*Works*, i. 92). Confining his attention to the appearances of objects, he regarded human nature as the capital of science, and boldly marched upon it (i. 8). He declared that all the perceptions of the mind may be divided into impressions and ideas (i. 15). He attempted to classify all the relations, natural and philosophical, by which our ideas are united (i. 30). He stigmatised the ordinary division of the acts of the understanding into three as a vulgar error, and endeavoured to show that judgment and reasoning were nothing but conception (i. 132). He denied that there was any necessity for supposing that every beginning of existence should be attended by a cause (i. 227); and he even professed that our perceptions may exist separately, and have no need of any substance to support their being (i. 299). But the speculations of the youthful sceptic had a wider reach. He examined the idea of *existence* (i. 95). "There is no impression nor idea of any kind, of which we have any consciousness or memory," he says, "that is not conceived as existent; and it is evident that from this consciousness the most perfect idea and assurance of *being* is derived" (*ibid.*). "From hence," he continues, "we may form a dilemma the most clear and conclusive that can be imagined, viz., that, since we never remember any idea or impression without attributing existence to it, the idea of existence must

either be derived from a distinct impression, conjoined with every perception or object of our
thought, or must be the very same with the idea
of the perception or object" (*ibid.*). That there
was no distinct impression from which it could be
derived he considered obvious, and accordingly
he concluded that " to reflect on anything simply,
and to reflect on it as existent, are nothing different
from each other"—that " any idea we please to
form is the idea of a being, and the idea of a being
is any idea we please to form "—in fine, that " the
idea of existence is the very same with the idea of
what we conceive to be existent" (i. 96). By the
same reasoning he came to the conclusion that *external existence* was nothing but a mere idea (i. 97).
"Let us fix our attention out of ourselves as much
as possible," he said—"let us chase our imagination to the heavens, or to the utmost limits of the
universe; we never really advance a step beyond
ourselves" (*ibid.*). The consequence of principles
such as these was obvious. According to the
Treatise, *Space* was nothing but " the manner in
which objects exist" (i. 62)—*Body* was nothing but
" a collection, formed by the mind, of the ideas
of the several distinct sensible qualities of which
objects are composed, and which we find to have
a constant union with each other " (i. 282)—*Mind*
was nothing but " a system of different perceptions, or different existences, which are linked to-

gether by the relation of cause and effect, and
mutually produce, destroy, influence, and modify
each other " (i. 331).

In broaching this system of absolute idealism,
however, Hume was not one of the men of bright
fancies who, to use his own simile, are like the
angels that Scripture represents as covering their
eyes with their wings. When the wing of the
angel was removed, no eye could be keener than his
in detecting the contradictions and imperfections of
his system; no man of common sense could be
readier to acknowledge its unsatisfying nature.
Philosophy such as this, he said, was mere philosophical melancholy and delirium of which nature
is the cure (i. 341); it was a mere dream, on waking
from which the philosopher would be the first to join
in the laugh against himself (iv. 187). But it was
in no such spirit that Fichte reproduced the philo-
sophemes of Hume. The Great Ego, as he was
styled by Goethe and by Schiller, is said to have
publicly imprecated everlasting damnation on himself if he ever swerved in the smallest degree from
any of the doctrines which he had propounded (*Reid*,
796). He submitted the question of external existence to the experiment to which Hume had previously
submitted it, and to which, for that matter, it had
been previously submitted by Berkeley. Try, he
said, the experiment of thinking any given object,
and then of thinking the ego, and you will infallibly
find that the object thought and the ego thinking

are the same (*Fichte*, 156).*   He rejects, with even
more contempt than Hume, "the wonderful assumption that the ego is something different from
its own consciousness of itself, and that something,
heaven knows what, lying beyond this consciousness, is the foundation of it" (*ibid.* 145).   The
ego, it is true, was the only substance; but substance was nothing but thought vicissitude in general (*Schwegler*, 267).   It was as thought vicissitude
in general that the ego comprehended the sum
total of reality, the entire compass of existence (*ibid.*).
The world of sense in short was nothing but a spontaneous conception of the ego when recoiling from
its own limitations (p. 268), and God was nothing
but the moral order of the universe (p. 274)—the
moral order of our own ideas.

But there is a breach of continuity in the speculations of Fichte, of which Hume at all events was
guiltless.   The ego from which Fichte's theory of
knowledge starts is nothing but the identity of the
conscious subject with the object of which it is conscious (*Fichte*, 149).   But Fichte goes on to say that
the ego referred to is not to be identified with the
individual or a person (p. 157).   All individual
finite spirits, he says, are merely modes of the infinite life, which is God (p. 203).   He holds in fine

---

* *Fichte,* by Robert Adamson, M. A., Professor of Logic in the Owens College, Victoria University, Manchester—a monogram published in the Blackwood Series which contains the most intelligible account of Fichte's philosophy which I have met with.

that " the one reality, the one life, the life of consciousness, which is the manifestation of God, breaks
itself up into an endless multiplicity of individual
forms—forms which in the experience of the finite
spirit must present themselves as independent self-
existing facts, but which for thought are only modes
of the one infinite life (p. 209). Panegoism is thus
exchanged for Pantheism, and the absolute idea of
Hegel is foreshadowed in the infinite life of which
all individual lives are modes.

Logic and Metaphysics, if thought be identical
with being, are different aspects of the same thing.
But even in the logical aspect of Hegel's system
there is little that is absolutely new. The principle that there is no thought without plurality
and contrast is as old as Heraclitus, and had been
made one of the commonplaces of philosophy by
Hobbes. The axiom that the science of opposites
is one dates back to the Stagyrite. The famous
dogma that all position is negation had been enunciated by Spinosa. The secret of the triple nisus,
the mystery that reasoning and judgment are only
forms of simple apprehension, had been revealed
by Hume. The paradox that Pure Being and Pure
Nothing are the same is merely a disguise for the
platitude that there is no such thing in the world as
pure Being, and even that had been propounded by
the brilliant Sophist. In declaring that to be un-
true means much the same as to be bad (*Log.* 306),

Hegel merely reproduces the theory of Wollaston that morality is conformity with truth; and in attacking the fluxions of Newton and the infinitesimals of Leibnitz he merely reproduces the *Analyst* of Berkeley.

Mr. Wallace tells us that the interpreters of Hegel have contradicted each other as variously as the commentators on the Bible (*Proleg.* xiii.). Nor is this matter of surprise. The metaphysical aspect of his system is constantly changing, and the true method of interpretation is to observe its changes. It is clear that he rejected the transcendental object and the transcendental subject and the transcendental ideality of Kant. The thing-in-itself, he said, whether mind of man or God, was a mere abstraction (*Log.* 77); and time and space, arising as they did in the negative movement of the mind, were nothing but negations. In like manner he repudiated the ego of Fichte and its anstoss. The anstoss, he said, was merely the transcendental object in disguise, and the ego being dependent on it for its impulse was not a free spontaneous force (p. 102). Accordingly, for the ego he substituted the " self-actualising universal," *Thought* (p. 30). This self-actualising universal, in its onward movement through the categories of being, relation, and development, evolved the *Notion* which constitutes the actual thing (*Proleg.* cxxiii.). In this manner external objects corresponded with our conceptions;

but our conceptions, if they were to be regarded as
expressions of the truth, should also correspond with
the *Idea* (p. 304). Up to this point the idealist was
consistent. Thought and existence had been treated
as the development of the self-actualising universal—subject and object had been identified—all
dualism had been consistently ignored. But here
occurs the fissure which has already been remarked
in Fichte. Over and above the specific system of
ideas which the self-actuating universal calls itself,
the idealist admits another system. " The *Absolute*" he says, " is the universal and one idea,
which, as discerning, or in the act of judgment,
specialises itself to the system of specific ideas,
which, after all, are constrained by their nature to
come back to the one idea where their truth lies "
(p. 305). Here the distinction between subject and
object once again emerges, and the transcendental
object looms before us in the form of the *Absolute
Idea*. And the very nature of phenomena seems
to undergo a change. They cease to be purely
subjective conceptions, hemmed in by the impenetrable barrier of Fichte (p. 207)—they cease
to be subjective intuitions moulded in the forms
of Kant—they become objective in their nature.
This, in contradistinction to the subjective ideal-
isms of previous philosophy, is *Absolute Idealism.*
This is the main point of difference between
Kant and Hegel, and the difference is stated by
Hegel in the following words:—" The things that

we immediately know about are mere phenomena, not for us only, but in their own nature and without our interference; and these things, finite as they are, are appropriately described when we say that their being is established not on themselves, but on the divine and universal idea" (*Log.* 79).

Before we consider this theory of absolute idealism in its metaphysical aspect, let us examine it in its relation to the categories of the understanding. In holding the categories to be nothing but anticipations of a course of nature which was determined by the operation of a transcendental cause, the critic of the reason found himself met with the question, how is it to be conceived that nature must regulate herself so as to agree with our anticipations? According to Kant, this was a transcendental enigma which he solved on the principle of a pre-established harmony, such as had been conceived by Leibnitz. A similar solution had been given by David Hume. Nature, he said, "has implanted in us an instinct which carries forward the thought in a correspondent course to that which she has established among external objects" (iv. 66)— she has constituted "a kind of pre-established harmony between the course of nature and the succession of our ideas" (iv. 65). This was not satisfactory either to Fichte or to Hegel. In getting rid of the transcendental object they fancied that they had got rid of the transcendental enigma also. The categories, they said, were nothing but the necessary modes of the action of the self-conscious ego viewed in an objective aspect (*Fichte*, 158). They were "not instruments which the mind *uses*, but elements in a whole, or stages in a complex process, which in its unity the mind *is* " (*Hegel*, 157). In a word, the categories were not the mere anticipations of experience—they were the essential *constituents* of thought.

But it is obvious that this is not a solution, but a mere evasion of the difficulty to be solved. Even if we suppose that nature is nothing but the evolution of a self-actualising universal, we must admit that nature has a course; and even if we suppose that such course is merely subjective and ideal, we must calculate upon its continuance, whether we engage in scientific inquiry or in action. Though we admit that there is no course of nature but the course of thought, the course of thought requires to be anticipated as much as the course of nature. The anticipation that to-morrow I shall have the idea of a sunrise is as much a preconception of the understanding as the anticipation that the sun will rise to-morrow. How is this anticipation to be explained? It cannot be explained by saying that the categories are constituents of thought. Thought may be developed according to the laws of thought, but what guarantee do we possess that the laws of thought will be continued? The acute thinker who first observed that the supposition of the continuance of the laws of nature could not be derived from experience, because

292 The Postulate of Mill.

all experimental conclusions presupposed it, observed also that it could not be regarded as matter
of demonstration, because it involves no contradiction that the course of things may change.
This reasoning, it is evident, is equally just, whether
we regard the course of nature as something which
exists without us, or as something which exists
within. If it be regarded as developed from within
we must anticipate our own development. Such an
anticipation cannot be regarded as the constituent of
that which ex hypothesi is not yet constituted—it
can only be regarded as a pre-conception, whether
we consider it as a mere instinct with Hume, or ele-
vate it to the rank of a category of the understanding with his successor Kant.

The impossibility of evading this conclusion is
conspicuous in Mill. Holding, as he did, that we
have knowledge of nothing but our sensations, and
the laws of their occurrence, Mill adopted an idealism
as absolute as that of Hegel. But while he held with
Hegel that "the whole variety of the facts of nature,
as we know it, is given in the mere existence of sensations, and in the laws or order of their occurrence"
(*Exam.* 257), he repudiated the Hegelian conclusion
that "the laws of physical nature were deduced by
ratiocination from subjective deliverances of the
mind" (p. 628). Nay, after many a bewildering
statement in the contrary sense, Mill ultimately
accepted the view of Hume and Kant, and among
the first principles on which his psychological theory

reposed was content to "postulate that the human mind is capable of *expectation*" (p. 225). "The real stumbling-block," he said, "is, perhaps, not in any theory of the fact, but in the fact itself"; and "the true incomprehensibility perhaps is, that something which has ceased, or is not yet in existence, can still be, in a manner, present; that a series of feelings, the infinitely greater part of which is past or future, can be gathered up, as it were, into a single present conception, accompanied by a belief of reality" (p. 248).

Nor was Hegel more successful with respect to the primary aim of his philosophy than with respect to the categories of the understanding. In contrasting the philosophy of Hegel with that of Locke and Kant, Mr. Wallace remarks that the latter philosophers admitted two independent centres in subject and object, and were puzzled, like other philosophers, in their attempt to get from one to the other (*Proleg.* lviii.). Hegel, it is true, by identifying subject and object, seemed to have escaped the puzzle; but it was only seeming. In declaring all objects to be merely the development of a self-actualising universal, he undoubtedly concentrates all objective existence in the subject. The rigorous result of this would be, as stated by Mr. Hodgson in his *Time and Space*, that "the world is produced and developed according to the laws which govern consciousness "—that " we make the world by knowing it" (p. 392). But Hegel shrinks from this rigorous result. He admits the existence of something antecedent to the world—a time when the earth was without form and void, and when darkness was on the bosom of the deep. While professing to have abolished the distinction between object and subject, he leaves the subject confronted by an object as independent of itself as matter. " The living being," he says, "stands face to face with an inorganic nature, and conducts itself as a power over that nature, and assimilates it to itself" (*Log.* 312). " The nature of the universe," he elsewhere says, " hidden and shut up as it is at first, has no power which can permanently resist the courageous efforts of the intelligence; it must at last open itself up; it must reveal all its depth and riches to the spirit, and surrender them to be enjoyed by it" (*Hegel*, 195).* But what is inorganic nature in the development of conscious thought? Here we are met with the most unintelligible of all the unintelligibilities of Hegel. Let us revert to Professor Graham for its exposition. The development of the self-actualising universal has been characterised by progress. The *Phenomenology* is a history of the successive stages through which consciousness has passed. Reason has advanced from the age when man made weapons of flint, to the age in which we live (*Ideal.* 37). But nature must

* *Hegel*, by Edward Caird, LL.D., Professor of Moral Philosophy, University of Glasgow—another admirable monogram, published in the Blackwood Series of Philosophical Classics.

have existed in geological periods long before the
advent of humanity—and how? As unconscious
thought (p. 23). And this explains the origin of the
world and man. Unconscious thought may cast up
existences as it did in those geological periods, albeit
there was no real existence till conscious thought
appeared (p. 65). Mr. Graham tells us we must
not try to refute Hegel, we must only try to understand him. Let the reader try. "It will be better,"
says Hegel, "if we use the term thought at all, to
speak of nature as the system of unconscious thought,
or, to use Schelling's expression, a fossilized intelligence" (*Log.* 39). This fossilized intelligence is
the new *materia prima*—nay, it is the *primum mobile*
as well. Such is the beginning of world in the
Genesis of Hegel, and Mr. Graham tells us that it
is only an example of his great principle, "that
being and non-being are the same" (*Ideal.* 65).

But it is not merely in the inorganic nature
which existed in the geological periods before the
advent of humanity that the Hegelian encounters
the inevitable object. He admits the existence of
self-actualising universals other than himself; and
it is perfectly clear that if there be a number of
self-actualising universals, every self-actualising universal other than himself is an object external to
himself, which escapes his apprehension as completely as any material or any transcendental object. The generations of men who preceded him,
mere systems of ideas as they are supposed to be,

were not *his* system of ideas.   The great battle,
amid the thunders of which the Phenomenology
was finished, was fought by spirits, to whom his
spirit was a stranger.   The past was the creation of
other minds than his; and the future is an object
which his mind may anticipate, but cannot possibly
evolve.   Above all, the Absolute Idea, in which he
supposes himself to live and move and have his
being, is a Being far transcending him, a God
whose thoughts are not his thoughts, and whose
ways are not as his.

Hegel at times gives a great elevation to his
language, and a great appearance of orthodoxy to his
doctrine, by dilating on the might and majesty of
God.   Indeed Mr. Graham informs us that "the
Hegelian sees God everywhere beneath the world of
nature, which is merely his woven veil, and knows
him in the high soul of man, which is the manifestation of his spiritual presence" (*Ideal.* 32); and Stirling goes so far as to say that Hegel, in vindicating
thought alone as the substantial element in the universe, has extended an immense support to every
spiritual influence, and supplied the most powerful
bulwark to religion (*Schw.* 443).   But the question
is not what Hegel believes or says, but what are his
principles, and what is the result to which they lead.
Let us therefore examine the theology of Hegel.

Mr. Wallace tells us that " the Hegelian system
has the all-embracing and encyclopaedic character
by which Scholastic thought threw its arms around

heaven and earth "; and that " Hegel's theory is
the explication of God, but of God in the actuality
and plenitude of the world, and not as a transcendent Being in the solitude of a world beyond "
(*Proleg.* xxvi.). Professor Caird adopts the same
metaphor, and tells us that " the essential unity
of all things with each other and with the mind
that knows them is the adamantine circle, within
which the strife of opposites is waged, and which
their utmost violence of conflict cannot break "
(*Hegel,* 141).* But how is the existence of this
Absolute Mind arrived at? The Absolute Idea,
transcending as it does all finite intelligence, is an
object as transcendent as the transcendental object
which it endeavours to supplant. Hegel tells us
that " when we hear the Idea spoken of we need
not imagine something far away beyond this mortal
sphere "—" the Idea is rather what is completely
present, and it is found in every consciousness,
although it may be in an indistinct and stunted
form " (*Log.* 306). But, before we can say that
the Idea is completely present, its presence must

* These metaphors may afford the
explanation of a seemingly absurd and
incongruous doctrine, which is attributed by Cicero to Parmenides, the
philosopher who first proclaimed that
thought and its object are the same.
Nam Parmenides commenticium quid-
dam *coronae* simile efficit—*stephanen*
appellat—continentem ardore [*qu:* ar-
dores] lucis *orbem,* qui cingit coelum,
quem appellat Deum (*De Nat. D.* i. 11).
The interpretation of this passage on
Hegelian principles is quite consistent
with what follows—Multaque ejusdem
monstra, quippe qui bellum, qui dis-
cordiam, qui cupiditatem, ceteraque
generis ejusdem ad Deum revocat. Al
these things, as existing realities, are
clearly comprehended in Hegel's Absolute Idea.

be proved, and before we can prove its presence we must prove that it exists. What, then, is Hegel's proof of God's existence? It is the old Cartesian proof. God, he says, " can only be thought as existing "—" his Notion involves Being "—" it is this unity of the Notion and Being that constitutes the only notion of God " (*Log.* 92). But the futility of this argument had been shown by Hume. " In the proposition, *God is,*" he said, " or indeed any other which regards existence, the idea of existence is no distinct idea, which we unite with that of the object, and which is capable of forming a compound idea by the union " (i. 132). The futility of the ontological argument had been still more clearly pointed out by Kant. The definition of the idea of existence showed that it was futile (*Kritik*, 367). The word *being* did not really predicate existence, it was merely the copula of logic (p. 368). The analysis of a conception could never establish the existence of its object (p. 392); and we might as well hope to increase our store of knowledge by the aid of mere ideas, as to augment our wealth by the addition of a multitude of noughts (p. 370).

But what is the nature of the God whose existence is supposed to be thus established? The Absolute Idealist informs us. " The Absolute," he says, "is intended, and ought to express God in the style and character of thought " (*Log.* 134). In the style and character of thought he is "the fulness of objectivity, confronted with which our particu-

lar or subjective opinions and desires have no truth
and no validity" (p. 289). "God, far from being
a Being or Essence, even the highest, is *the* Being
or Essence" (p. 180). In fine, " God, who is absolutely infinite, is not something out of, and beside
whom, there are other essences"—" all else out of
God, if separated from him, possesses no essenti-
ality" whatever (p. 180). But what is the relation
between this transcendent essence and our own?
Professor Caird tells us that the universe of Hegel
is " a universe in which every thought is a truth,
and every particle of dust an organisation—a ma-
crocosm made up of microcosms, which is all in
every part " (*Hegel*, 179). If we accept this proposition in the literal sense, then God would seem
to be merely the sum total of the infinitesimals of
finite thought, a mere integration of existence ; and
war, and discord, and lust, and every evil thought,
as Cicero said of Parmenides, must be referred to
God. But if God is not the integral of humanity,
is man an infinitesimal of God? Every individual
being, Hegel tells us, is some one aspect of the Idea ;
and he tells us that in God we live and move and
have our Being. This is the language of Malebranche—the language of Berkeley—the language
which was borrowed from Epicharmus by St. Paul.
But language so variously applied means anything
or nothing. Let us take some intelligible utterance
of Hegel. The universal and one idea, he says,
specialises itself to a system of specific ideas, which

after all are constrained by their nature to come
back to the one idea where their truth lies (*Log.*
305). This would seem to be merely another form
of the infinite impersonal life of Fichte. If this
be the case, Hegel would seem, like Fichte, to be
merely an idealised Spinosa. For what is the doctrine of Spinosa? Spinosa holds that there is one
infinite and extended substance of which all finite
existences are modes—waves, as it were, of the
ocean of being, which rise and swell and subside,
but never really are (*Schw.* 173).* If we eliminate
the ideas of substance and extension from this conception, we may form some dim adumbration of the
Absolute Idea. But if this be the true conception, what is God? According to Stirling himself,
nothing but a shadowy universal (*Schw.* 435). And
if God be nothing but a shadowy universal, what
is man? Let Professor Graham answer. Something as unsubstantial as the cloud, something as
evanescent as the foam (*Ideal.* 45).

---

* Goethe, though he changes the metaphor at the close, would seem to have
had this idea of Spinosa's in his mind, when he put the following words into
the mouth of the Spirit of the Earth:—

> In the floods of life, in the storm of strife,
>   On the crest of the wave,
>   In the depths of the sea,
>   I am birth and grave
>   Eternally !
>   As I weave my tissues,
>   Life glows and issues ;
> For the thunderous loom of time is mine,
> Which clothes the world with its life divine !
>
> *Faust,* p. 37.

But even here the difficulties of the Hegelian
system do not end. A doctrine which insists upon
the co-existence of the Absolute Idea and specific
systems of ideas is as dualistic as the doctrine which
assumes the mutual co-operation and correspondence of a transcendental object and a transcendental subject. Here the criticism of the Absolute
Idealist recoils upon himself. " In every dualistic
system," says Hegel, " and especially in that of
Kant, the fundamental defect makes itself visible
in unifying at one moment what a moment before
had been explained to be independent and incapable
of unification " (*Log.* 98). But things may be similar
in essence without being unified in thought ; and notwithstanding any similarity of essence, the question
of dualism recurs—How can I know any essence
but my own ? The Absolute Idea is something
supersensible, and Hegel admits that " the rise of
thought beyond the world of sense, its passage from
the finite to the infinite, the leap into the supersensible which it takes when it snaps asunder the links
of the chain of sense—all this transition is thought,
and nothing but thought " (*Log.* 87). But if thought
leaps into the supersensible, the supersensible into
which it leaps is not something out of and beyond
itself. Out of and beyond itself not even thought
can leap. What thought as thinker thinks, on the
principles of Hegel, it creates. If it thinks a Being
or Essence which is God, then God himself is its
creation. And it is in this sense that Fichte must

be understood when he proclaimed to his astonished
audience that in his next lecture he was going to
create God. But if this be so, the Hegelian system is absolutely inverted and reversed. The mind
of man does not exist in God; on the contrary,
God exists only in the mind of man. Pantheism
is thus metamorphosed into Panegoism—the ego is
declared to be the All—the world, the soul, and God
are nothing but imaginations of the ego—and the
ego is nothing but a system of shadowy ideas,
without any existence in space or time, and without
any ground of existence in substance or in cause.

The Absolute Idealism of Hegel, notwithstanding its pretensions, is, in fact, the metaphysical
lunacy which Reid attributed to Hume (*Reid*, 127,
209). Nor, after all, can it be more graphically described than in the homely language of the sage of
common sense. Like the Treatise of Human Nature the Logic discards spirit and body from the
world and leaves impressions and ideas the sole existences in nature (p. 109). Its ideas are as free and
independent as the birds of the air, or as the atoms
of Epicurus when they pursued their journey through
the vast inane (*ibid.*). They are set adrift in the
world without connexion or support (*ibid.*). "But
why," said Reid, "should we seek to compare them
with anything, since there is nothing in nature
but themselves? They make the whole furniture
of the universe; starting into existence, or out of
it, without any cause; combining into parcels, which

the vulgar call minds, and succeeding one another by fixed laws, without time, place, or author of those laws " (*ibid.*).

How then have the promises of Hegel been fulfilled? Has he exhibited the diamond net in which the universe is held? Has he given an exposition of God in his eternal essence? Has he exhibited truth without her veil? He has done none of these things. He professes to have displayed the diamond net in which the universe is held; but he has only shown that the universe is a mere evanescence with no diamond net to hold it. He professes to have given an exposition of God in his eternal essence; but he has only shown that God in his eternal essence is a shadowy universal. He professes to have exhibited the form of truth without a veil; but like the Grecian painter, it is only the veil itself that he has painted. And what of the sphinx enigmas of existence, and the problem of the painful earth? Hegel solves the enigma by declaring there is no enigma to be solved. He finds no difficulty in conceiving that things may subsist without a substance and originate without a cause. He assumes the existence of our sensations without inquiry as to where they come from, and how it is that they arise. He assumes their co-existences and their successions and their laws without asking how the co-existences and successions are determined, by what power those laws have been imposed. The logic of Hegel gives no answer to the questions which cannot be evaded by the philosopher any more than they can be evaded by the common man. " Where am I, or what ? From what causes do I derive my existence, and to what condition shall I return ? Whose favours shall I court, and whose anger must I dread ?" Hume asked himself these questions, and professed himself to be confounded (i. 340). Kant asked them, and left reason trembling on the verge of the abyss of necessity, which he regarded as the ultimate support of all existing things (p. 376). These questions the philosophy of Hegel ignores ; it ignores the very craving of intelligence by which they are suggested. He is content to regard God as a shadowy universal with no existence but a shadow's ; he is content to regard the universe as only another name for that shadowy universal ; and oscillating between Pantheism on the one hand and Panegoism on the other, he is driven to regard man as either a mere shifting shadow of a shade, or an unessential essence which constitutes the universe of things.

AN IDEAL OF SYSTEMS:

OR

THE NEW KRITIK.

AN IDEAL OF SYSTEMS:

OR

THE NEW KRITIK.

———◆———

*Sed jam, ut omni me invidia liberem, ponam in medio sententias philo-
sophorum; quo quidem loco convocandi omnes videntur, qui quae
sit earum vera judicent.*—DE NAT. DEOR.

THE advent of Hegel, as we have seen, was regarded
as the advent of a new Messiah ; and in the hour of
his triumph all Germany hailed him with hosannas.
But the hosannas were followed by a crucifixion.
A reaction set in against the absolute philosophy.
Unbelievers began to ridicule its empty abstractions, its shadowy universals, its artificial tricho-
tomies, its affectation of omniscience, and its
wearisome iteration of barbaric and unintelligible
terms.* Heine described the Hegelian system as
a harlequinade of thought; and Schopenhauer
derided its author as a philosophical acrobat,

---

* The following details are derived
from a very interesting work—HEGEL
et SCHOPENHAUER, Études sur la
Philosophie Allemande Moderne depuis
Kant jusq'a nos jours. Par A. Foucher
de Careil. Paris, 1862.

who had the misfortune to have lost his body.
Schopenhauer went still further—further perhaps
than he was justified in going. He denounced
Fichte, Schelling, and Hegel as three sophists who
made a trade of philosophy, and were the intellectual mercenaries of the state—ready to abandon
pantheism for pietism if adequately paid, and, like
Bottom the weaver, equally prepared to roar as the
lion or to whisper as the sucking dove.

Schopenhauer professed to have supplied an element which he said was wanting in Hegel's theory
of the evolution and self-development of *thought.*
"My great discovery," he said, "is a Thebes with
a hundred gates; it is that, at the base of all things,
there is a *force* which is one and identical, always
equal and eternally the same; and that this force,
which slumbers in the plant, which awakes in the
animal, and which becomes conscious of itself in
man, is *will.*"* But Stirling is right (*Schw.* 446).
Although Schopenhauer must take a high rank
among German philosophers, it is clear that German
philosophy is closed with Hegel. The shadowy universal, with no existence in space or time and with

* Goethe, who was a friend of Schopenhauer, probably had this theory in
view when he makes Faust hesitate as to how he should translate the λόγος of
the famous passage of St. John :—

Is it mere *thought* evolves all nature's course ?
Surely in the beginning there was *force* !
Still as the word is traced beneath my hand,
A something warns me not to let it stand.
The Spirit aids me—all is now exact—
I write, In the beginning was the *act* !—*Faust*, p. 73.

no ground of existence in substance or in cause, was the last word of idealism. Even the power of absurdity, which Hobbes regards as the privilege of reason, could go no further.

The history of philosophy from Berkeley to Hegel would seem to justify the positive philosopher in his prophecy that the educated intellects of the future would abandon all metaphysical speculation, and devote themselves exclusively to the study of the phenomena of nature and their laws. But as Schopenhauer remarks—and the remark had previously been made by Kant—there is a metaphysical instinct in human nature which is as ineradicable as any of its other instincts. The energetic intellect of youth, when it feels the first stirrings of intellectual life, conceives everything to be open to its efforts, and with unconscious audacity looks the mystery of existence in the face and fancies it can solve it. It may be that this is a mere beating of the air, but it is the beating of the air which develops the muscles of the athlete. Nor is this the only factor in the case. In every free state—and this is the most obvious indication of its freedom—there will ever be men who, by the bias of their genius, will devote themselves to philosophy, as others devote themselves to poetry and art; and as poetry and art are never exhausted, so philosophy will everlastingly assume new forms. The object which the philosopher sets before him may be as far beyond the reach of human knowledge

as the grand arcanum or the great elixir. But the
spirit of metaphysics never dies. Its destruction
is as illusory as that of the visionary maid which
Dryden's Theodore beheld when " more than a mile
immersed within the wood." The hounds may
fasten on her side and the knight may plunge his
sword into her back; but an irrevocable sentence
has been past. The pursuit must for ever be continued, and the phantom is no sooner slain than
it revives—

> Renewed to life, that she might daily die,
> We daily doomed to follow, she to fly.

But is philosophy, after all, the visionary pursuit that is imagined ? As Hume has remarked, it
is no inconsiderable part of science to know the
different operations of the mind, to separate them
from each other, to classify them under their appropriate heads, and to remove all the seeming disorder
in which they are involved, when made the subject
of reflection (iv. 12). But there is an element of
science, even in the books of metaphysics, which the
sceptic wished to burn. In the attempt to solve the
metaphysical problem of the world a number of
hypotheses have been framed by philosophers, and
though none of these hypotheses can claim to rank
as science, yet in their totality they possess a scientific value. In themselves they may be the mere
play of philosophic imagination, the romance of
reason. But reason, confronted with the great mystery of existence, cannot choose but make its guesses

at the riddle. Every philosophy is such a guess; and a complete system of philosophies will constitute the sum total of the guesses which reason is competent to make. Such a system, even as a matter of curiosity, would be interesting, and, as a fact expressive of the limitation of the powers of reason, would come within the strict domain of science. Nor is it impossible to imagine such a system. In every department of mental philosophy a conspectus of the various theories which have been invented may be made. The theories as to the origin of knowledge, or as to the nature of universals, or as to the true character of the process of induction, may be contabulated so as to see where they diverge, how far they differ, and in what respect they are expressions of the truth. Such a synopsis of systems would not only facilitate study, but would go far to remove the opprobrium of philosophy— the fatal differences of opinion which seem to exist among its masters. For truth is a polygon, and not a point; and apparent differences of opinion are caused by the different sides of the polygon on which the attention of philosophers is fixed. It is thus that a Kritik of Systems is required to supplement the Kritik of Reason. Let us see whether on the subject of the great cosmological problem the outlines of such a Kritik can be traced.

"It seems evident," says Hume, "that men are carried by a natural instinct or prepossession to repose faith in their senses, and that without any reasoning, or even almost before the use of reason, we always suppose an external universe which depends not on our perception, but would exist though we and every sensible creature were absent or annihilated." While we are under the influence of this natural instinct, not only do we suppose an external universe, which depends not on our perception, but we suppose that we immediately perceive it. It appears to us as if sense actually apprehended things out of itself and in their proper space. We make no distinction between the object existing and the object known. We presume not only that the world exists, but that we know it as existing. We presume that we know it not as a mere cause, but as an object. This is the conclusion to which we are led by the instinct of our nature; and this instinctive determination of the human race is *Natural Realism* in its only intelligible sense.

" But," as Hume continues, " this universal and primary opinion of all men is soon destroyed by the slightest philosophy, which teaches us that nothing can ever be present to the mind but the image or perception, and that the senses are only the inlets through which these images are conveyed, without being able to produce any immediate intercourse between the mind and the object." And in this, as a statement of the fact, the philosopher is right. The blue of the ocean and the sky, the green of the forest and the field, all the variegated colours of creation, are admitted to be mere sensations. Everything which seems presented from without by vision is admittedly projected from within. What we take to be reality turns out to be a mere conception of the mind. It is the idea of which we are conscious, and not the actual thing. But with the instinct of reality still strong upon us, we are unable to accept the doctrine of a pure, unqualified idealism, which admits the existence of nothing but the mere idea. Convinced that in the perception of the distant we are only conscious of an idea, we nevertheless regard the idea within as representative of the thing without. The theory of Representative Perception thus emerges. We suppose the existence of a reality which our idea represents, and *Hypothetical Realism*, to employ the phrase of Sir William Hamilton, is the first conclusion which we adopt when we abandon common sense and instinct for philosophy and reason.

But how can we know that our ideas are representative of objects which are thus assumed to be unknown? The question did not escape the Atomists of old, and their answer is given by the poet who beautified the sect which was otherwise inferior to the rest. We are told by Lucretius that, stripped from the surface of external things, light films are incessantly emitted, which, borne upon the air, are received by the various appliances of

sense, and are the *Sensible Eidola*, which represent
the realities from which they come.

> The slender form and effigy of things,
> By things emitted, from their surface springs ;
> Membranes, or films, they bear, whate'er their name,
> The image of the thing from whence they came,
> The species similar—the form the same.

Such was the theory which Democritus bequeathed
to Epicurus—such was the theory which Reid attributed to all philosophers from Plato down to
Hume. And undoubtedly there is an element of
truth in this, the earliest of the theories of perception. Unless the rays of light impinge upon
the retina of the eye, unless the tympanum of the
ear be struck by the vibrations of the air, unless
there be an effluvium of the particles of odour soli-
citing the membrane of the nose, we neither see,
nor hear, nor smell. But a material antecedent is
not of necessity a material efflux ; and a material
efflux is not of necessity a material film ; and the
presence of a material film is one thing, and the
sensation of which it is the antecedent is another.
How, then, is the mental fact, the fact of consciousness, to be explained ? This was a question to
which the theory of Democritus, as far as we are
acquainted with it, gave no answer. An answer was
essayed by Aristotle. Perception, the Stagyrite
said, is the reception not of a material film, but of
an immaterial form. The mind receives the form
of things perceived without the matter, just as

wax, when impressed by a seal, receives nothing but the mere impression. What we are conscious of is not a sensible eidolon, which is a modification of matter, but a *Sensible Idea*, which is a modification of the mind itself. Here, too, there is an element of plausibility or truth. As far as appears, our organs of sense stand in relation to certain specific qualities of body, and each sensation receives its development, its form, from the operation of the quality to which it corresponds (*Reid*, 827). But the rationale of the doctrine escaped the apprehension of the men who proclaimed themselves the followers of the great master. The form with which he conceived the mind to be impressed they seem to have regarded as a matterless efflux from matter. A system of entities, distinct from matter and from mind, was thus devised; and the material films of Democritus were superseded by the *Intentional Species* of the schoolmen. A simpler doctrine, one perhaps identical with that of Aristotle, was afterwards embraced. The sensible idea was regarded as a mere act of sense; the act of sense was conceived to be determined by the secret powers of matter; and thus, with a minimum admixture of hypothesis, was developed the theory of *Physical Influence or Influx*.

A film emitted, a form impressed, a fact of consciousness determined, such are the three aspects under which our ideas of sensation may be regarded as the representatives of material things. But the difficulties of the case were not exhausted.

A deeper and more serious question arose. Matter and mind, it was said, are different in their nature; they are separated by the whole diameter of being. Not only must philosophy explain how the mind can perceive matter at a distance— it must explain how mind can perceive matter in contact, or at all. The hypothesis of a *Plastic Medium*—a medium which was neither mind nor matter, but which had affinities with each— was excogitated in order to bring the two discordant elements into relation. But the Plastic Medium was a mere hypothesis, with nothing in experience to suggest it; and the interposition of a medium between mind and matter scarcely disguised and did not solve the problem. To solve the problem the Alexandrine philosophers devised the theory of *Gnostic Reasons*. They supposed certain forms and representatives of things which, prior to the act of perception, have a latent existence in the soul;* and they held that on the occasion of the impression made on the external organ by the object, the mind, being roused to action, mingles the image from without with the

* Tum mentis vigor excitus,
  Quas intus species tenet
  Ad motus similes vocans,
  Notis applicat exteris,
  Introrsumque reconditis
  Formis miscet imagines.

It is strange that Hamilton, in citing these verses of Boethius, should have failed to observe the approximation of the theory of Gnostic Reasons to the Kantian doctrine of the Forms of Sense, although he observed its approximation to the hypotheses of Descartes and Leibnitz (*Reid*, 263). The Alexandrine theory was adopted by Kant's immediate predecessor, Wolff (*Log.* i. 6).

form within, and elicits into consciousness the representation through which the reality is known (*Reid*,
263). In thus mingling the image with the form,
the theory of gnostic reasons, it is obvious, approximates to the transcendental ideality of Kant.
But its defects are obvious. It assumes the existence of the external world, for our knowledge of
which it professes to account; and while admitting
the action of matter on the living body and the
stimulated mind, it in effect merely gives a statement of the difficulty which it was invented to
explain.

It was at this point the discussion of the question
was resumed in modern times. The material world,
it was conceded, was not given as an *object;* the
question was, could matter be regarded as a *cause.*
Matter, it was said, is conceived as passive and
inert; how, then, can it be conceived as cause? It
is conceived as essentially unthinking; how, then,
can it be conceived as the cause of thought? Re-
stricting the conception of causation to that of efficiency, and assuming that the conceptions of the
human mind are the measure of the possibilities of
things, philosophy once more embarked on the sea
of speculation. Though matter be conceived as in
its own nature incapable of thinking or producing
thought, might it not be regarded as invested by
Omnipotence with powers which it did not of itself
possess? This was the theory of Locke. We may
conceive that God, if he pleases, can superadd to

matter a faculty of thinking; and though motion, according to the utmost stretch of our ideas, can produce nothing but motion, we may still allow it to produce sensation, if we attribute it wholly to the good pleasure of our Maker (*Essay* IV. iii. 6). Philosophy thus effected an alliance with Theology, and the first fruits of the connexion was this theory of the *Hyperphysical Influence of Matter*. But this conception, it is plain, could scarcely stand the test of logic. If motion can produce nothing but motion, if the production of sensation is resolved into the good pleasure of our Maker, it is God and not matter that is the cause of thought. A new hypothesis was therefore started. God, said the Cartesian, by the incessant action of his omnipotence, produces all the changes in material things, but he does not operate on matter so as to enable it to manifest itself to mind; he operates on mind so as to enable it to take cognizance of matter. On the occasion of the presence of the material object, God, as the efficient cause of thought, determines the mind to the formation of a representative idea. Such was the theory of *Occasional Causes* or *Divine Assistance*. But this theory also was open to attack. According to its opponents it postulated a perpetual miracle. It condemned the Creator to create for ever. In the vigorous phrase of Aristotle, it compelled the Deity to put his hand to everything. It degraded the Demiurgus to a drudge. In opposition to the theory of the incessant agency of God, it was maintained that the series of causes and effects spontaneously evolves itself as a consequence of the original constitution of the world. The music of the spheres was not that of an organ on which the musician strikes every note, nor that of a cylinder which the maker was himself obliged to turn: it was that of a mechanism which the great artist had cunningly contrived, and which, when once set going, never ceased its chime. There was a *Pre-established Harmony* between mind and matter. According to Leibnitz the mind of man was a monad, a unit of substance, endowed with a representative power, and the various representations which it evolves were pre-adjusted so as to correspond with the pre-adjusted evolution of material monads. The soul and the world were clocks with independent springs, and set to correspond. But this theory, like its predecessors, failed to satisfy the exigencies of speculative thought. It introduced the principle of mechanism into incorporeal things. It postulated what it did not prove, the existence of the world. It postulated what it did not prove, the existence of a God. It did not even solve the difficulty which it was framed to solve. If, as the Leibnitzian averred, everything goes on in mind as if there were no matter, and everything goes on in matter as if there were no mind, the chasm between mind and matter, it is evident, remains unbridged, and philosophy stands helpless on its verge. To bridge the chasm, recourse was had to theology once more.

Philosophy accepted from theology not merely the agency of a God, but the existence of a revelation, to enable it to solve its problem. On the authority of revelation it assumed the existence of an external world, and then it had recourse to reason to explain the knowledge of the existence so assumed. "In the beginning God created the heavens and the earth "—and therefore, said Malebranche, the heavens and the earth have a material existence. Of that material existence we can have no knowledge, for mind cannot take cognisance of matter. But God takes cognisance of the world, the existence of which he has revealed, and he can communicate that cognisance to us. In him we live and move and have our being. Our sensations are the production of his power; our perceptions are a participation of his knowledge. What he sees we see, what he thinks we think—we are parts of him. We are partakers of his heavenly vision, and the world of sense is the *Vision of the Universe in God.*

Matter operated on by God so as to reveal itself to mind; mind operated on by God so as to take cognisance of matter; matter and mind each operated on by God so that their modifications should correspond; mind admitted by God to a participation of his knowledge of material things—such are the four great forms of *Theological Realism*—a realism which recognises the existence of a world of matter, but professes itself unable to explain our knowledge of that existence without the intervention of a God. From such a realism the transition to a pure *Theological Idealism* was as inevitable as it was obvious. If, as Malebranche said, God produces our sensations— why not allow him to produce our perceptions also ? If all that the mind is conscious of is a series of conceptions; if that series of conceptions in the mind can never be produced by matter; if the Deity must be invoked to account for the appearances of sense— why suppose the existence of material things? Their existence could not possibly be proved. True, there must be some cause of the continual succession of ideas which we experience; but that cause must be an incorporeal active substance other than ourselves (*Prin.* xxvi.). The existence of a Spirit infinitely wise and powerful and good is sufficient to explain all the appearances of nature (§ lxxii.). But if we come to the conclusion that there is "a mind which affects us every moment with all the sensible impressions we perceive" (*Dial.* ii.), the consequence is clear. The soul does not exist in the world; the world, on the contrary, exists only in the soul. Space cannot exist without the mind, and its idea is a mere abstraction (*Prin.* cxvi.); even time itself has no existence abstracted from the succession of our thoughts (§ xcviii.).

Berkeley fondly imagined that with materialism and atheism he had also banished *Scepticism* from the world. But his idealism in reality evoked the sceptic. This was shown by Hume. The arguments

Y

of Berkeley, he said, admit of no answer, and produce no conviction (iv. 181). Nature, by an absolute and uncontrollable necessity, has determined us to judge as well as to be ache and feel (i. 240), and if we listen to the dictates of nature, the existence of body must be taken for granted in all our reasonings (i. 245). As an agent, he said, I am quite satisfied with this; but as a philosopher I want to learn the ground of my belief (iv. 47). The ground of the belief, according to Berkeley, was a mere illusion arising from our consciousness that our sensations are imprinted from without. The tenet in question involved a contradiction. Strictly speaking, there was and could be no belief in the existence of objects independent of the mind (*Prin.* lvi.). This, it is evident, was a new departure. In recognising the existence of matter, preceding philosophers had deferred to the authority of common sense; in denying the existence of matter, Berkeley committed common sense and philosophy to an internecine conflict. If we wish to know the issue of the conflict, we have only to pursue the history of idealism from its rise with Berkeley to its culminating point in Hegel.

Hume prepared the way for Kant. His unknown cause (iv. 178) was in reality the transcendental object. His principle, that nothing can be inferred from experience which every inference from experience presupposes (iv. 46) was the principle of the categories of the understanding. Above all, his position that the ideas of space and time are not separate and distinct ideas, but merely those of the manner in which objects exist (i. 62), was, in effect, a declaration that space and time were transcendentally ideal. The transition from positions such as these to the *Transcendental Idealism* of Kant was but a step. If space and time be merely ideas of the manner in which sensible appearances exist, why should we postulate their absolute existence? If space and time are presupposed in all sensible experience, why should we not regard them as the forms of sense? The things which we intuite in space and time are nothing but phenomena, and phenomena are nothing but representations moulded in the forms of sense, which have no self-subsistent existence apart from human thought (*Kritik*, 307). It is true we must suppose the existence of some transcendental object as an originating cause which stimulates our sensibility; but the nature of that object is essentially unknown. We know not whether it exists within ourselves or whether it is to be found without. Such was the reasoning of Kant. The Deity of Berkeley was superseded by a *nescio quid;* his abstractions were declared to be the constituent forms of sense; and, in spite of his consciousness that our sensations are imprinted from without, it was held that the ideal world, in part at least, was originated from within.

The *Subjective Idealism* of Fichte was the outcome of the Transcendental Idealism of Kant. Where was

the necessity for assuming a transcendental object ?
If a cause for the world of sense must be assumed,
why should we seek the cause beyond ourselves ?
The activity of the ego was manifest in consciousness. In its action it evolved all the conceptions
with which philosophy was concerned : why should
we deem it insufficient to account for the appearances of sense ? In its onward movement, it is
true, it seemed to encounter an insurmountable
obstacle which drove it back upon itself. But this
obstacle was merely an *anstoss* which, like the sense
of incubus, had its origin within. It was this which
induced the ego to form the notion of a thing without ; it was thus that it formed the conception of
objects occupying space. But all this was nothing
but conception. The objects which appear to be
external were the various breakings of the action
of the ego against an incomprehensible obstacle
(*Schw.* 268) — they were the mere spray of the
billow when recoiling from its bound.

The subjective idealism of Fichte, after its brief
hour of triumph, gave way to the *Absolute Idealism* of
his rival. The incomprehensible obstacle of Fichte,
it was said, was merely the transcendental object in
disguise (*Log.* 102) ; his idealism left us hemmed in
by an impenetrable barrier, and confined us to our
subjective conceptions for a world (p. 207). The
transcendental object, whatever form it might assume, was nothing but a mere abstraction (p. 77).
The things which we immediately know were phe-

nomena, it is true; but phenomena were neither
subjective intuitions moulded in our forms of sense,
nor subjective conceptions formed by our understanding in its recoil from nothing; they were
simple appearances existing in their own nature,
and without our interference (p. 79). Genuine
idealism was in fact the *Transcendental Realism* which
the critic of the reason had rejected (*Kritik*, 307).
Phenomena were things subsisting in themselves
(*ibid.*). There was no essence behind or beyond
the appearance; existence was nothing but appearance, and appearance was all that essentially exists
(*Log.* 206). Appearances supplied the content of the
absolute idea (p. 307); of this absolute idea every
individual was an aspect (p. 305); and in these
aspects "God, who is the essence, lends existence
to the passing stages of his own show in himself,"
and is "the infinite kindness which lets its own
show freely issue into immediacy, and graciously
allows it the joy of being" (p. 206).*

But even Fichte and Hegel recoiled from the
rigorous results of their respective systems. Their
common purpose was to solve the problem of objec-

---

* Goethe, who was the friend and benefactor of Hegel, would seem to have
had some such idea as this in view when writing the closing words of the *Pro-
logue in Heaven* :—

> But ye, true Sons of God, surrender
> Your spirits to the rich and living Splendor!
> The teeming Whole which ever works and lives
> Bind you together with its blessed linking!
> And all the shifting shows its essence gives
> Substantiate by unremitted thinking !—*Faust*, p. 24.

tive knowledge by abolishing the difference between the subject and the object. Rejecting the dogma that the non-ego produces the ego, Fichte propounded the counter dogma that the ego produces the non-ego, and regarded the object as a mere conception of the subject. Rejecting the dogma that the object is a mere conception of the subject, Hegel propounded the dogma that there is no objectivity apart from universal thought, and regarded the subject as an aspect of the object. But objectivity remained. The subjective idealist recognised an infinite life, of which every individual is a mode; the absolute idealist recognised an absolute idea, of which every individual is a phase. Both of them admitted that personality is inconceivable, unless we assume the existence of a multiplicity of persons; and each of them, accordingly, assumed the existence of a system of egos coexistent with himself (*Fichte*, 182, 202). But on the slope of speculation the descent of down-lapsing thought is not to be arrested. To the reflecting ego a system of egos other than itself is as much an external object as an external world of matter. If consciousness is unable to transcend itself, then the infinite life and the absolute idea are as far beyond its reach as the most transcendental, the most transcendent, object. It is in vain to resolve the elements of the universe into thought, and to exclaim, Alles ist Ich; that is a position which cannot be consistently maintained unless we are prepared to hold that Ich ist Alles. *Egoistic Idealism*, therefore, with its world of subjective conceptions, is the bourne for which all idealism is ultimately bound. This is shown by the philosophy of Fichte in its earlier form. There the Deity was nothing but the moral order of the universe (*Schw.* 274); the universe was merely the sum total of the conceptions of the ego (p. 267); and the ego itself was merely thought vicissitude in general (*ibid.*). The ego was thus converted into the egomet; the egomet declared itself to be the All; and *Panegoism* was the last expression of the "philosophical delirium" of Hume.

Yet not the last. For what is Panegoism itself when the ego is destitute of substance? On the acknowledgment of Fichte it is merely *Nihilism* in disguise. "The sum of all", he says, "is this. There is absolutely nothing permanent either without me or within me, but only an unceasing change. I know absolutely nothing of any existence, not even of my own. I myself know nothing, and am nothing. Images there are; they constitute all that apparently exists, and what they know of themselves is after the manner of images; images that pass and vanish without there being aught to witness their transition—that consist, in fact, of the images of images without significance and without an aim. I myself am one of these images; nay, I am not even thus much, but only a confused image of images. All reality is converted into a marvellous dream, without a life to dream of, and without a mind to dream—into a dream made up only of a dream of itself. Perception is a dream; thought—the source of all the existence, and all the reality which I imagine to myself of my existence, of my power, of my destination—is the dream of that dream". That is the last word which idealism has to utter. That, according to one of the greatest of the idealists, is the sum of all.

Such is the natural and almost the historical development of the various theories which have been propounded to explain the phenomena of sense. Like the unquiet spirit in the gospel, for two thousand years and more, the spirit of speculation has wandered to and fro through the wilderness of thought, seeking evermore for rest and finding none. Impelled by an unreflecting instinct, we first imagine that we grasp the thing; instructed by awakened reason, we are fain to confess that what we are conscious of is nothing but the idea. With the instinct of reality still strong upon us, we are prompted to regard our ideas as representatives of things, and forthwith atoms, forms, and films are invented as intermediaries between the reality without and the conception of the reality within. Baffled in the endeavour to conceive the nature of the relation between mind and matter, in our inability to explain the inexplicable, we invoke the Deity, and speculation enters the domain of hyperphysical influences, miraculous causes, imaginary harmonies, and theosophic visions. The Deity having being invoked to account for our knowledge of the world of matter, the existence of the world of matter is ignored as unnecessary to the operation of the Deity, and our ideas of sense are conceived to be excited in our minds by the unassisted agency of God. But as the world was superseded by God, so God in his turn is superseded by the soul. The mind, which first rushed into materialism, then burst into the region of theology, falls back exhausted on itself. It first declares space and time to be mere forms of sense; it next denies the existence of all external causes; and, finally, it ignores all substance. It resolves the universe into unsubstantial thought, and hails this unsubstantial entity which trembles on the verge of non-existence as the All.

What, then, is the impression left upon the mind by the contemplation of so many shadowy and shifting systems? In these lofty solitudes of thought we see nothing but the mists which boil around the glaciers, and, like Manfred on the summit of the Jungfrau, we are giddy. But it is not in vain we have reached these silent heights. It is something to have climbed the mountain; it is something to have seen the mists. We have tried our powers; we have satisfied our curiosity; we are content. But is this the only benefit that those high speculations are calculated to confer? By no means.

They have shown us our ignorance, it is true, but in ascertaining our ignorance we have increased our knowledge. We know what we may aspire to know, and we know what cannot possibly be known. To use the phrase of Locke, we have learned the length of our tether, and we are satisfied to sit down in quiet ignorance of the things which lie beyond the reach of our faculties of knowledge. And our ignorance as to these subjects is quiet because it is complete. We have learned to regard with indifference any new demonstrations of the old indemonstrable dogmas. We know that it is as impossible to prove thought to be a function of matter as it is to prove matter to be a phantasy of thought. We know that the materialist cannot prove the existence of the molecules which he would substitute for ideas—nay, that he cannot prove the very existence of that matter by means of which he would fain supersede the necessity of recognising any spiritual existence either within us or beyond us. But what is this absence of knowledge of which the agnostic so bitterly complains? In reality it is of no significance whatever. We are so constituted, that upon those all-important subjects which we cannot know we are compelled to think; and in thinking on them there are things which we cannot but believe; and even in the absence of grounds for unwavering belief there are probabilities on which, as reasonable men, we may well be satis-

fied to act.* For probability is the guide of life.
In enterprises of the highest moment we are constantly compelled to take action in the midst of
uncertainty and doubt. The great practical intellects which have swayed the minds of men and
shaped the destinies of nations have been the most
conspicuous for the promptitude with which they
calculated probabilities and took their chance. And
in the same spirit they were ready to take their
chance in higher things. Bacon would rather believe all the fables of the Legend, the Talmud, and
the Koran, than that this universal frame was without a mind; and Napoleon, looking up into the
star-lit heavens, appealed to the principle of final
causes as confidently as Butler or as Paley.

The fact is, we hold the possessions of our higher
life by the same tenure as that on which we hold
our possessions in the world of sense. And it is
here that philosophy, even in its negative or agnostic side, has rendered a service to religion. It has
shown that we can live upon a world the existence
of which we cannot prove. It has shown that we
can safely calculate on the continuance of a course
of nature in the future which we do not know.
It has shown that we can associate and act with

* Tum Catulus, Egone? inquit—ad
patris revolvor sententiam, quam quidem ille Carneadeam esse dicebat, ut
percipi nihil putem posse, assensurum
autem non percepto (*Acad.* iv. 48). Is
quoque qui a vobis sapiens inducitur,
multa sequitur probabilia non compre-
hensa, neque percepta, neque assensa,
sed similia veri, quae nisi probet om-
nis vita tollatur (*Ibid.* 31). This is
alike the language of Butler and of
Hume.

a multitude of fellow-creatures whose existence is as incapable of demonstration as that of the Deity himself. It has shown, in fine, that in the most ordinary events of life, as in the deepest mysteries of religion, we live by faith and not by sight. For the whole universe is concealed from us by the veil of our ideas. What is it that exists beyond the veil? That is a question which we can neither answer nor evade. The mind of man is haunted by the supposition of something, he knows not what, which is beyond him. It is in this sense of the unknown that all philosophy and all religion have their source. But the highest intelligence is as helpless as the lowest when it tries to grasp it. The mystery of existence is as inscrutable to the modern philosopher as it was to Plato; and it was as inscrutable to Plato as it was to the ignorant Egyptian who forty centuries ago bowed before the Veiled Statue of Isis, and worshipped the symbol of existence as the Unknown God.

APPENDIX.

APPENDIX.

NOTE A.

LOCKE, as his philosophy for two hundred years has been under-stood, is the father of modern empiricism, and as such the source to which we must trace the sensualism of Condillac, the selfish-ness of Helvetius, and the atheism of La Mettrie and Mirabaud. In opposition to this view, I published the *Intellectualism of Locke*, in which I endeavoured to show that Locke, when properly un-derstood, is to be ranked with Reid and Kant, and not with Helvetius and Condillac. As that work has long been out of print and may never be republished, I propose in this note to recall the reasons which conducted me to that conclusion.

The purpose of Locke, as he himself expresses it, was " to in-quire into the original, certainty, and extent of human knowledge, together with the grounds of belief, opinion, and assent " (*Essay* i. i. 2). As the basis of his inquiry he assumes that no object is pre-sented to the understanding but *ideas*, and, accordingly, he makes the word idea "stand for whatsoever is the object of the under-standing when a man thinks" (i. i. 8). *Knowledge* he subsequently defines to be " the perception of the connexion and agreement, or disagreement and repugnancy, of any of our ideas " (iv. i. 2). In order to ascertain the origin of knowledge, therefore, it is necessary to ascertain the origin of ideas, and, accordingly, Locke's first inquiry is, how ideas come into the mind (i. i. 8).

The controversy raised by Reid and continued by Hamilton

as to the nature of Locke's *ideas* may happily be considered obsolete. No one now-a-days contends with Reid that Locke's idea was a *tertium quid*, existing in the mind like a wafer in a box ; everbody believes it to be, what Locke persistently asserts it to be, an act of perception (II. x. 2)—a modification of thinking (II. xix. 1)—a mere act or affection of the mind (II. xxvii. 25). How, then, do these actual perceptions or modifications of thinking first arise ?

The first book of the Essay contains a negative answer to this question—we have none that are *innate*. The criticism of Leibnitz on this doctrine of Locke is well known, and it supplies a key to all the misunderstandings and misrepresentations which have followed. " Experience is necessary, I admit", says Theophilus to Philalethes, in the *New Essays*, "in order that the mind should be determined to such or such thoughts, and in order that it should take note of the ideas that are in us ; but what of the means by which experience and the senses are competent to supply ideas ? Is the mind a window ? Does it resemble a tablet ? Is it like wax ? It is clear that all who think thus make the mind material. I shall be met with the received maxim, that there is nothing in the soul which comes not from the senses ; but we must make an exception in favour of the soul itself and its affections. *Nihil est in intellectu quod non fuerit in sensu—nisi intellectus ipse*". But on this point there is no difference between Locke and Leibnitz. The exception, so far as it has any real significance, Locke readily admits. He admits that the mind possesses certain " inherent faculties " (I. ii. 2), certain " powers intrinsical and proper to itself " (II. i. 24), certain " natural propensities of thought " (I. iv. 11), certain " principles of common reason " (I. iv. 10), certain principles of " common sense " (I. iii. 4 ; IV. viii. 2 ; IV. xviii. 11). All he denies is the existence of innate principles in the form of " characters, as it were, stamped upon the mind of man, which the soul receives in its very first being, and brings into the world with it " (I. ii. 1). He does not deny the modern principle of ' heredity '; but he denies the pre-existence of Pythagoras (II. xxvii. 14), the reminiscence of Plato (I. iv. 20), the latent modifications of Leibnitz (I. ii. 5), the innate ideas commonly attributed to Descartes—in brief, the " cognita adtulit" which Cicero adopted from Plato (*Tusc.* i. 24), and which Locke regarded as the " established opinion" of the times (i. ii. 1). It may be that the controversy in which Locke thus engaged was in a measure verbal. He repeatedly admits that it was (i. ii. 5 ; i. ii. 27 ; i. iii. 13). But it is one thing to contend against misleading phraseology, and another thing to contend against the truth. Locke admits everything for which any reasonable advocate of innate principles can contend. The capacity is innate, he says, though the knowledge is acquired (i. ii. 5). The admission of self-evident principles, he says, depends not on "native inscription" (i. ii. 11), but on their " native evidence " (iv. vii. 10), and the " immediate intuition " of their truth (iv. ii. 1). " Locke", says Reid, " endeavours to show that axioms or intuitive truths are not innate " (*Reid*, 465). " He does more", says Sir William Hamilton—" he attempts to show that they are all generalisations from experience ; *whereas* experience only affords the occasion on which the native, not innate, or a priori cognitions virtually possessed by the mind itself actually manifest their existence " (*ibid.*). Strange to say, this is the very language of Locke himself in his reply to Lowde. Locke objects to the phraseology of Lowde as " misleading men's thoughts by an insinuation, as if those notions were in the mind before the soul exerts them, *i. e.* before they are known ; *whereas* truly", he says, " before they are known there is nothing of them in the mind but a capacity to know them when the concurrence of the circumstances which this ingenious author thinks necessary in order to the soul's exerting them brings them into our knowledge".

The passage with which Kant commences the Kritik of the Reason may be regarded as the expression of the doctrine with which Locke commences the second book of his Essay on the Understanding :—" That all our knowledge begins with *experience* there can be no doubt ; for how is it possible that the faculty of cognition should be awakened into exercise otherwise than by means of objects which affect our senses, and partly of themselves produce representations, partly rouse our powers of understanding to compare, to connect, or to separate them, and so to convert the raw material of our sensuous impressions into a knowledge of objects, which is called experience". What, then, is the function of *experience*, in the philosophy of Locke, and what is its nature and extent? Not only does it supply the chronological condition for the development of knowledge, but it supplies its material content. In answer to the question, Whence has the mind all the materials of reason and knowledge? Locke replies, "in one word, from experience; in that all our knowledge is founded, and from that it ultimately derives itself" (II. i. 2). This one word unfortunately supplies the sum and substance of all that the critics seem to know of the philosophy of Locke; and they never ask themselves what the one word means. In the first place, what are the materials which experience supplies? The answer of Condillac and his followers is, *sensations* only. But the theory of transformed sensations ignores the fact that, on its own showing, sensations are transformed. It ignores the fact that if sensations are transformed, they can only be transformed by certain operations of the mind. It ignores the fact that of these operations of the mind the mind itself must sooner or later, in point of time, take notice. It ignores the fact that the mind could not take note of its own operations, unless it possessed a capacity of *reflection*. None of these considerations were ignored by Locke, and accordingly he agrees with Kant in regarding the fountain of experience as comprising two sources, sensation and reflection (II. i. 2), or, as he elsewhere terms them, in the very language of the Kritik, *external and internal sense* (II. i. 4; II. xi. 17).

But Locke went further in the path of Kant. In the Kritik it is laid down that our knowledge springs from two main sources in the mind, sensibility and understanding—the one a "receptivity for impressions," the other a "spontaneity in the production of conceptions." Does Locke recognise the spontaneous production of conceptions by the *understanding*? It is here that the philosophy of Locke has been in a peculiar manner misunderstood; and it is here that his own language has most materially contributed to the misunderstanding. Locke undoubtedly lays it down that "simple ideas, the materials of all our knowledge, are suggested and furnished to the mind only by the two ways, sensation and reflection " (II. ii. 2); he undoubtedly lays it down that " all relation terminates in, and is ultimately founded on, those simple ideas we have got from sensation or reflection " (II. xxviii. 18); nay, he says that " external and internal sensation are the only passages he can find of knowledge to the understanding " (II. xi. 17). But this says nothing more than Kant himself has said. Locke's simple ideas, being merely the ideas which the mind passively receives through sense (II. i. 25), correspond with the sensible intuitions of the Kritik ; and in holding that these constitute " the materials " of all our knowledge, Locke merely holds with Kant that the senses external and internal supply " the matter", as distinguished from the form of thought. True, he holds that if a conception of the understanding be " removed from all simple ideas quite, it signifies nothing at all" (II. xxviii. 18); but in this he merely holds with Kant that without material content thoughts are void. For Locke, to do him justice, has abundantly explained himself. Though he tells us that the simple ideas of sense are " the materials and foundations of the rest," he also tells us that there are other ideas which, though not " simple", but " complex", are uncompounded (II. xii. 1), and which the understanding, when " employed about " the simple ideas of the senses, must inevitably " attain unto " (II. xii. 8). Not only does he admit that the understanding can separate, compound, and compare the ideas with which it has been furnished by the senses (II. xii. 1), but he admits that, over and above the simple ideas which the understanding gets from the senses, " there are others it gets from their comparison with one another " (II. xxv. 1). These are the ideas of relation which are " added by the mind " (III. iii. 11). Such is the idea of causation which the mind " collects" in observing the constant changes which occur around it (II. xxi. 4 ; II. xxvi. 1). Such is the idea of substance, which the mind " supposes ", when we find that " we cannot conceive" how the simple ideas of which substances are composed can possibly subsist alone or in each other (II. xxiii. 4). Such also are the ideas of identity and diversity which we " form " on comparing a thing with itself, and " never finding or conceiving it possible that two things of the same kind should exist in the same place at the same time " (ii. xxvii. 1). These ideas of relation, it is true, " terminate in and are concerned about " ideas of sensation and reflection (ii. xxv. 9), but, in their abstract nature, they are neither ideas of sensation nor ideas of reflection—*they are " the inventions and creatures of the* UNDERSTANDING " (iii. iii. 11).

Nor is this seeing in Homer more than Homer saw. Locke has not left himself at the mercy of the careless reader or the hostile critic. The point was presented to him in a manner which it was impossible for him to evade. The question of the co-operation of the understanding with our faculties of sense in the development of knowledge was forced upon him in his correspondence with the Bishop of Worcester. Stillingfleet raised the question of the origin of ideas and the origin of knowledge as explicitly as Reid or Stewart, as explicitly as Kant or Cousin. In the course of the discussion, Locke admits that the principle of causation is " *a true principle of reason*", on the ground of our " perceiving that the idea of beginning to be is necessarilyconnected with the idea of some operation, and the idea of operation with the idea of something operating which we call a cause" (*Works*, iii. 61). But it is on the question of substance that he is most explicit. It was the idea which Stillingfleet had selected in proof that sensation and reflection were insufficient to explain " the ideas necessary to reason " (iii. 11). " If the idea of substance be grounded upon plain and evident reason", said Stillingfleet, " then we must allow an idea of substance which comes not in by sensation or reflection " (iii. 19). Locke admits the fact, but says, " *I am sure the author of the Essay of Human Understanding never thought, nor in that Essay hath anywhere said,* that the ideas which come into the mind by sensation and reflection are all the ideas that are necessary to reason, or that reason is exercised about " (iii. 11). " *I never said that the general idea of substance comes in by sensation and reflection, or that it is a simple idea of sensation or reflection,* though it be ultimately founded on them ; for it is a complex idea, made up of the general idea of some thing or being with the relation of a support to accidents. *For general ideas come not into the mind by sensation or reflection, but are the creatures or inventions of the* UNDERSTANDING, *as I think I have shown"* (iii. 19). Locke is not content with even this. He makes a further effort to explain himself. " To explain myself and clear my meaning in this matter", he says, "all the ideas of all the sensible qualities of a cherry come into my mind by *sensation;* the ideas of perceiving, thinking, reasoning, knowing, &c., come into my mind by *reflection:* the ideas of these qualities and actions, or powers, are perceived by THE MIND to be by themselves inconsistent with existence; or, as your Lordship well expresses it, ' we find that we can have no true conception of any modes or accidents, but *we must conceive* a substratum, or subject, wherein they are, *i. e.* that they cannot exist or subsist of themselves'. Hence the MIND perceives their necessary connexion with inherence, or being supported, which being a relative idea, *superadded* to the red colour in a cherry, or to thinking in a man, the mind frames the correlative idea of a support. *For I never denied that* THE MIND *could frame to itself ideas of relation, but have shown the quite contrary in my chapters on Relation"* (iii. 21).

Let us now consider Locke's views on the origin of knowledge. Our knowledge, he says, is of two kinds—one relating to the agreement or disagreement of our ideas, the other to the correspondence of our ideas with external objects (IV. xi. 13). As to the agreement or disagreement of our ideas with each other, the key-note of misrepresentation has again been struck by Leibnitz. "If Locke", says Leibnitz, "had sufficiently considered the truths which are necessary and demonstrative, and those which we infer from induction alone, he would have perceived that necessary truths could only be proved from principles which command our assent by their intuitive evidence, inasmuch as our senses can inform us only of what is, not of what must necessarily be". Yet, not only did Locke consider the necessary and demonstrative truths in question, but the consideration of them pervades the whole of the fourth book of the Essay Concerning Human Understanding. He repeats, till the reader is weary of the repetition, that all demonstration must be based

on " intuitive principles", which are " irresistible as sunshine"
(IV. ii. 1)—which are known by their "native evidence" (IV. vii. 10)
—which " neither require nor admit of proof " (IV. vii. 19). Not
only does he distinguish between what is and what must necessarily be, but he gives the criterion by which they are to be distinguished—the absence or presence of " necessary connexion",
of "necessary coexistence", of "necessary dependence and visible
connexion", of " evident dependence, or necessary connexion", of
" the necessary connexion of the ideas themselves" (IV. iii. 14).
Kant himself has not more accurately distinguished between
a priori and a posteriori knowledge than Locke has done. He
contrasts the " necessary dependence" which is discoverable in
our ideas themselves with "the constant and regular connexion "
of ideas which we attribute to the " arbitrary determination " of
the Creator, and which are discoverable only by " experience "
(IV. iii. 28 . " In some of our ideas", he says, " there are
certain relations, habitudes, and connexions, so visibly included in the nature of the ideas themselves that we *cannot
conceive* them separable from them by any power whatsoever,
and in these only we are capable of *certain and universal knowledge* " (IV. iii. 29) ; because, as he proceeds to argue, " the
things that, as far as our observation reaches, *we constantly find* to
proceed regularly, we may conclude do act by a law set them,
but yet by a law we know not, whereby, though causes work
steadily, and effects flow from them, yet their connexions and dependencies being not discoverable in our ideas, we can have but an
experimental knowledge of them" (*ibid.*). Or, take another passage.
" General and certain truths", he says, " are only founded in the
habitudes and relations of abstract ideas", and "a sagacious and
methodical application of our thoughts, for the finding out these
relations, is the only way to discover all that can be put with
truth and certainty concerning them into general propositions"
(IV. xii. 7). " What, then", he asks, " are we to do for the improvement of our knowledge of substantial beings ?" " Here", he says,
" we are to take a quite contrary course ; the want of ideas of their
real essences sends us from our own thoughts to the things themselves as they exist—EXPERIENCE *here must teach us what* REASON

cannot, and it is by trying alone that I can certainly know what other qualities coexist with those of my complex idea " (IV. xii. 9).

What is it then that Locke, on the principles of Kant, has left undone ? He distinguishes between objective and subjective knowledge (IV. iv. 3 ; IV. xi. 13). He distinguishes between analytic and synthetic propositions (IV. viii. 8), and lays down the "infallible rule" by which they are to be distinguished (IV. viii. 13) He distinguishes between synthetic a priori and synthetic a posteriori judgments (IV. iii. 29 ; IV. xii. 7). He distinguishes between experience and reason (*ibid.*). And hence it is that he is enabled to accomplish his design and to give an answer to the inquiries with which he started (I. i. 2). The "original" of knowledge is to be discovered in experience (II. i. 2) ; its "certainty" is based on intuition (IV. ii. 2) ; its "extent" is determined by our perception of the identity, co-existence, and relation of our ideas, and the existence of their corresponding objects (IV. iii. 7), so far as it is revealed to us by intuition on the one hand, or by experience on the other (IV. iii. 29). On these principles Locke holds that mathematics, as based on ideas the agreement or disagreement of which may be "intuitively perceived", is capable of demonstration (IV. ii. 9). On these principles he shows that moral science may be deduced "from self-evident propositions, by necessary consequences as incontestable as those in mathematics" (IV. iii. 18). On these principles he contends that the existence of God may be proved by "a regular deduction of it from some part of our intuitive knowledge," with an "evidence equal to mathematical certainty" (IV. x. 1). Such is the empiricism—such is the sensualism of John Locke. But, unfortunately for philosophy, the error as to his true character has become inveterate. It is embodied in all the histories of philosophy. It is stamped with the authority of great men, whose writings are in every hand, and whose names are upon every tongue. For two hundred years Locke has been regarded as a mere empiric ; and it is to be feared that, in spite of all that may be said to the contrary, he will be so regarded to the end of time.

NOTE B.

HOBBES : ON GENERAL REASONING.

No exposition of the philosophy of either Locke or Berkeley would be complete without a consideration of their opinions as to abstract ideas and general names ; and to discuss this question with effect we must go still farther back, and examine the views of the founder of modern Nominalism—Hobbes.

The life of Hobbes was unusually protracted. He was born at Malmesbury in 1588, the year of the Armada, and he died at Hardwicke, in 1679, the year of the Exclusion Bill. He lived under five sovereigns. He was the amanuensis of Bacon. He was twenty-eight when Shakspere died. He was twenty when Milton was born, and he survived him. He died when Locke was forty-seven. His life therefore covers the whole period from the Novum Organum, which he translated into Latin, to the Essay Concerning Human Understanding, which was in preparation when he died. In the interval Hobbes wrote and published the *De Cive*, the *Leviathan*, and the *Human Nature*. Though he did not commence his philosophical writings till he was close upon the verge of sixty, he produced the most powerful effect, not only upon his own age but upon succeeding ages. He was the founder of modern political philosophy. In enunciating the principles of the utilitarian system he anticipated Bentham. In all that is essential to the science of jurisprudence he anticipated Austin. The influence of his philosophy is visible in Locke, in Berkeley, and in Hume. But his passion for paradox was so great, and he clothed the most innocent truisms in such obnoxious forms, that he aroused a feeling of personal hatred so violent that not only was the whole church militant thundering on his head-piece during his life, but nearly two hundred years afterwards an election mob greeted the editor of his works with the cry " No

Obbes!" As usual, detraction followed in the footsteps of dislike, and no philosopher in the annals of misrepresentation has been so systematically misrepresented as the founder of the Nominalism of modern times.

The controversy between the Realists and Nominalists is one of the most remarkable in the history of the world. The schools resounded with its discussion; but the discussion was not confined to the limits of the schools. It was maintained by rival theologians, who mutually accused each other of the unpardonable sin. It procured the martyrdom of Huss. It deluged the streets of Paris with blood. Like the controversy of the Guelfs and Ghibellines, it distracted medieval Europe. Emperors and kings took up arms on the question of universals *a parte rei;* and, according to John of Salisbury, more money was expended on the contest than was laid up in the treasure-house of Croesus, more time was consumed in its discussion than was required to consolidate the empire of the Caesars.

To the ordinary reader the dispute as to the nature of universals which thus convulsed the middle ages is apt to suggest the dispute as to the primitive way of breaking eggs which embroiled the Emperor of Lilliput and the Emperor of Blefuscu. But to the philosopher it suggests topics of interest, which, even in these days when physical science is predominant, continue to agitate the minds of men. The question as to the origin of species is only another form of the inquiry as to the nature of universals *a parte rei;* and though the hypothesis of protoplasm and evolution has taken the place of the hypothesis of substantial forms, they equally belong to that metaphysical aspect of the question which every physical science of necessity presents. The questions as to the origin of language, again, which within the last few years have been popularised by the ability of Max Müller, are only a phase of the question raised by the Nominalists as to the origin of general terms. These questions, however, belong to the domains of physiology and philology rather than to the domain of abstract thought; and the question in which the mere philosopher is interested relates exclusively to the nature of universals in the mind. What is the object present to the mind in its general reasonings? Is it a thing, an idea, or a name? Is the Realist or the Conceptualist, or the Nominalist, right?

Unfortunately, such are the ambiguities of language, that before we can discuss the subject we must consider the preliminary question, What are the doctrines which the Realist, the Conceptualist, and the Nominalist actually held? This question is exhaustively discussed by Brown, and we cannot do better than take the opinions attributed to the contending sects from him. According to Brown, the Realist maintained that the universal a parte mentis is a " species distinct from the mind, which, of course, could not be particular, like the sensible species, but universal, so as to correspond with the universality of the notion and the generic term" (*Lect.* ii. 458). The Nominalist is supposed not only to deny the existence of intelligible species, but also to " deny the existence of that peculiar class of feelings or states of mind which have been denominated general notions, or general ideas, asserting the existence only of individual objects perceived, and of general terms that comprehend them, without any peculiar mental state denoted by the general term" (p. 464). The Conceptualist, in his turn, is supposed to maintain that the object of the mind in reasoning is not an arbitrary symbol, but an abstract idea, " a notion of an object uniting at once all the qualities of the individual objects, yet excluding every quality which distinguishes each from each " (p. 483).

But the more absurd a doctrine appears to be, the less likely is it to have been actually held by any reasonable man; and when a critic, however intelligent, conceives a great philosopher to have been a fool, it is within the limits of possibility that the fool after all may be, not the philosopher, but the critic. Before we ridicule we should refute, and before we refute we should strive to understand, and before we can understand we must carefully weigh the language of our author. Let us try, then, in the first place to understand what was meant by the *intelligible species* of the schools. As the type of modern Realism we may take the modern Platonist, who was the greatest of the antagonists of Hobbes. Cudworth, like his master, holds that " the immediate

The General Names of Hobbes.   347

objects of intellection and science are eternal, necessarily existing, and incorruptible". But he immediately proceeds to obviate
the misconception into which Brown was betrayed upon the
point. He tells us that "the rationes and essences of things are
not dead things, like so many statues, images, or pictures hung
up somewhere by themselves alone in a world : neither are
truths mere sentences and propositions written down with ink
upon a book " (*ibid*). He tells us that, on the contrary, " the
rationes, intelligible essences, and verities of things, are nothing
but noemata, that is, objective notions or knowledge, which are
things which cannot exist alone ; but together with that actual
knowledge in which they are comprehended they are the modifications of some mind or intellect " (*ibid*). As modifications of
intellect or mind, in other words, as cognitive acts, intelligible
species were not denied by the founders of Nominalism (*Reid*, 954),
and accordingly on this point Cudworth and Ockham are agreed.

The criticism of Leibnitz upon the sage of Malmesbury is one
of the commonplaces of the history of philosophy. According to
Leibnitz, Hobbes was *plus quam Nominalis*—a Nominalist and
something more—*non contentus enim cum Nominalibus universalia
ad nomina reducere, ipsam rerum veritatem ait in nominibus consis-
tere, ac, quod majus est, pendere ab humano arbitrio, quia veritas pen-
deat a definitionibus terminorum, definitiones autem terminorum ab arbitrio humano*. Now Hobbes, in his *Computation*, undoubtedly
states that "the first truths were arbitrarily made by those that first
of all imposed names upon things, or received them from the
imposition of others " (*Works*, i. 36). But his paradox that all
truth is arbitrary is of a piece with his paradox that no law can be
unjust. All depends on what we are to understand by truth and
law. The fact is, that each proposition is a platitude rather than
a paradox. If truth be thought expressed in words, and if words
be arbitrarily selected, then it is an identical proposition that
truths are arbitrarily made. The whole mystery is cleared away
in the *Leviathan*. Though "true and false are attributes of
speech, not of things", and though, "where speech is not, there
is neither truth nor falsehood", yet "*error* there may be, as when
we expect that which shall not be, or suspect what hath not

been", albeit, " in neither case can a man be charged with *un-truth*" (iii. 23). Whether Hobbes was right or wrong in consi-dering language to be arbitrary, he is undoubtedly right in his conception of the relations which subsist between the thing, the idea, and the name. " A name is a word taken at pleasure, to serve for a mark which may raise in our mind a thought *like* to some thought we had before, and which, being pronounced to others, may be to them a sign of what thought the speaker had, or had not, before in his mind" (i. 16). But names are " signs of our conceptions" (i. 17); and, " one universal name is imposed on many things for their *similitude* in some quality or other accident" (iii. 21). Accordingly Hobbes tells us that " a man that seeketh precious truth had need to remember what every name he uses stands for, and to place it accord-ingly, or else he will find himself entangled in words, as a bird in lime-twigs—the more he struggles the more belimed" (p. 23). He tells us " that in the *right* definition of names lies the first use of speech, which is the acquisition of science" (p. 24); and he concludes his discussion with the weighty apophthegm, that " words are wise men's counters, they do but reckon by them; but they are the money of fools, that value them by the authority of an Aristotle, a Cicero, or a Thomas, or any other doctor whatsoever, if but a man " (p. 25).

What then were the views of Locke upon the subject? The philosopher of the revolution was no admirer of the philoso-pher of the restoration. He professed to be but slightly ac-quainted with his works, and seems to have thought so slightly of them that, in enumerating the works on the original of society, and the extent of political power, which had appeared within the previous sixty years, he is silent on the *Leviathán* and the *De Cive*, and mentions only the Ecclesiastical Polity of Mr. Hooker, the Discourses on Government of Mr. Alger-non Sydney, and a Treatise of Civil Polity by Mr. Paxton (*Works*, ii. 408). But the similarity of the views of Hobbes and Locke on the question of universals is not to be concealed. Locke holds that " truth and falsehood properly belong to propo-sitions " (II. xxxii. 1). He holds that mixed modes are arbitrary

(III. v. 3). He "would not be thought to forget, much less to deny, that nature in the production of things makes several of them alike"; but he thinks "we may say the sorting of them under names is the workmanship of the understanding, taking occasion, from the *similitude* it observes among them, to make abstract general ideas and set them up in the mind, with names annexed to them, as patterns or forms to which as particular things existing are found to agree, so they came to be of that species, have that denomination, or are put into that classis" (III. iii. 13); or, as he elsewhere expresses it, are determined to be of that "sort" (III. iii. 6, 12). "Ideas", he says, "become general by separating from them the circumstances of time and place, and any other ideas that may determine them to this or that particular existence" (III. iii. 6). This process of abstraction he regards as the prerogative of man; and he delights in magnifying the difficulties that attend it. "General ideas", he says, "are fictions and contrivances of the mind, that carry difficulty with them, and do not so easily offer themselves as we are apt to imagine". "Does it not require some pains and skill", he asks, "to form the general idea of a triangle (which is yet none of the most abstract, comprehensive, and difficult), for it must be neither oblique, nor rectangle, neither equilateral, equicrural nor scalenon; but all and none of these at once"—"in effect it is something imperfect that cannot exist; an idea wherein some parts of several different and inconsistent ideas are put together" (IV. vii. 9).

But it is never with impunity that a writer sacrifices precision to point. Locke's abstract idea of a triangle is as enigmatical as the Aelia Laelia Crispis of the schoolmen; and accordingly from the first it has been the butt of philosophers and wits. Arbuthnot, in the Memoirs of Scriblerus, could find no parallel for it but Crambe's Abstract of a Lord Mayor. Berkeley, in the Introduction to his Principles of Human Knowledge, found it hard to imagine that a couple of children could not prate of their sugar-plums and rattles till they had tacked together a number of inconsistencies and framed abstract general ideas (*Intr.* xiv.). Brown considers the passage as unworthy of its great

author, and as abundantly ridiculous (*Lect.* xlvii.); while
Hamilton declares that Locke held the conceptualist doctrine in
its most revolting absurdity, contending that the general notion
must be realised in spite of the principle of contradiction (*Lect.*
ii. 300). But Locke's critics, to use Locke's metaphor, have all
been lost in the great wood of words. They have failed to
observe that parts of inconsistent ideas are not necessarily inconsistent, and that ideas may be obtained by abstraction without being capable of being imaged in the abstract. The
abstract idea is not so much an idea as a "measure of name"
(iii. iii. 14), and it is the very essence of a definition that it should
comprehend all particulars and be identified with none. Locke,
in fact, repudiates the absurdity with which he has been
charged. "If", he says, "I put in my ideas of mixed modes
or relations any inconsistent ideas together, I fill my head also
with chimeras; since such ideas, if well examined, cannot so
much as exist in the mind, much less any real being ever be
denominated from them " (iii. x. 33).

The doctrine which Hume attributes to Berkeley is, that
"all general ideas are nothing but particular ones annexed
to a certain term, which gives them a more extensive signification, and makes them recall upon occasion other indivi-
duals which are similar to them "; and Hume looks on this as
"one of the greatest and most valuable discoveries that had been
made of late years in the republic of letters" (i. 34). But Berkeley
said nothing which had not previously been said by Locke. He
says it is true in fancied opposition to Locke that he does not
"deny that there are general ideas, but only that there are any
abstract general ideas " (*Intr.* xii.), and that " it is one thing for
to keep a name constantly to the same *definition*, and another
to make it stand everywhere for the same *idea* " (§ xviii.).
But these are mere verbal misunderstandings. Berkeley
acknowledges that " a man may consider a figure merely as
triangular without attending to the particular qualities of the
angles or relations of the sides " (§ xvi.). He holds that " an
idea, which considered in itself is particular, becomes general
by being made to represent or stand for all other particular

ideas of the same *sort*" (*Int.* xii.).   He insists it is true that
"it is not necessary, even in the strictest reasonings", that
" significant names which stand for ideas should, every time
they are used, excite in the understanding the ideas they are
made to stand for " (§ xix.).   But on this point Locke agrees
with Berkeley.   He admits everything for which a Nominalist
can reasonably contend.   He concedes that "most men, if not
all, in their thinking and reasonings make use of words instead
of ideas " (iv. v. 4).   He does not contend that " a man need
stand to recollect and make an analysis " of the meaning of the
word every time he happens to employ it (iii. xi. 9)—all he
insists on is, " that he have so examined the signification of that
name, and settled the idea of all its parts in his mind, that he
can do it when he pleases " (*ibid.*)

How then are we to arbitrate between the contending sects ?
The materials for an arbitration exist, and, if not obvious, yet
when pointed out must be admitted by reasonable men.   It must
be admitted that in our general reasonings we employ words,
without any conscious reference to their meaning, and merely as
algebraic symbols.   It must be admitted, at the same time, that,
if our reasonings are not to end in nonsense, our words must
have a meaning, and that their meaning must be determined
by their definition, whether denominated abstract idea, scheme,
or concept.   It must be admitted, moreover, that if our general
reasonings are to conduct to any practical result, our conceptions
should not be mere chimeras, but should accord with the facts of
nature and the realities of things.   But then again it must be
admitted that everything which exists, whatever may be the physical cause that determines the mode of its existence, is *particular*.
At the same time it cannot be denied that in contemplating a
multitude of particulars the mind is struck with a sense of their
resemblance, and that it selects the point of resemblance by a process of abstraction and combines them into a scheme or concept.
But can this scheme or concept be present to the mind as an
image or idea ?   No ; and even if it could be, it would be parti-
ticular.   The only means of *generalising* it and keeping its abstracted elements together is by the imposition of a name.   The

name, the idea, and the thing, are thus relegated to their natural rights, and are placed in their natural relations. What, then, is each party called on to renounce? Nothing but the privilege of attributing absurdity to its opponents. The mental facts are all agreed on, and nothing is to be abandoned but the *un*intelligible species attributed to Scotus, the unmeaning symbolism attributed to Hobbes, and the self-contradictory ideas attributed to Locke.

NOTE C.

BACON : ON INDUCTIVE REASONING.

THE three first names in English philosophy are Bacon, Hobbes and Locke ; and it is hard to say which of these great men has been most generally magnified, and, at the same time, most generally misunderstood.   In one point Locke and Bacon have been subjected to a common error.   Both have been regarded as champions of the *Empiricism* which, according to the critics, is characteristic of their nation (*Schw.* 153, 181).

So far was Bacon from being a mere empiric, that the whole object of his philosophy, as stated in his *Distributio Operis*, was to effect a reconciliation between the rational and the empiric faculties, the divorce of which, he said, had thrown all human affairs into confusion.   The true process of science, he said in his *Novum Organum*, was neither that of the ant, which merely stores what it has collected from without, nor that of th spider, which spins everything from within, but that of the bee, which gathers its material from the flowers of the garden and the field, and by its own faculty digests them and converts them into honey.   The influence of reason in the development of science from experience is never for a single moment either denied or ignored by Bacon.   In his *Philosophia Prima* he anticipates Kant, and attempts to enumerate the transcendental axioms and notions which are assumed in all physical investigation. In his *Topica Particularis* he adopts the words of Plato, and declares that he who seeks anything in nature must comprehend it in some general notion, in order to recognize it when he finds it.   In his *Interpretatio Naturae* he analyzes the process by which the form is elicited by reason from the facts furnished by experience, and makes mental anticipation the first step in the process of induction.

2 A

The nature of the inductive process has been the subject of bitter and long-continued controversies. But the fact is, the word induction, like every other philosophical term, is used in a variety of senses, and this occasions an apparent variety of opinions where, in reality, none exists. *Logical Induction*, as it may be called, is a process which goes upon the self-evident fact, that what belongs or does not belong to all the constituent parts, belongs or does not belong to the constituted whole. It is merely the converse of the syllogistic process, and belongs exclusively to the domain of logic. A like remark may be made with respect to the *Psychological Induction*, as it may be termed, of Mill, who defines induction to be " the operation of the mind, by which we infer that what we know to be true in a particular case, or cases, will be true in all cases which resemble the former in certain assignable respects " (*Log.* i. 319). But this inference from the known to the unknown is merely an expression of our belief in the continuance of the laws of nature ; and this belief, though the basis of all our experimental inquiries, and the condition of their application, is not so much an inference from experimental data as an anticipation of experience ; and whether it be regarded as an instinct, as a category, or as a transcendent, it must be relegated to psychology, as the logical induction was to logic. The object of induction, as Bacon conceived the process, was to ascertain the laws of nature, and not to explain our belief in their continuance. The cause, the law, or, to use Bacon's term, the form, of any set of phenomenon can only be elicited from the facts ; and the facts can only be ascertained by a patient interrogation of nature, conducted on a preconceived plan (topica particularis), the results of which, to be available, should be methodically recorded (experientia literata). But the interpretation of nature should follow its interrogation ; and the form which explains the facts ascertained by observation and experiment must be discovered by induction. This process may be styled *Physical Induction*, for the purpose of distinction ; and, according to Bacon, there are two ways in which it may proceed. The form being unknown can, in the first instance, be merely matter of conjecture ; but

when the mind has formed its conjecture it must proceed to test
its truth by a reference to the facts. This it may do, in a hasty
and perfunctory manner, by an enumeration of the particular
instances in which the form appears to exist, without inquiring
into the analogous instances in which it does not exist, and so
conclude that it is the form. This is the *Induction by Simple
Enumeration* which Bacon considered a precarious method of
inquiry—a method leading to results which may be neutralized
by the first contradictory instance that presents itself—a method
which affords no exit from the labyrinth of facts into the light of
law. Precario concludit, et periculo ab instantiâ contradictoriâ
exponitur, et consueta tantum intuetur, nec exitum reperit.
In opposition to this, he insists on the employment of an *Induction by Exclusion*—a form of induction quae experientiam solvat
et separet, et per exclusiones ac rejectiones debitas necessario
concludat—a process which considers the facts that experience
has furnished, forms hypotheses as to their laws, rejects every
hypothesis which is inconsistent with the facts observed, and
inducts the true hypothesis after the rejection of those which are
d emonstrably false

In his *Impetus Philosophici* Bacon supplies a formula to determine whether any given hypothesis for the explanation of a set
of observed phenomena should be rejected. Omnes naturae quae
aut datâ naturâ praesente adsunt, aut datâ naturâ absente adsunt, ex formâ non sunt ; atque post rejectionem aut negatio-
nem completam manet forma et affirmatio. This, he said, was
a brief remark, but it embodied a conclusion at which he had
only arrived by a long and patient course of thought. In the
Novum Organum, however, after still deeper meditation on the
subject, he gives a formula more comprehensive and correct.
Invenienda est enim super comparentiam omnium et singularium
instantiarum natura talis, quae cum naturâ datâ perpetuo adsit,
absit, atque crescat et decrescat (II. xv.). These formulae, it is
plain, are a compendious expression of Mill's canons of agreement, difference, and concomitant variations, and they show how
completely Bacon, in the infancy of physical science, anticipated
all the logical principles on which, in its maturity, it proceeds.

Instead of illustrating the Baconian method by trivial or ridiculous instances, let us illustrate it by the process which conducted physical investigation to its greatest triumph—the discovery of the laws which regulate the planetary movements. The facts of the celestial motions had been observed from the earliest times, and records of those observations had been made generations ago by the Assyrian, the Egyptian, and the Greek.   But what was the law of those familiar motions? It was not known; and in the first place it could only be provisionally guessed.   Was the motion in a line, a spiral, or a curve?   Did the earth revolve around the heavenly bodies, or did the heavenly bodies revolve around the earth?   The hypothesis of sidereal revolution was embraced.   It explained the more obvious phenomena of the heavens; but fact after fact was observed which it was incompetent to explain.   It was in vain that astronomers strove to modify the original hypothesis by subsidiary hypotheses, and imagined " cycle and epicycle, orb on orb".   In the felicitous language of Whewell, the conception could not colligate the facts.   Accordingly, the hypothesis of Hipparchus was at last rejected; and Copernicus, in order to explain the facts of the celestial movements, embraced the hypothesis that the earth revolved around the planets in a circle.   But though the circular hypothesis explained a multitude of facts, there were facts which even it was unable to explain.   It was in vain that Copernicus again introduced the epicycle in the form of an equalizing circle; his hypothesis was in its turn rejected.   After so many rejections a new hypothesis was formed by Kepler—the hypothesis of an elliptic orbit.   The problem of the heavens was solved.   The hypothesis of an elliptic orbit explained every phenomenon that had been observed. The infinitesimal calculus was invented by Newton; astronomy was converted into a branch of mathematics; and, after so many anticipations and so many rejections, the great cosmical hypothesis was inducted to its place of honour as the highest type of science.

It is evident from what has been said, that in point of logic the Baconian induction is a disjunctive syllogism, of which the major premiss is the sum total of the hypotheses which the mind can form in order to explain the facts. The law of the phenomena must be either this or that or the other theory; it is neither this nor that; therefore it must be the other. The major is thus supplied by the anticipations of the mind; the minor is the rejection of all anticipations which are inconsistent with the facts of nature; the conclusion is the induction. As Bacon himself expresses it, a variety of opinions are formed; all volatile opinions disappear as smoke; and the true solid and affirmative result remains.

The mention of syllogism suggests another matter in which injustice has been done to Bacon. According to Mill, he "leaves no room for the discovery of new principles by way of deduction"; and he adds, that "it is not to be conceived that a man of Bacon's sagacity could have fallen into this mistake, if there had existed in his time among the sciences which treat of successive phenomena one single deductive science, such as mechanics, astronomy, optics, acoustics, &c., now are" (*Logic*, ii. 451). This is as curious a misrepresentation as could well be made. In Bacon's correspondence there is a letter to the Redemptorist Father Baranzan, in which he distinctly states that when the original facts and primary laws of nature have been ascertained by induction the syllogistic method may be used. In physicâ prudenter notas, et idem tecum sentio, post notiones primae classis, et axiomata super ipsas per inductionem bene eruta et terminata, tuto adhiberi syllogismum, modo inhibeatur saltus ad generalissima et fiat progressus per scalam convenientem. Nay, so far was Bacon from being betrayed intò the alleged mistake by the fact that no deductive science existed in his time, that he actually *predicts* the advent of the very sciences which were destined to form the proudest triumph of the deductive method. Multae naturae partes, nec satis subtiliter comprehendi, nec satis perspicue demonstrari, nec satis dextre et certo ad usum accommodari, possunt sine ope et interventu mathematicae; cujus generis sunt perspectiva, musica, astronomia, cosmographia, machinaria, et nonnullae aliae. Caeterum in mathematicis mixtis integras aliquas portiones deside-

ratas jam non reperio, sed multas in posterum *praedico* si homines
non ferientur ; prout enim physica majora indies incrementa
capiet, et nova axiomata educet, eo mathematicae operâ novâ in
multis indigebit, et plures fient mathematicae mixtae (*De Aug.*
iii. vi.).

One word still remains to be said. The tendency of Lord
Macaulay's celebrated essay on Bacon is to give his philosophy a
far more material and utilitarian aspect than it really bears.
We are told that Bacon indulged in no rants about the fitness
of things, or the dignity of human nature—that he said nothing
about the grounds of moral obligation or the freedom of the
human will—that he paid no attention to the casuistical sub-
tleties which occupied the attention of the keenest spirits of the
age. Nothing could be more misleading. The book of the *De Augmentis*, which he devotes to moral philosophy, contains a refutation
of all these statements. He praises the philosophers, for the manner in which they had treated ideal excellence. He regards
them, however, as surpassed by the pious and strenuous diligence
of the theologians, in their treatment of the moral virtues and
cases of conscience, and the delimitations of sin. He speaks of
the higher power and dignity of the *bonum communionis* and the
bonum activum, as compared with the selfish cares and passive
enjoyment of life. He speaks of an approach to the divine or
angelic nature as the perfection of our moral form ; and with
Aristotle, he proposes heroic and divine virtue as the scope of
all our moral aims. The two words, says Lord Macaulay,
which are the key of Bacon's philosophy are, utility and progress. Even this is not correct. The key of his doctrine was
not utility and progress, but utility and *truth.* Propositum a
nobis est, non rerum pulchritudinem sed usum et veritatem
sectari. Nay more, the great experimental philosopher places
truth before utility in his estimate of their relations. In his
Aphorisms he asserts that the contemplation of truth is something for higher and worthier than any mere utility—esse
contemplationem veritatis omni operum utilitate et magni-
tudine digniorem et celsiorem (*Nov. Org.* i. lxxiv). And in
his *Essays* are the words, which every man of education has by

heart : " Howsoever these things are in men's depraved judgments and affections; yet truth, which only doth judge itself,
teacheth, that the inquiry of truth, which is the love-making
or wooing of it ; the knowledge of truth, which is the presence of
it ; and the belief of truth, which is the enjoying of it ; is the
sovereign good of human nature".

NOTE D.

SIR JAMES MACKINTOSH, in his Dissertation on the Progress of Ethical Philosophy, which still maintains its time-honoured place in the Encyclopædia Britannica, regards Hume as a profes- sor of UNIVERSAL SCEPTICISM, and remarks that " the Sceptic boasts of having involved the results of experience and the elements of geometry in the same ruin with the doctrines of religion and the principles of philosophy " (*Works*, i. 137). How erroneous this criticism is we have already seen. We have seen that Hume systematically distinguishes between the results of experience and the elements of geometry (iv. 190)—that he protests against confounding the principles of philosophy with the principles of action (iv. 47)—that he maintains we are under the necessity of acting upon beliefs which no reasoning is able either to produce or to prevent (iv. 56), and that he holds the fundamental doctrines of religion to be based on the principle of natural and necessary faith (iv. 192 .

Sir James Mackintosh, still speaking of Hume, remarks, with reference to his views on NATURAL RELIGION, that " to those who are strangers to the seductions of paradox, to the intoxica- tion of fame, and to the bewitchment of prohibited opinions, it must be unaccountable, that he who revered benevolence should, without apparent regret, cease to see it on the throne of the uni- verse " (i. 135). But to those who are strangers to the bewitch- ments of criticism it must be equally unaccountable that Mackintosh should have been betrayed into such a miscon- ception of Hume's opinions, and that he should have considered it necessary to deprive natural religion of the authority of the most profound metaphysical thinker that these countries have produced. Twice has Hume written on the subject of Natural

Religion, once in his *Natural History*, and again in the *Dialogues* which were posthumously published, and in each of those works he repudiates the atheism which is attributed to him by his critic. In his Natural History of Religion he protests that " the whole frame of Nature bespeaks an Intelligent Author", and that " no rational inquirer can, after serious reflection, suspend his belief a moment with regard to the primary principles of genuine Theism and Religion " (*Works*, iv. 435). In his Dialogues concerning Natural Religion he is still more emphatic. Cleanthes, whose opinions he accepts (ii. 548), maintains that " the most agreeable reflection which it is possible for human imagination to suggest is that of genuine Theism, which represents us as the workmanship of a Being perfectly good, wise and powerful, who created us for happiness, and who, having implanted in us immeasurable desires of good, will prolong our existence to all eternity, and will transfer us into an infinite variety of scenes, in order to satisfy those desires, and render our felicity complete and durable " (ii. 543). He insists on " the curious adapting of means to ends", which is found " throughout all nature", as supplying an argument by which we prove at once the existence of " the Author of Nature " and his wisdom (ii. 440). He says that the conscience of the Sceptic or Atheist must be scrupulous, indeed, if he refuses to call the universal unknown cause a Deity or God (ii. 459). And, finally, in the following passage he lays aside the philosophic calm which he generally affects, and bursts into an impassioned strain of eloquence, which might well be mistaken for one of the pious rhapsodies of Berkeley. " The order and arrangement of nature, the curious adjustment of final causes, the plain use and intention of every part and organ, all these bespeak in the clearest language an intelligent cause or author. The heavens and the earth join in the same testimony. The whole chorus of nature raises one hymn to the praises of its Creator. You [the Sceptic] alone, or almost alone, disturb this general harmony. You start abstruse doubts, cavils, and objections. You ask me what is the cause of this cause? I know not ; I care not ; that concerns not me. I have found a Deity, and here I stop my inquiry " (ii. 465, 6).

These passages reflect a vivid light on Hume's opinion on the general subject of Causation. " Mr. Hume's theory of causation", says Mackintosh, " is used as an answer to arguments for the existence of the Deity, without warning the reader that it would equally lead him not to expect that the sun will rise to-morrow " (*Works*, i. 138). Here again we have a criticism which not only misrepresents Hume, but involves a number of philosophical questions in confusion. Hume, as we have seen, recognises the principle of *efficient causes* as the ground of our belief in the existence of a God, while he recognises the principle of *final causes* as the ground of our belief in his intelligence and goodness. As regards *natural causes*, he has the conspicuous merit of being the first to popularise, if not to establish, what is now an accepted truth, that the sole object of the physical inquirer is to ascertain the *constant conjunction* of phenomena in the vast sequence of changes which constitute the laws of nature. This is Hume's theory of causation in the proper sense. But the existence of these constant conjunctions in the past is no guarantee for their continuance in the future. That the sun rose yesterday is no proof that he will rise to-morrow. Our belief in the *future continuance* of the conjunctions which we have experienced is not to be accounted for by mere experience, according to Hume, but by an instinct of our nature called into play by the recurrence of the phenomena which we have experienced, and supplying a fresh instance of the principle of final causes (iv. 65).

Hume's theory of causation naturally suggests a topic which has subjected him to greater obloquy than even his supposed scepticism—his views as to the nature of Miracles, and the evidence by which they are supported. He defines a miracle to be " a transgression of a law of nature by a particular volition of the Deity, or by an interposition of some invisible agent " (iv. 134). Let us consider the question in its philosophic aspect merely. Recognising as he does the existence of a Deity, Hume, by the principles of his philosophy, is bound to admit that there is no a priori objection to accepting a mere volition for a cause. " If we reason a priori", he says, " anything may appear able to produce anything "—" the falling of a pebble may, for aught we know, extinguish the sun, or the wish of a man control the planets in their orbits " (iv. 191 ; i. 315). The existence of any matter of fact, on his theory, is incapable of demonstration ; and all arguments for its existence must be based upon experience alone (iv. 191). In short, it is a " general maxim " with Hume, " that no objects have any discoverable connexion together, and that all the inferences which we can draw from one to another are founded merely on our experience of their constant and regular conjunction " (iv. 130.

Let us then view the matter a posteriori. " A miracle", says Hume, " is a violation of the laws of nature, and as a firm and unalterable experience has established these laws, the proof against a miracle is as entire as any argument from experience can possibly be imagined " (iv. 133). But this, surely, is a mere begging of the question. For in the first place, is a miracle a *violation* of a law of nature ? On Hume's theory of causation nature is a mere series of antecedents and consequents, and the expression of a law of nature is simply this—the antecedent A, in our past experience, has been constantly followed by the consequent B, the death of a man, for instance, by the dissolution of his body. A miracle is confessedly an unusual occurrence, and on the theory of observed sequences its expression would be this —the antecedent X, has been followed by the consequent Y, the volition of a divine person, for instance, by a resurrection from the dead. Here a new antecedent has been introduced, and a new consequent has followed, This, it is evident, is not a violation of the old sequence, but the introduction of a new one. If the new consequent, the resurrection from the dead, be regarded as an interference with the old consequent, the dissolution of the body, even this cannot be regarded as a violation of the laws of nature, for it is a contingency to which every law of nature is subject—the intervention of a counteracting cause.

To say, then, that the laws of nature are established by an *unalterable* experience is misleading. Dr. Haughton, in his admirable Lectures on Physical Geography, published in the Dublin University Series, describes the scientific law of the uniformity of nature as " a shallow creed " refuted by the science of Geology, "from which we learn that the present is unlike the past, and will probably be still more unlike the future" (p. 75). But neither Hume nor Dr. Haughton, as I venture to think, has formed a true conception of the law in question. Its true expression is to be found in the opening chapter of the *Analogy*. "There is in every case a probability," says Butler, "that all things will continue as we experience they are, in all respects, *except* those in which we have some reason to think they will be altered".

" It is a miracle that a dead man should come to life", says Hume, "because that has never been observed in any age or country" (p. 134). Again, this begs the question. The question we are discussing is whether a resurrection, such as that of Lazarus, has been observed. This can only be determined by the testimony of observers. Hume lays it down as " a maxim that no human testimony can have such force as to prove a miracle" (iv. 150). But a miracle, after all, as distinguished from a law of nature, is merely an extraordinary occurrence. It may well be that, if we were admitted to a wider view of the universe, as Butler suggests, we might find that the occurrence of miracles is subjected to a law as rigorous as, for instance, the secular appearance of a comet. All we can say is, that a miracle, if it occurred, was an extraordinary, or, if you will, a singular occurrence. But if a singular occurrence cannot be established by testimony, nothing can be so established. The repeated occurrence of the most ordinary event is merely the repetition of a series of singular occurrences, and if the evidence for each of them be regarded as a cypher, it is plain that no multiplication of cyphers will constitute a unit.

This brings us to the real point of the whole matter. What is the *evidence* in favour of miracles, and how is that evidence to be regarded? Hume lays down another " general maxim " (iv. 134). He says that " no testimony is sufficient to establish a miracle unless the testimony be of such a kind that its falsehood would be more miraculous than the fact which it endeavours to establish" (p. 134). This is merely a play on the word miraculous. The true statement of the case is made by Mr. Mill. " The improbability, or, in other words, the unusualness, of any fact is no reason for disbelieving it, if the nature of the case renders it certain that either that or something equally improbable, that is, equally unusual, did happen" (*Log.* ii. 168). "All, therefore, which Hume has made out", again to use the words of Mr. Mill, "is that no evidence can prove a miracle to anyone who did not previously believe the existence of a being or beings with supernatural powers ; or who believes himself to have full proof that the character of the Being whom he recognises is inconsistent with his having seen fit to interfere on the occasion in question" (p. 162). But Hume, with all his dogmatism, never pretended to be furnished with any such proof ; and Hume, with all his scepticism, was a firm believer in the being and attributes of God.